THE STORY OF NORTH DEVON BOXING

Volume..Two

Part 3

A Very
Story of
Tragedy
treet

ave Made The

Some Of The Ill
Following Page
Rough State B
North Devon
And Would
Fights!

Everythi
Asking

NORTH DEVON

First published 2017
DICK BROWNSON
TORRIDON HOUSE
CHUBB ROAD
BIDEFORD
EX39 4HF
DEVON
U.K.
Telephone..
01237 700901
email..
brownson7@aol.com

ISBN: 978-0-9954686-7-2

THE STORY OF NORTH DEVON BOXING
Volume...2

DICK BROWNSON

Typeset, printed and bound by
DB Associates
PO BOX 55
BIDEFORD
EX39 3WB
DEVON
U.K.

BOXING GYM TALK

I have used the descriptive term TRAINER throughout this book and not the modern word COACH. My old trainer heard this word used to describe his job in the early 1950's and the result was a bout of hysterics from him.
'Another***Yankee word left here, coach is a posh name for a*** bus!'
That was the first time I heard the word COACH described in that way, many times since.
Nevertheless, I'll stick with TRAINER!
PS...The British Boxing Board of Control Ltd., founded in 1929, STILL issue a TRAINER licence.

BOXER SCRAP-BOOKS.

These should always be compiled by a PROUD MOTHER or SISTER ! They carefully cut out the newspaper reports on the family member, adding the date and source. This is, sad to say, a rare occurrence but I have included almost all NEWSPAPER CUTTINGS that came in as they are of such great interest and historical value to the boxing enthusiast. Some are difficult to read but persevere, the content is well worth the effort.

PHOTOGRAPHS

A few group photos. have been duplicated in this book. This was necessary because the only known image of a particular BOXER was in that group and he has been identified.

Please read...
For DICK BROWNSON..DB
For the NORTH DEVON JOURNAL..NDJ
For the NORTH DEVON GAZETTE..NDG

DID IT NOT SEEM REAL?

NIKKI BROWNSON — SHADOWSMEDIA

CARL HAWKINS — HAWK MEDIA

Their expert advice with the technical problems of compiling this book was invaluable.

My thanks to all the boxers and officials of NORTH DEVON CLUBS who helped me during my extensive research for this book.

A big thank-you to the NORTH DEVON JOURNAL and the NORTH DEVON GAZETTE for use of their reports on NORTH DEVON BOXING.

ACKNOWLEDGEMENTS

PART...3 CONTENTS...

Bideford Amateur Boxing Club

Proudly Presents

An Event of skills Boxing

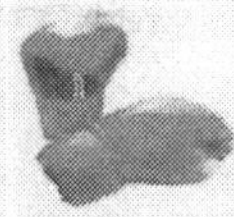

27th September 2015

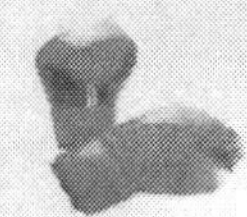

Door open 1pm

Show Starts 2pm

Bideford, Barnstaple and Torrington Boxing Clubs
Together with other Devon Clubs are hosting a Fund Raising afternoon of Skills Bouts and Sparring Sessions in Aid of a North Devon Charity Appeal.

North Devon Children's Holiday Foundation.

The Charity started for the benefit and support of numerous children and families from North Devon

Raffle on the day

Bar and refreshments ava...

All Money raised ...
to North Dev...
Holiday ...

Appledore ...
(Ro...

Tic...
(Apple...

...ckets
Adult £5
Children
£2.50

BIDEFORD ABC
CONTINUED

...teur Boxing Club
...nk you for your
Support
and welcome Sponsors

SPORT ENGLAND

NIKKI BROWNSON and SYLVIA WREY.

Running order for Sunday, all 3 x 1 minute rounds except Ross *Chard and Rob Squires 3 x 2.*

Reece Hollingsworth (Bideford) VS Zack Oloughin (Tiverton)

Billy Heard (Bideford) VS Freddie Wright (Bideford)

John Penfold (Tiverton) VS Edd Cross (Barnstaple)

Jacob Stevenson (Bideford) VS Ned Pettifer (Torrington)

Jed Davies (Barnstaple) VS Trai Sheppard (Torrington)

Grace Short (Bideford) VS Daisy Burdett (Torrington)

Edward Fry (Tiverton) VS Jack Pledger (Torrington)

Alfie Betts (Torrington) VS Charlie Golder (Torrington)

Connor Woods (Barnstaple) VS Matt Grey (Torrington)

Frank Blackmore (Bideford) VS Fergus Mclean (Torrington)

Josh Short (Bideford) VS Robbie Moore (Torrington)

Ross Chard (Tamar) VS Rob Squires (Barnstaple)

Ryan Gumbley (Bideford) VS Billy Parsons (Bideford)

Pete Macdonald (Bideford) VS Ben Owen (Bideford)

Andy Short (Bideford) VS Alex Downie (Bideford)

...ACTION IN THE RING.

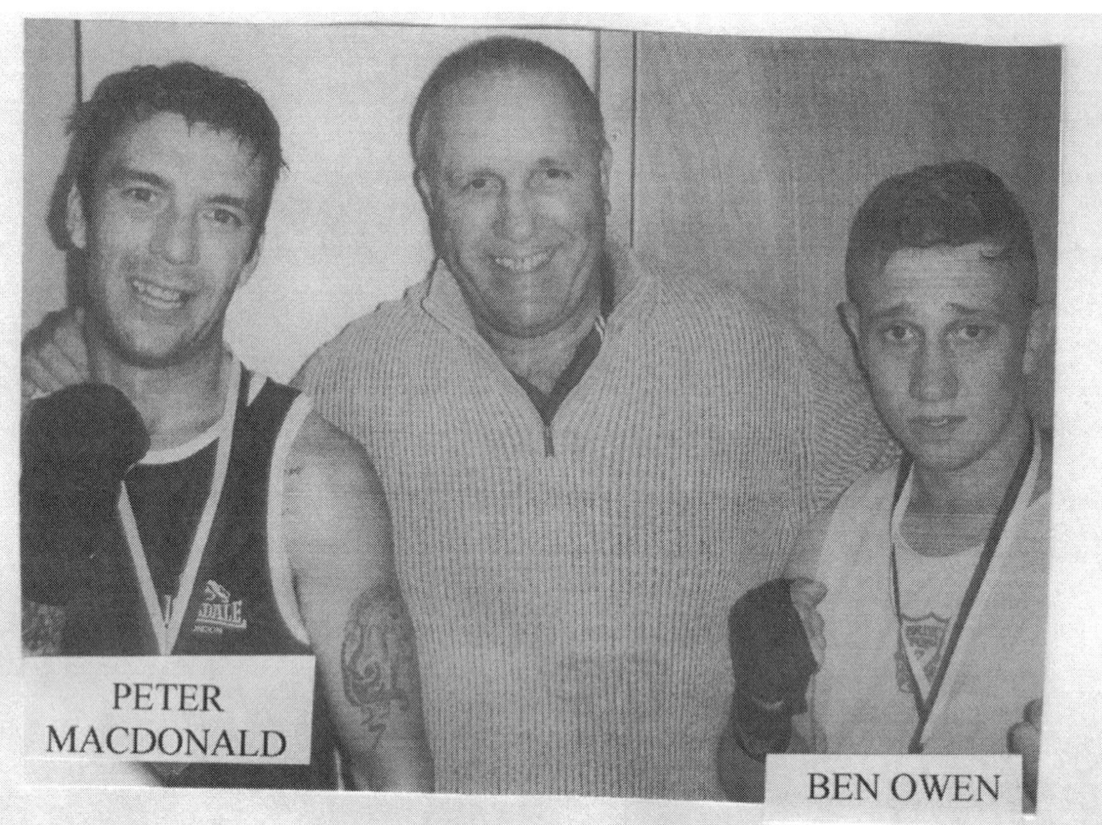

PETER MACDONALD

BEN OWEN

Former BRITISH AMATEUR HEAVY-WEIGHT BOXING CHAMPION, GLENN ADAIR presents COMMEMORATIVE MEDALS at the APPLEDORE CHARITY SHOW.

BILLY PARSONS

RYAN GUMBLEY

Wednesday, October 14, 2015 | North Devon Gazette

Bideford's Vitali is national champion

■ Aiden Vitali celebrates with coach Richard Grigg. Picture: SUBMITTED

BOXING

Bideford ABC has another national champion to add to the club's list in 15-year-old Aiden Vitali.

He became the junior national development welterweight champion following the long trip to Rotherham for the final against Joel Smith from Salisbury, Liverpool.

Vitali started in his usual quick way, cutting the ring off and working the head and body. Smith tried to box and move but continually had Vitali in his face.

In the second, the pace began to tell as Vitali continually found the target and a flurry on the ropes wobbled Smith and forced the referee to step in and give him a standing count in a dominant round.

Vitali, known for his killer instinct, went straight in for the finish, but Smith showed grit to see out the round.

Vitali kept the pace up in the last, using his feet and head movement to push Smith to the ropes then unleash with fast and hurtful flurries and several big uppercuts which saw the Bideford lad win all three rounds in a dominant display, winning gold in his first attempt at a championship.

Bideford coach Richard Grigg said: "It's a great achievement for the club and more so for Aiden.

"Since joining the club he has had the discipline in the gym and knuckled down, trained very hard and channelled his energy and aggression in the right direction, which has changed him as a person and landed him his first title in a short space of time."

Thursday October 15, 2015 **The Journal**

Vitali is a champion after first title fight

BOXING

BIDEFORD ABC have a new national champion after Aiden Vitali triumphed at the England Boxing Junior Development Championship Finals.

The 15-year-old won a unanimous points decision against Joel Smith, of Liverpool's Salisbury ABC, in Rotherham.

It was a dominant display from Vitali to win the welterweight gold in his first attempt at a championship.

■ GOLD MEDAL: Aiden Vitali with coach Richard Grigg.

Bideford coach Richard Grigg said: "It's a great achievement for the club and more so for Aiden.

"When he came to the club he was going down a bad route – drinking, smoking and getting in trouble on the streets.

"Since then he has had the discipline in the gym, knuckled down, trained very hard and channelled his energy and aggression in the right direction, which has changed him as a person and landed him his first title in a short space of time."

Vitali made his usual fast start, cutting the ring off and working the head and body.

Smith tried to box and move but continually had Vitali in his face.

In the second round, the pace began to tell as Vitali continually found the target.

A flurry on the ropes wobbled Smith and forced the referee to step in and give him a standing count. Known for a killer instinct, Vitali went straight in for the finish but Smith showed grit to see the round out.

Vitali's pace stayed high in the last round, battering Smith around the ring. The Bideford lad used his feet and head movement to push his opponent to the ropes before unleashing fast, hurtful flurries and several big uppercuts.

Vitali and Kyle England will fight for the first time since becoming national champions during Bideford's annual dinner show at the Durrant House Hotel on November 20.

England, who is returning to the ring after a break from the sport, won the England ABA Senior Novice Championships bantamweight title in 2012.

Limited tickets for the show are available from Dick Kersey on 07841 846552.

N.D.J. 28/11/2013

Stanbury in final

BOXING

BILLY STANBURY is through to the National Ambition Championships final.

The Bideford ABC member recorded a convincing win over Abdi Omar, of Earlsfield ABC, in the semi-finals at Newbury.

Stanbury, known for his all-action style, showed good movement to leave the London boxer missing the target with big shots in the early exchanges.

After edging ahead with a succession of straight punches, Stanbury went through the gears in the second round, landing combinations to head and body.

He continued to dictate in the final round and Omar, despite a wide points defeat, showed a strong chin to go the distance.

Stanbury, the only boxer from the Western Counties to reach a final, will box for the national title in Portsmouth on Saturday, December 7.

North Devon Gazette | Wednesday, December 9, 2015

Bideford boxers return with rewards

■ From left: Jacob Stevenson, Frank Blackmore and Callum Cunningham. Picture: SUBMITTED

BOXING

Bideford ABC travelled to Port Talbot for its annual visit to the Baglan Bulldogs show.

Callum Cunningham put in a career-best performance to beat Gwent boxer Jack Davies and receive the award for best visiting boxer.

Cunningham went straight out in the first round and completely dominated, scoring shots with his greater hand speed and showing impressive defensive skills.

Towards the end of the second, he went on the front foot and rallied away, nearly taking Davies out with a barrage of hooks. But Cunningham settled for a wide unanimous points victory.

Another award came Bideford's way as they featured in the bout of the night: a rematch from the show at the Durrant hotel two weeks earlier between Tom Baldwin and Nathan Bantwick.

Baldwin went on the front foot from the bell, drawing blood as he split Bantwick's nose.

In the last, both boxers showed loads of heart as they traded blows.

The tight decision this time went the way of the home boxer by split decision.

Jacob Stevenson continued his progression as he made it three wins in four weeks, this time beating George Cook of Penarth ABC.

Stevenson showed the winning mentality and made Cook miss with fast feet and step back into range with combinations catching him out. He won on a unanimous points decision.

Frank Blackmore also featured against one of the home club's boxers, Jordan Horrell.

Horrell took the first, getting through with combinations. Blackmore relaxed in the second and used his superior reach and strength in a big round.

Blackmore used his fitness in the last, landing combinations as Horrell's pace dropped to win a points decision.

WILL JAMES...another boxer who left the gym all too soon.

A very young RAY PENFOLD on his left.

Father BILL JAMES who 'did a bit' himself, outside the SILVER STREET GYM with DB.

ADAM VAN EMMENIS

CHRIS SAUNDERS

BIDEFORD BOXING CLUB PRESENTATION NIGHT.

BIDEFORD BOXING CLUB PRESENTATION NIGHT.

■ IN ACTION: Bideford's Ricky Dymond (in black) lands a punch on Joe Simpson, from Pilgrims.

■ OPPONENTS: Bideford's Jake Hatch (in black) with Billy Stanbury, from Combe Martin.

RICHARD 'DICKY' JONES
...ALL ACTION, NEVER IN A DULL FIGHT !

Bideford success at six counties

THREE Bideford boxers won through the six counties Southern Division section of the ABA Junior Championships at Broad Plains in Bristol at the weekend.

Young Ray Penfold gave a masterly display of controlled boxing to dominate his opponent throughout the three rounds and end with an 8-1 points victory.

Jack Langford and Matt van Emmenis were both given walk-overs into the next round.

Clubmate Ben Owen was unlucky, narrowly losing a great bout 8-7, while Kyle England went even closer with a draw – but losing out on the ABA 'countback' scoring system.

RICHARD GRIGG, his BOXING CAREER OVER all too soon.
Here with his SPONSOR, ALAN BLIGHT after a WINNING bout.

A young TOMMY LANGFORD

CLIVE WHITMORE

A thoughtful moment at the STEVE CLARKE GYM.

A busy corner, KEN MANLEY and TAFFY EDWARDS give instructions.

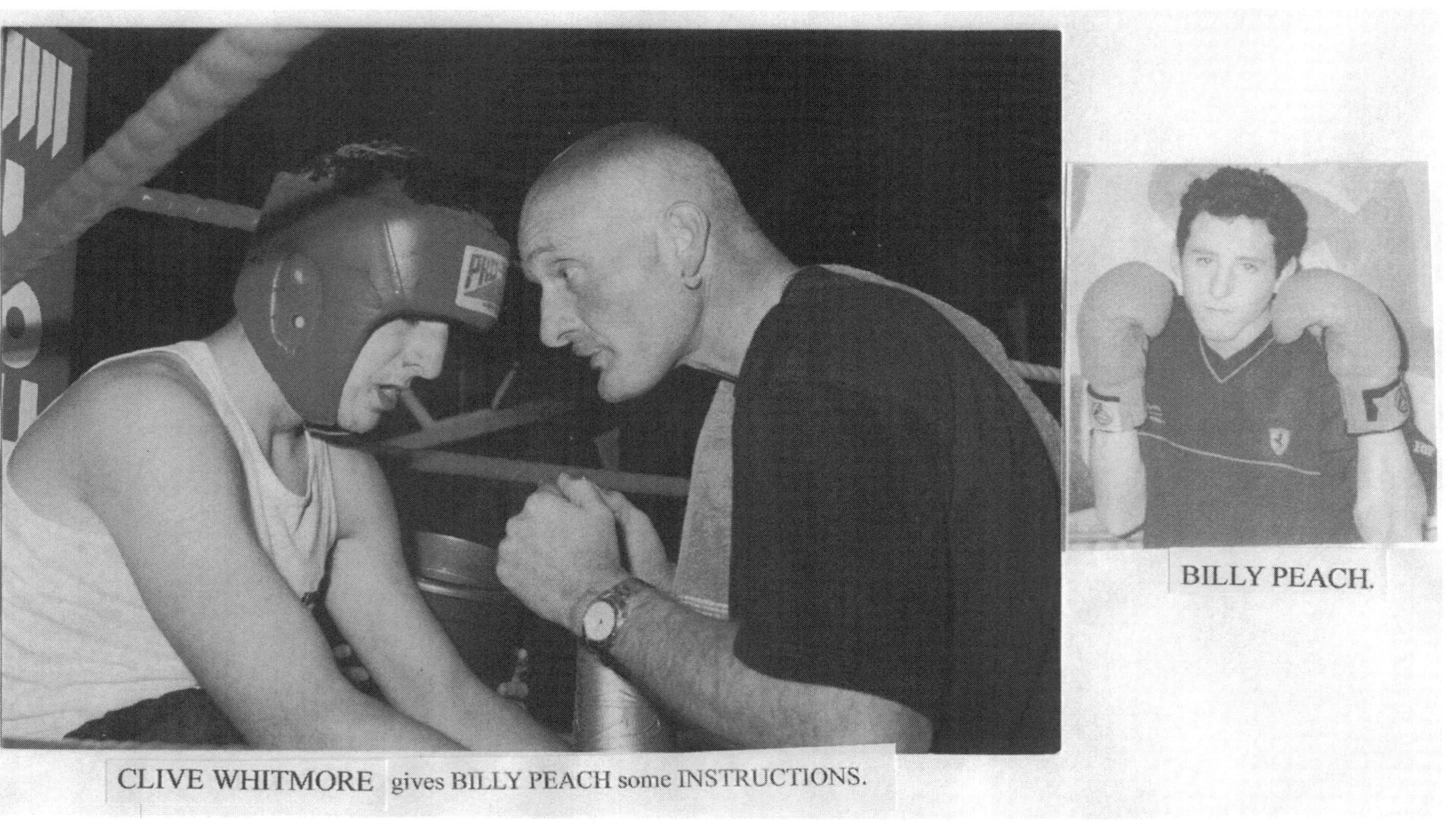

CLIVE WHITMORE gives BILLY PEACH some INSTRUCTIONS.

BILLY PEACH.

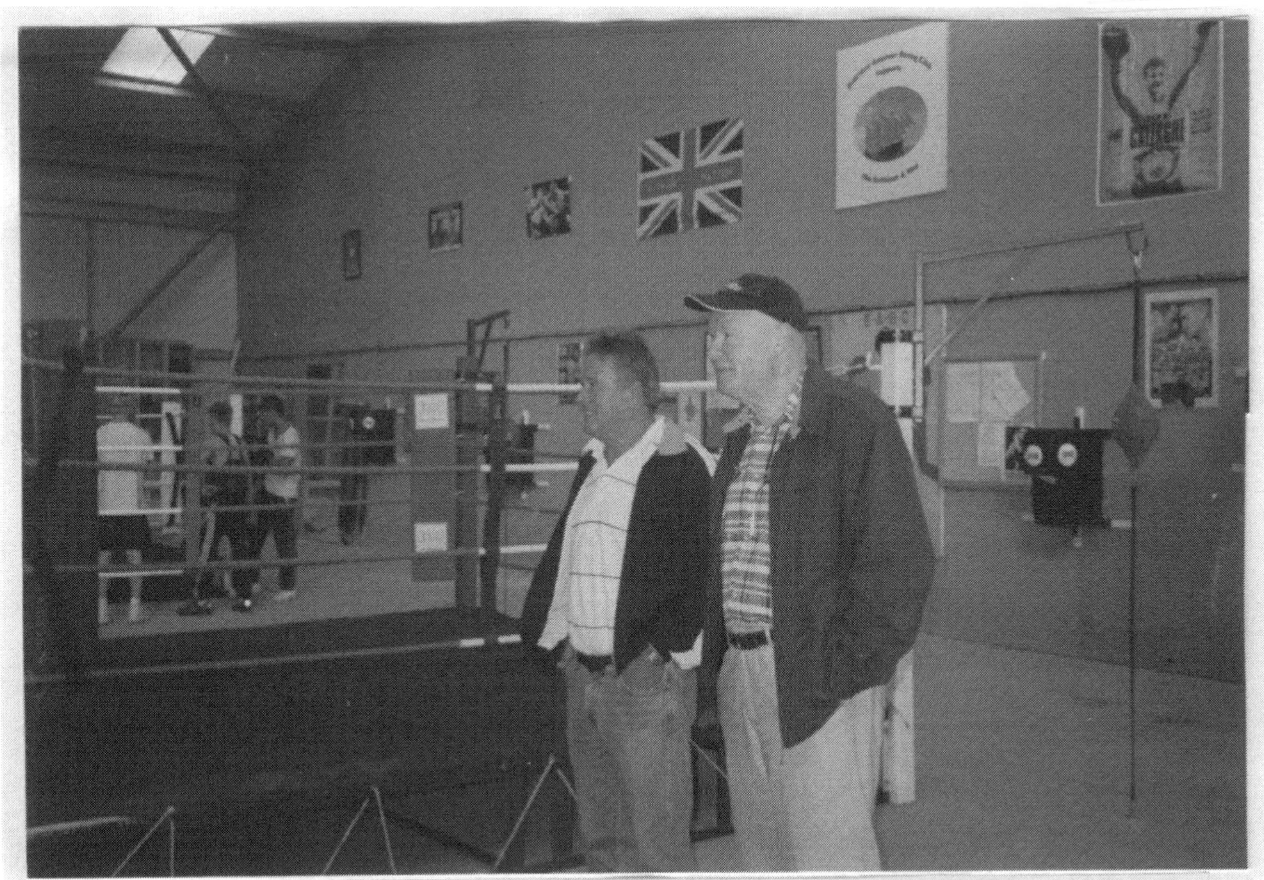

DICK KERSEY and DICK BROWNSON keep a watchful eye on training...

....DISCUSSION TIME !

SILVER STREET GYM.

Just a few identified here...from the left...
MICHAEL HIGGINS, JAMIE 'SNOWY' SHORT, CLIVE WHITMORE and far right ...trainer ROLAND 'TAFFY' EDWARDS.

MARK HICKEY

SILVER STREET, GYM.

SILVER STREET GYM.

SILVER STREET GYM.

SILVER STREET GYM.

SILVER STREET GYM.

SILVER STREET GYM.

TAFFY EDWARDS, CLIVE WHITMORE, KEN MANLEY, DICK KERSEY
and a young boxer at the SILVER STREET GYM.

SILVER STREET GYM.

SILVER STREET GYM.

SILVER STREET GYM.

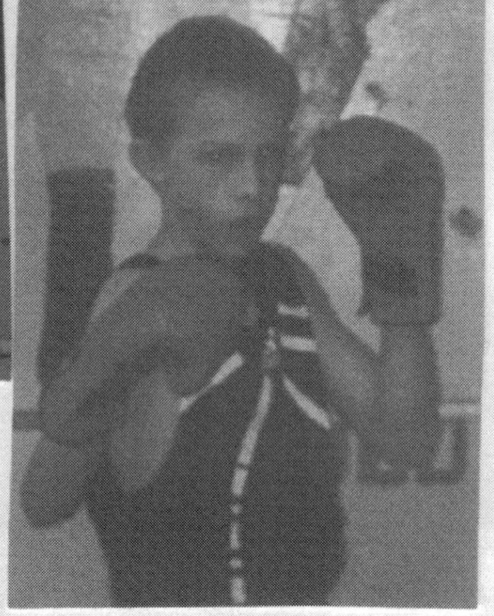

SILVER STREET GYM.

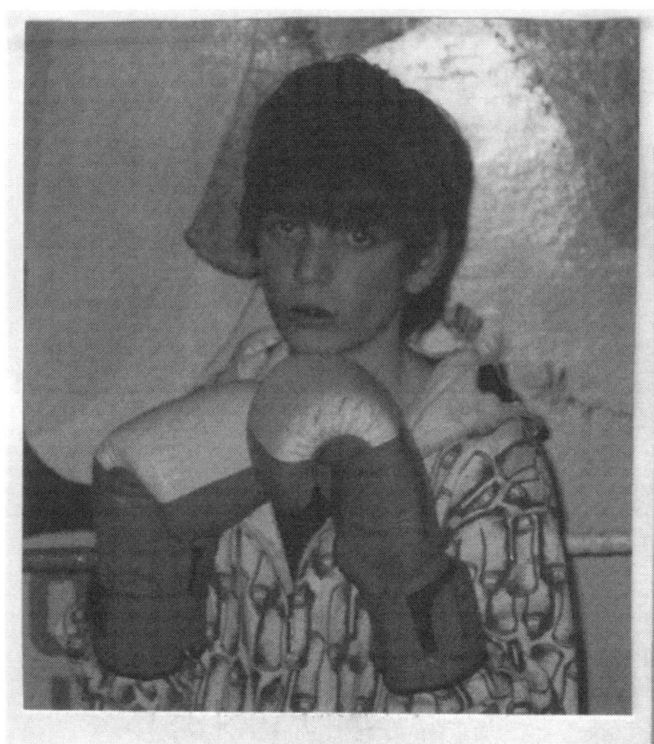

SILVER STREET GYM.

SILVER STREET GYM.

DICK KERSEY shows KINGSTON MALANGA a FEW MOVES !

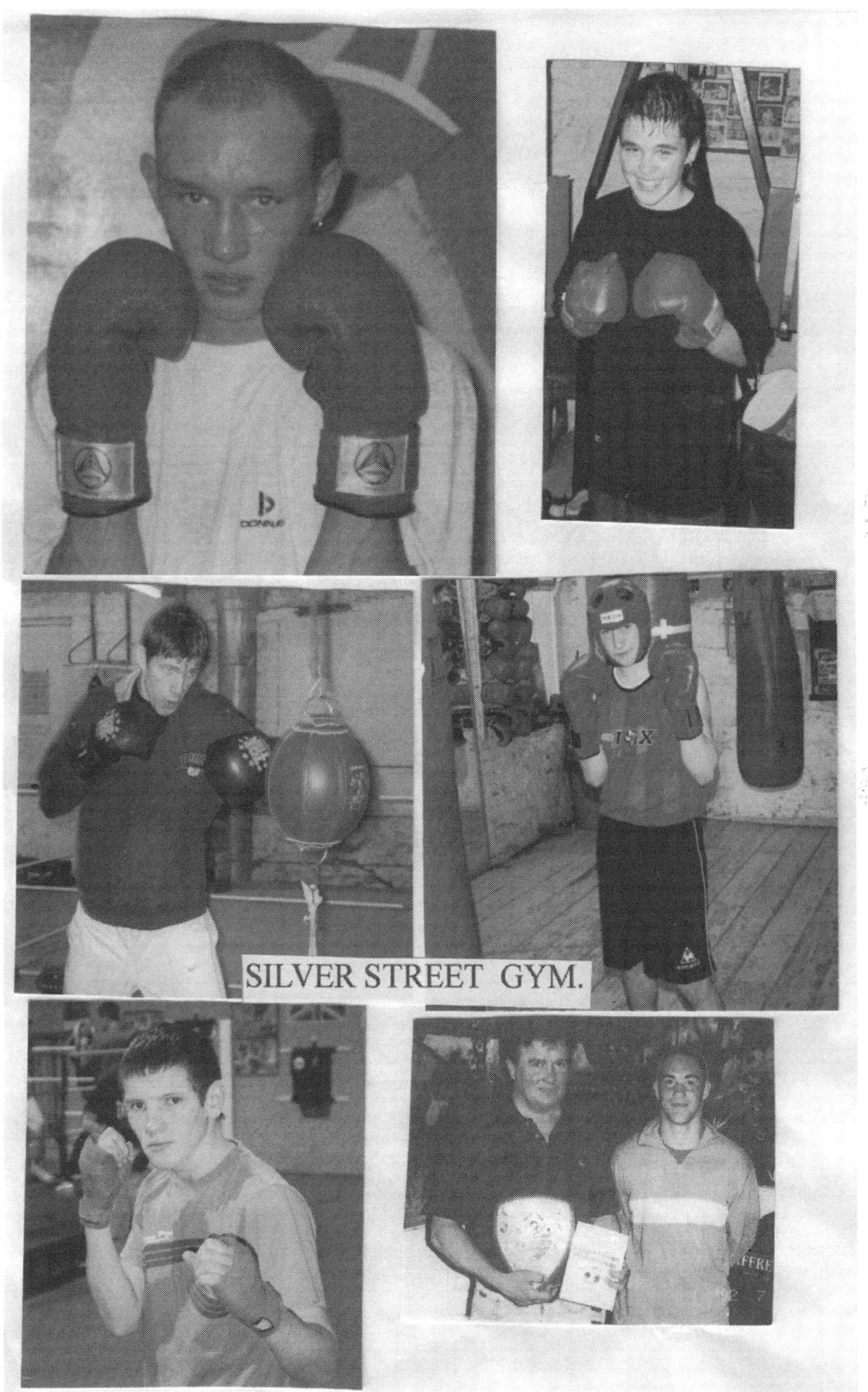

SILVER STREET GYM.

Thursday October 15, 2015 The Journal

Vitali is a champion after first title fight

BOXING

BIDEFORD ABC have a new national champion after Aiden Vitali triumphed at the England Boxing Junior Development Championship Finals.

The 15-year-old won a unanimous points decision against Joel Smith, of Liverpool's Salisbury ABC, in Rotherham.

It was a dominant display from Vitali to win the welterweight gold in his first attempt at a championship.

■ GOLD MEDAL: Aiden Vitali with coach Richard Grigg.

Bideford coach Richard Grigg said: "It's a great achievement for the club and more so for Aiden.

"When he came to the club he was going down a bad route – drinking, smoking and getting in trouble on the streets.

"Since then he has had the discipline in the gym, knuckled down, trained very hard and channelled his energy and aggression in the right direction, which has changed him as a person and landed him his first title in a short space of time."

Vitali made his usual fast start, cutting the ring off and working the head and body.

Smith tried to box and move but continually had Vitali in his face.

In the second round, the pace began to tell as Vitali continually found the target.

A flurry on the ropes wobbled Smith and forced the referee to step in and give him a standing count. Known for a killer instinct, Vitali went straight in for the finish but Smith showed grit to see the round out.

Vitali's pace stayed high in the last round, battering Smith around the ring. The Bideford lad used his feet and head movement to push his opponent to the ropes before unleashing fast, hurtful flurries and several big uppercuts.

Vitali and Kyle England will fight for the first time since becoming national champions during Bideford's annual dinner show at the Durrant House Hotel on November 20.

England, who is returning to the ring after a break from the sport, won the England ABA Senior Novice Championships bantamweight title in 2012.

Limited tickets for the show are available from Dick Kersey on 07841 846552.

N.D.J. 28/11/2013

Stanbury in final

BOXING

BILLY STANBURY is through to the National Ambition Championships final.

The Bideford ABC member recorded a convincing win over Abdi Omar, of Earlsfield ABC, in the semi-finals at Newbury.

Stanbury, known for his all-action style, showed good movement to leave the London boxer missing the target with big shots in the early exchanges.

After edging ahead with a succession of straight punches, Stanbury went through the gears in the second round, landing combinations to head and body.

He continued to dictate in the final round and Omar, despite a wide points defeat, showed a strong chin to go the distance.

Stanbury, the only boxer from the Western Counties to reach a final, will box for the national title in Portsmouth on Saturday, December 7.

JAMIE 'SNOWY' SHORT sparring at the SILVER STREET GYM.

At a CLUB SHOW, still a keen supporter of local boxing.

STEVE CLARKE GYM.

STEVE CLARKE GYM.

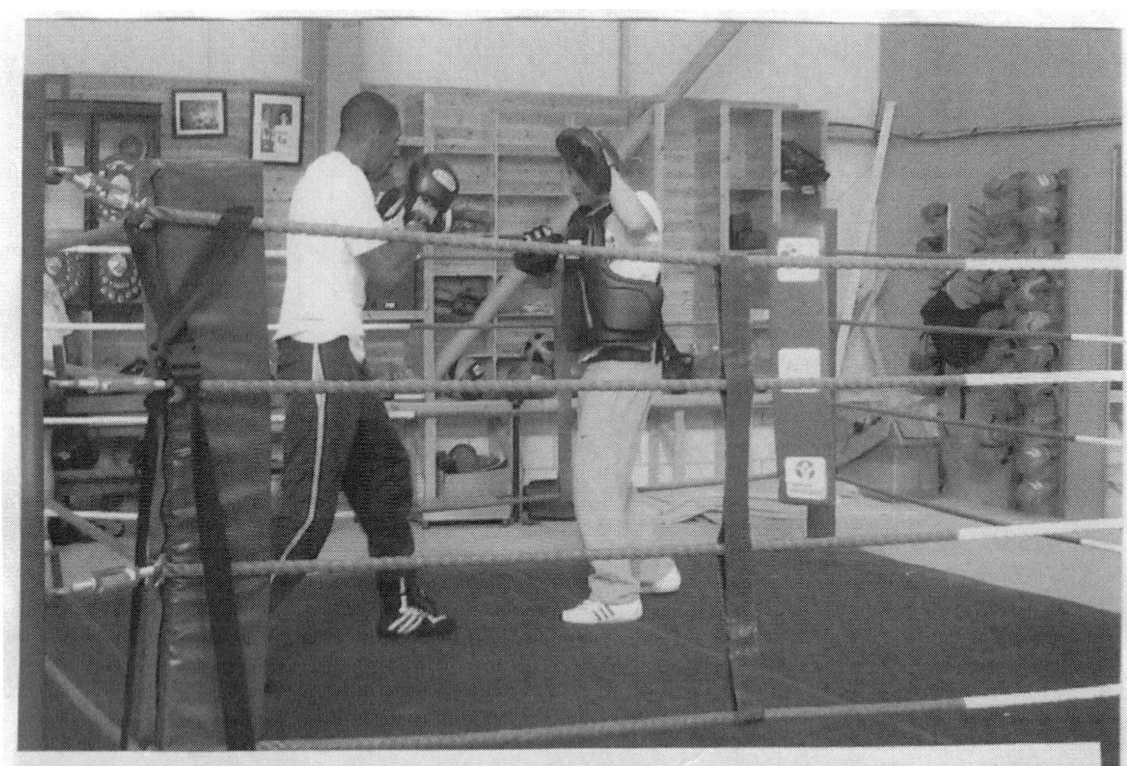

BIDEFORD ABC always made other boxing clubs welcome for training sessions.
This is the STEVE CLARKE GYM.

ROLL-CALL at the STEVE CLARKE GYM.

In the NEW GYM, courtesy of STEVE CLARKE.

JEFF FACEY, RICHARD GRIGG, DB, CLUB PRESIDENT RAY PENFOLD, DICK KERSEY, CHRIS FRIENDSHIP.

BIDEFORD and BARNSTAPLE BOXING CLUBS with a VISITING TEAM in a joint training session at the STEVE CLARKE GYM.

RON HERNIMAN in the RING, BIDEFORD PANNIER MARKET.

It was always a great pleasure to work with RON, a true professional and so sadly missed.

DB with Ron.

Thursday, October 25, 2001

BOXING DAVE PEDLER

Ron Herniman began his 50th year as the "voice of boxing" on Saturday night.

The man with the microphone has been compering tournaments all over Devon for half a century.

And he won't be handing it over just yet . . . it wasn't long ago that he bought a new dinner jacket!

Nice to see DAVE PEDLER'S name on the sheet, the doyen of all NDJ Boxing Reporters.

BIDEFORD PANNIER MARKET.

BIDEFORD PANNIER MARKET.

The facilities could hardly be called 'PLUSH' but the atmosphere made up for any shortcomings.

Some photographs from a BIDEFORD PANNIER MARKET promotion, 1990's.
Not too clear but worth viewing.

BIDEFORD PANNIER MARKET, a great venue for boxing.

BIDEFORD PANNIER MARKET.

PHIL VANSTONE,
PAST PRESIDENT of BIDEFORD ABC.
An untiring worker and organiser for the CLUB.
He gave his time and financial support to
ALL BOXING in NORTH DEVON.

...supporting PROFESSIONAL BOXING.

PHIL the SHOWMAN.

CHRISTINA VANSTONE with EDDIE
her
FRENCH BULLDOG.

Howard to be guest of honour

MERTHYR'S Howard Winstone will be the guest of honour at the Bideford Amateur Club's Boxing Tournament on January 19.

The club sent a representative, Mr. John Armstrong, to Merthyr to invite the former world champion and they are pictured together above, with one of Howard's trophies.

WINSTONE GOES WALKABOUT FOR BIDEFORD BOXERS

BIDEFORD Boxing Club, 21-years-old this year, is making a determined effort to put itself back on the Westcountry boxing map.

Eight years ago the club looked doomed when its committee resigned, but a determined coach, Bob Ellis, kept it going almost single-handed and gradually put it back on its feet.

There is now a committee of 17, which includes a husband and wife, Martin and Cherry Sainty, and the people of the town are beginning to show that they want a boxing club.

As part of its birthday celebrations, the club is staging a tournament at the Kingsley Leisure Club, Westward Ho! on January 19, when the guest of honour will be the former world featherweight champion, Howard Winstone.

He will present the trophies at the tournament, and the following day he and his wife will go on a walk-about in Bideford.

Boxers from Bideford, Exeter, Exmouth, Lympstone, Sherborne, Teignmouth, and Barnstaple will be taking part in the tournament, which starts at 8 p.m., and includes cabaret.

The club is also planning a tournament for October 20 or 27, which will see the best young boxers in Devon pitted against those from Wales.

TOP FIGHTERS AT BIDEFORD

Some of the top boxers in Devon and South Wales enter the ring at the Kingsley Leisure Club, Westward Ho, on Saturday when the county take on Merthyr Tydfil.

The tournament is being organised by Bideford Amateur Boxing Club and is being regarded as their biggest show since their match against Poland a decade ago.

The team from Wales is being brought over by former world featherweight champion Howard Winston and former Welsh flyweight title holder Donald James.

Devon will be represented by international boxers from HMS Raleigh at Plymouth and from the Royal Marine Commandoes at Lympstone as well as by local men from the Bideford and Barnstaple clubs.

At least ten bouts are scheduled, climaxed by an international class heavyweight contest.

The Bideford club, now 21-years-old, are aiming to regain their status of the 1960s under Stan Fishleigh.

From the MARTIN & CHRIS SAINTEY scrapbook.
BIDEFORD ABC

SIMON LITTLE, still looking fit!
Now running a successful scaffolding business.

Southern Division Western Counties
Junior A.B.A.

CHAMPIONSHIPS

PRESENTED BY

BIDEFORD AMATEUR BOXING CLUB

ON

SATURDAY 7TH APRIL 1979

AT THE

KINGSLEY LEISURE CLUB

WESTWARD HO!

SCALES BY COURTESY OF AVERY

BIDEFORD ABC

HELLO CHAMP. Former world featherweight champion Howard Winstone (second right) with Bideford boxers and club officials before Friday's tournament at Westward Ho.

BOXING

Weather fails to KO Bideford Club tournament

ALTHOUGH the weather failed to knock out Bideford Amateur Boxing Club's tournament at the Kingsley Leisure Centre, Westward Ho! it curtailed the programme, with two visiting clubs and many would-be spectators unable to attend.

Apart from the absence of the Plymouth Mayflower and Lympstone boxers there was a danger at one stage that the tournament would have to be cancelled because of a lack of ABA officials. Former Bideford club secretary Stan Fishleigh stepped into the breach and the tournament went ahead with 10 bouts instead of 15.

Prizes were presented by former world featherweight champion Howard Winstone, who was accompanied by the former Welsh flyweight champion Donald James.

Three of the five Bideford boxers scheduled for bouts were in action, Keith Owen winning the trophy for the best boxer of the evening with a fine performance in his junior bout against P Phillips of the Riviera Club, Torquay. Roger Piper and Robert Davies of Bideford, who were both boxing in their first competition, were both stopped.

Results: D Bovey (Riviera) bt C Dawson (Exmouth) on points; P Kingsbury (Exmouth) bt R Piper (Bideford) rsb; J Rickard (Exmouth) bt R Davies (Bideford) rsb; H Hardy (Riviera) bt C Brown (Barnstaple) pts; C Norrish (Exmouth) bt S Huxtable (Barnstaple) pts; K Owen (Bideford) bt P Phillips (Riviera) pts; D Thomas (Barnstaple) bt V Heard (Exeter) pts; A Haggar (Exeter) bt V Edgcombe (Riviera) pts; D Kendall (Riviera) bt B Hawkins (Barnstaple) pts; exhibition match — Jones (Riviera) stopped Vinnicombe (Riviera).

Bideford Boxing Club members (left to right). Robert Davis, Richard Arnold, Colin Prouse, Keith Owen and Roger Piper, who will be competing in Friday's tournament. In the foreground is their trainer Roland Edwards.

Former world featherweight champion guest at Westward Ho! tournament

Former world featherweight champion Howard Winstone will be guest of honour and will present the awards at Bideford Amateur Boxing Club's tournament at the Kingsley Leisure Centre, Westward Ho ! on Friday, which is being organised in conjunction with Devon ABA.

The Bideford club is also issuing souvenir programmes containing the life history of Howard Winstone MBE from the outset of his boxing career at the age of 10 to the achievement and five defences of the world title.

Winstone, who will be staying at Tapeley as the guest of Miss Rosamund Christie, is well known for his charitable work, particularly for young people. While in Bideford he will be visiting the boxing club's headquarters in Silver Street and will be accompanied on a walk through the town by members of the club.

Boxing

World champ Winstone at Bideford

FORMER world featherweight champion Howard Winstone is to be the guest of honour at Bideford Boxing Club's tournament at the Kingsley Leisure Centre on January 19.

Winstone, who holds the MBE for his services to the sport, will spend three days in North Devon, staying at Tapeley Park, Instow.

He will present the trophies at the tournament on Friday night and, the following morning, he and his wife plan a walk-about in Bideford to meet the townspeople and sign autographs.

Five Bideford boxers are on the tournament bill, Robbie Davis, Richard Arnold, Keith Owen, Roger Piper and Colin Prouse will all meet opponents from other Devon clubs.

The Bideford club, founded in 1958, has suffered from a lack of local interest in recent years but is now pushing forward confidently with their boxers making progress under the guidance of trainer Roland Edwards and coach Robert Ellis.

Blizzard beaters

BIDEFORD Amateur Boxing Club went ahead with its planned tournament at the Kingsley Leisure Club, Westward Ho on Friday night despite doubts right up until the last minute.

The afternoon blizzard caused immense problems, not the least the non-arrival of competitors from Plymouth and Lympstone because of road conditions.

This meant a total re-arrangement of the 15 bouts scheduled, and instead, a hastily-contrived programme of 10 bouts was substituted.

Guest of honour was former world featherweight champion Howard Winstone who presented the awards, and the ex-Welsh flyweight champion Don James was also a guest.

In the best junior contest of the night, Bideford's Keith Owen beat Phillips of the Riviera club, Torbay on points.

The two best senior bouts saw victories go to Barnstaple's D. Thomas at featherweight and Riviera's D. Kendall.

Thomas outpointed Exeter's V. Herd and Kendall edged out Barry Hawkins of Barnstaple at welterweight.

The Kingsley has been booked for two more major tournaments. On April 7, the South Western Counties junior ABA championships will be staged, and on October 28, the Pick of Devon meet Wales.

BOXING

Local youngsters in schoolboys' championships

SIX young Bideford boxers travel to Torquay this week-end to take part in the national schoolboys' boxing championships.

All members of Bideford Amateur Boxing Club, they are Keith Owen, Graham Clarke, Simon Little, Dave Keen, Paul Squires and Paul Estep.

Last week-end Paul Squires and Mike Higgins of the Bideford club competed in a tournament at Gunnislake and Dave Keen, Paul Estep and Simon Little fought at Ottery St Mary.

Higgins made a fine impression in his first bout, stopping his opponent in the opening round, while Squires won on points.

At Ottery Dave Keen stopped his opponent in the second round, Paul Estep was unlucky to lose on a split decision in his return with P Coleman of Ottery and Simon Little also lost on points.

BIDEFORD AMATEUR BOXING CLUB

present

BOXING

on

Wednesday, March 26th, 1980

at

THE PLOUGH THEATRE TORRINGTON

Featuring a combined team from

BIDEFORD and BARNSTAPLE

v.

DEVON

WEIGH-IN 6.45 p.m. BOXING COMMENCES 7.30

TICKETS at £2 and £3 available from THE PLOUGH THEATRE or

M. J. Saintey, 4, Bullgarden, Street, Bideford

BOOKING BY TELEPHONE BIDEFORD 3591

BIDEFORD ABC

Boxing club has two county champs

TWO TEENAGE members of Bideford Amateur Boxing Club at the week-end won county titles without throwing a punch.

Keith Owen (15) of Appledore was given a walk-over in his Devon schoolboys' final when his opponent came in overweight and David Keen (14) of Bideford also had a walk-over when his opponent failed to pass the medical examination.

Both boxers will now fight in the Devon and Cornwall championships at Truro a week tomorrow.

A third Bideford boxer to reach the county finals, Simon Little, lost on a majority points decision after a particularly hard-fought contest.

Continuing one of their most active seasons for many years, the Bideford club also has another five boxers in action within the space of 10 days. Graham Clarke took part at a Plymouth tournament on Wednesday night, Mike Powe boxes at Exmouth next Wednesday and on February 9 Simon Little, Paul Estep and Paul Squires all fight at Barnstaple.

INTERNATIONAL BOXING

DEVON v. WALES

Presented by Bideford Amateur Boxing Club on

SATURDAY, 20th OCTOBER

at 7.30 p.m. at the

KINGSLEY LEISURE CLUB, WESTWARD HO!

Tickets £6.50 including meal. Men only. Supporting cabaret.

Bookings and tickets available from the Kingsley Leisure Club; Rotary Kiosk, Jubilee Square, Bideford; or by telephone Bideford 3591.

BOXING

TOP AWARD IN FIRST BOUT

Taking part in his first bout ever 14-year-old Neil Lacey of Bideford not only won in convincing style at Beaminster boxing tournament at the week-end, but also took the trophy for the best boxer of the night.

One of four young boxers from the Bideford Amateur Boxing Club, Neil gave a superb display in outpointing D Connolly of Sydenhem.

The body punching of Keith Owen enabled him to gain an easy win over R Gwyther of St Aldhelms School, the referee stopping the contest in the second round.

Paul Squires gave a below-par performance and was beaten on points by D Chant of Beaminster and Peter Shortridge, who was competing in his first competition, lost on points to R Doran of Minehead.

On Monday night two more Bideford club members took part in a tournament organised by the Virginia House Boxing Club of Plymouth.

Simon Little beat D Meade on points in a particularly close contest, but Dave Keen was outpointed by F Long.

YOUNG BOXERS IMPRESS

Only one of five young Bideford boxers won his bout at the Exmouth ABA junior tournament, but all gave displays belying their lack of experience.

In only his second fight Roger Piper of Bideford gained revenge over Paul Kingsbury of Exmouth, who beat him at Westward Ho! last month.

Bideford's Colin Prouse, who is only 10, made a tremendous debut in the ring, being only narrowly defeated by a taller and much more experienced opponent in P Collins of Ottery St Mary.

Keith Owens was beaten on the narrowest of decisions by Alan Smith of Exmouth; Roger Arnold was beaten by P Coulan of Lympstone and Robert Davis lost for the second time to John Rickard of Exmouth.

Next date for local boxers is April 7 when the Bideford Club stages the South Western Counties junior ABA championships and also provides the supporting bouts.

BOXING

Three reach Devon schoolboys finals

THREE Bideford Amateur Boxing Club members have won their semi-final bouts to reach the finals of the Devon Schoolboys' Boxing championships, which are being held in Plymouth tomorrow.

Simon Little stopped his semi-final opponent K Robinson of Paignton in the first round of his semi-final at Torquay at the week-end and on the same bill his Bideford colleague Keith Owen stopped A Bowers of Paignton in the third round to also reach the finals.

Making up the trio of Bideford finalists David Keen was given a semi-final walk-over.

Three other Bideford boxers all reached the semi-final stage before being eliminated.

Paul Squires had an unlucky draw and had to fight two bouts on the same evening. After beating S Huxtable of Barnstaple in a hard-fought quarter-final he was beaten on a majority points decision by R Bowen of Torquay in the semi-final.

Paul Estep also lost on points and Graham Clarke lost when the referee stopped his bout in the opening round.

FOR A GREAT EVENING'S ENTERTAINMENT
IT'S A WINNER!

After the Knock-out response from our last Boxing Tournament we are pleased to say we are holding another at

THE PLOUGH

FORE STREET, TORRINGTON Tel 2553

Wednesday 26 March 1980

7.30 pm

BIDEFORD AMATEUR BOXING CLUB
presents

BOXING TOURNAMENT

BIDEFORD & BARNSTAPLE
v
DEVON

Tickets from The Plough — Torrington 2553 and Mr Saintey — Bideford 3591

Late Bar applied for ● Refreshments ● Doors 7 pm

★ *SEATS £2* *TIERED SEATING £3* ★

(Under ABA Rules)
ROAR

World champ helps local boxers

FORMER world featherweight boxing champion Howard Winstone is to help Bideford Amateur Boxing Club in their campaign to raise funds towards the provision of new headquarters.

On Thursday he will be attending the Kingsley Leisure Club at Westward Ho! to show films of his world title fights against Terry Spinks and Vincent Salvador and to meet visitors and sign autographs—all proceeds going to the local boxing club.

Next month he is bringing a South Wales team to Westward Ho! to meet a Devon representative side at a dinner-jacket tournament that the Bideford club is promoting at a cost of £1,250.

The Devon team will include Bideford teenager Keith Owen.

Such has been the growth of the Bideford club over the past year that from only a few boxers it now has 43 youngsters training regularly. This means even more pressure, however, on their present limited headquarters—a 39 feet square room above a paint spraying shop in Silver Street, Bideford.

Pictured during a training session are the two Torridgeside schoolboys—David Keen, 14 (right) from Bideford and Keith Owen, 15, from Appledore—who both lost in their finals in the Schoolboy Amateur Boxing Association Western Counties championships at Sherborne in Dorset at the weekend.

David had his match with Michael Walsh from the Channel Islands stopped in the second round, and Keith lost on points to Peter Leslie from Bournemouth in a closely-fought contest.

Both lads are members of the Bideford Amateur Boxing Club and both did extremely well to reach this stage.

BARNSTAPLE AMATURE BOXING CLUB

(President K. N. Abrahams Esq.)

presents

GRAND BOXING TOURNMENT

at

Braunton Road Motel

Saturday 9th. February 1980

Commencing 7-30p.m.

OFFICIALS

Official in Charge	A. French
Referees	B. Polland, V. Christian
Judges	J. Upton, R. Phillips
	J. Butson, G. Beecham
	N. Parsons, L. Wetherill
Clerk of the Scales	V. Christian
Medical Officer	Mr. D.G. Lloyd-Davies F.R.C.S.
Medical Officer's Assistant	R. Bravery
Time Keeper	G. Fogwell
M.C.	R. Herniman

OFFICIAL PROGRAMME PRICE 10p.

<u>Schoolboy</u> BOUT 1
M. Roode, Barnstaple v P. Estep, Bideford
3 x 1½

<u>Schoolboy</u> BOUT 2
D. Swain, Newton Abbot v P. Southcott, Calstock
3 x 1½

<u>Schoolboy</u> BOUT 3
H. Francis, Newton Abbot v N. Wakhem, Calstock
3 x 1½

<u>Schoolboy</u> BOUT 4
S. Huxstable, Barnstaple v P. Squires, Bideford
3 x 1½

<u>Schoolboy</u> BOUT 5
R. Tweedie, Newton Abbot v S. McArthy, Torbay
3 x 1½

<u>Junior Class B</u> BOUT 6
D. Guyler, Calstock v A. Clook, Bideford
3 x 2

<u>Junior Class A</u> BOUT 7
A. Paddon, Barnstaple v S. Little, Bideford
2 x 1½
1 x 2

<u>Middle</u> BOUT 8
H. Davie, Barnstaple v P. Draper, Exeter
3 x 2

<u>Light</u> BOUT 9
M. Sanders, Barnstaple v F. Curtis, Camborne
3 x 2

<u>Light Welter</u> BOUT 10
S. Brown, Barnstaple v E. Miles, Camborne
3 x 2

<u>Light Welter</u> BOUT 11
G. Lane, Barnstaple v S. Pedley, Torbay
3 x 2

<u>Welter</u> BOUT 12
A. N. Other v D. Johns, Camborne
3 x 2

<u>Light Welter</u>, BOUT 13
M. Ferrero, Torbay v M. James, Camborne
3 x 2

<u>Middle</u> BOUT 14
M. Griffiths, Barnstaple v A. Stout, Watchet
3 x 2

Hard hitting Barum boys win five out of seven

BARNSTAPLE'S boxers, roared on by an enthusiastic home crowd, won five of their seven bouts on the Club's Saturday bill at the Barnstaple Motel to set the seal on a night of skilful and hard-hitting entertainment.

And one of them, light welterweight Steve Brown, provided the highlight of the evening with a points win over E. Miles of Camborne in a memorable battle over three action-packed rounds.

From the first bell both men set out to dominate the fight and the result was a titanic, toe-to-toe tussle with neither prepared to give an inch.

Brown's fitness earned him the verdict as his opponent tired in the third round.

The two "local derbies" between Barum and Bideford schoolboys ended with honours even.

Simon Little's punching power persuaded the referee to stop his bout with Barnstaple's Andrew Paddon in the first round but Stephen Huxtable restored the club's pride in his return bout with Paul Squires.

Two Bideford boxers hope to take another step towards the national schoolboy championships when they fight at Sherborne on Saturday. Keith Owens and David Keen both won titles in the Devon and Cornwall finals.

Squires won their first meeting three weeks before but his rival turned the tables on Saturday with a splendid display of left hand boxing.

Mark Sanders showed his attacking intent against Camborne's T. Curtis with an immediate two-handed attack to head and body. And he maintained the pressure so powerfully that the referee stepped in half way through the first round of their lightweight bout.

Middleweight Mike Griffiths took longer to finish his bout against the experienced M. Bullay of Newton Abbot but it was a fine performance nevertheless.

He caught his man almost at will with fast jabs followed by left hooks and some well-timed right hands and with Bulley hardly getting in a good counter, the referee stepped in towards the end of the third.

Barnstaple's other winner was light welterweight Gary Lane. He outpointed S. Pedley of Torbay with a good display of boxing.

And their second defeat came when Michael Roode was beaten on points by K. McKerman of Torbay.

*** Two dates for the diary: Metropolitan Police provide the opposition for Barnstaple's next bill, a dinner/stag night on March 12; and Barnstaple and Bideford will combine their talents to take on the rest of Devon at Torrington's Plough Theatre on March 26.**

STRAIGHT SWAP. Bideford's Paul Squires of Bideford (left) takes a straight left from Stephen Huxtable of Barnstaple as he lands one of his own. Huxtable reversed a previous decision by winning a points verdict over his rival at the Barnstaple Club's bill on Saturday.

	RED		BLUE
	Junior 3 x 1½ Minutes		
1)	M. Roode (Barnstaple)	v	B. Cridge (V/H)
2)	S. Bryant (Lympstone)	v	H. Kibby (Newton Abbot)
	Senior 3 x 2 Minutes		
3)	R. Adams (V/H)	v	D. Manley (Barnstaple)
	Junior 3 x 1½ Minutes		
4)	A. Hill (Lympstone)	v	V. Birchall (Station)
	Senior 3 x 2 Minutes		
5)	S. Copp (Ford)	v	A. Bond (Dawlish)
	Junior 3 x 1½ Minutes		
6)	W. Lynch (Ford)	v	S. Little (Bideford)
7)	P. Coulam (Lympstone)	v	P. Squires (Bideford)
	Senior 3 x 2 Minutes		
8)	C. Brown (Barnstaple)	v	M. James (Camborne)
	Junior 3 x 1½ Minutes		
9)	T. Burgess (Lympstone)	v	S. Huxtable (Barnstaple)
	Senior 3 x 2 Minutes		
10)	K. Trivett (Station)	v	A. Cloke (Bideford)
11)	F. Bovey (Riviera)	v	D. Saunders (Dawlish)
12)	C. Bailey (Exeter)	v	M. Masters (Camborne)
13)	D. Johns (Camborne)	v	M. Seaward (Riviera)
14)	M. Delves (Camborne)	v	T. Haggar (Exeter)

****

Lympstone
Amateur Boxing Club

BOXING

CABARET & DANCING

EXMOUTH PAVILLION

Wednesday November 5th 1980 8pm to 1am

Guest of Honour - Alan Minter
Undisputed Champion of the World

Admission £2.00

Dave is champ!

Nineteen year old Dave Kersey, an apprentice plumber at the yard, is the 1973 featherweight champion of Devon, Dorset and Cornwall A.B.A.

He won the coveted Three Counties title at Paignton by outpointing George Georgieu, of Portland.

But it was a disappointing tournament for electrical draughtman Bob Ellis. He reached the final of the middleweight championship only to lose to another Portland boxer, C. Tozer.

The defeat left Bob bitterly disappointed. Passed fit to box by the doctor only a few hours before, he won his semi-final bout in convincing style and although slowed down slightly in the final because of a badly bruised arm, he was convinced he had done enough to win his first Three Counties title.

Dave paved the way for his championship win with a fine start, scoring points well with some penetrative attacks. The Portland boxer came back well in the last round but Dave staged such a great rally that he had his opponent almost out on his feet in the dying seconds.

Dave, who has been boxing for six years, was Devon champion at the age of 17 and he estimates that of the 50 or so bouts he has fought, he has won about 35.

Unfortunately Dave failed in his bid to add the Six Counties title to his record, his fight against Mike Lawrence (Bristol) being stopped in the first round.

Dave has no aspirations to become a professional: the ambition he would most like to achieve would be to box for his country.

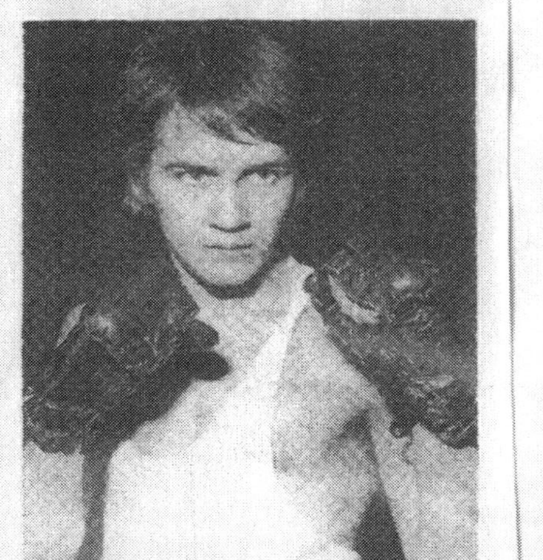

Dave Kersey

For Dave read Dick

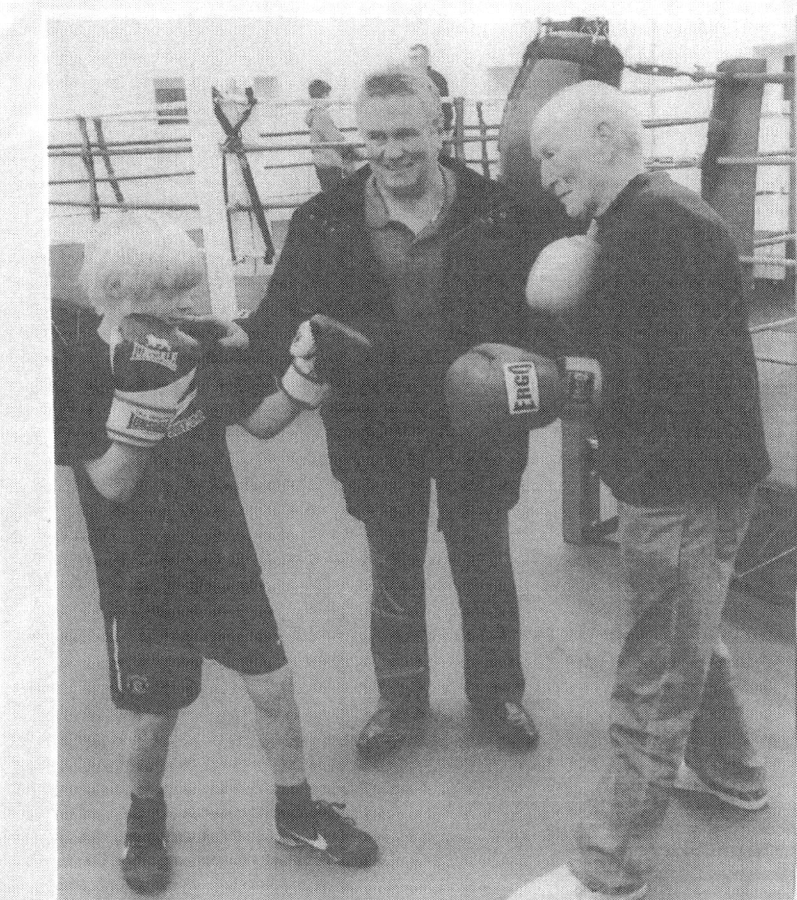

BIDEFORD ABC boss, DICK KERSEY, still at the Club 40 years later!

JACOB STEVENSON, DK, SAMMY WREY.

BIDEFORD ABC...rescued by STEVE CLARKE.
At the NEW GYM.
DICK KERSEY, DB, RICHARD GRIGG, RAY PENFOLD, CHRIS FRIENDSHIP.

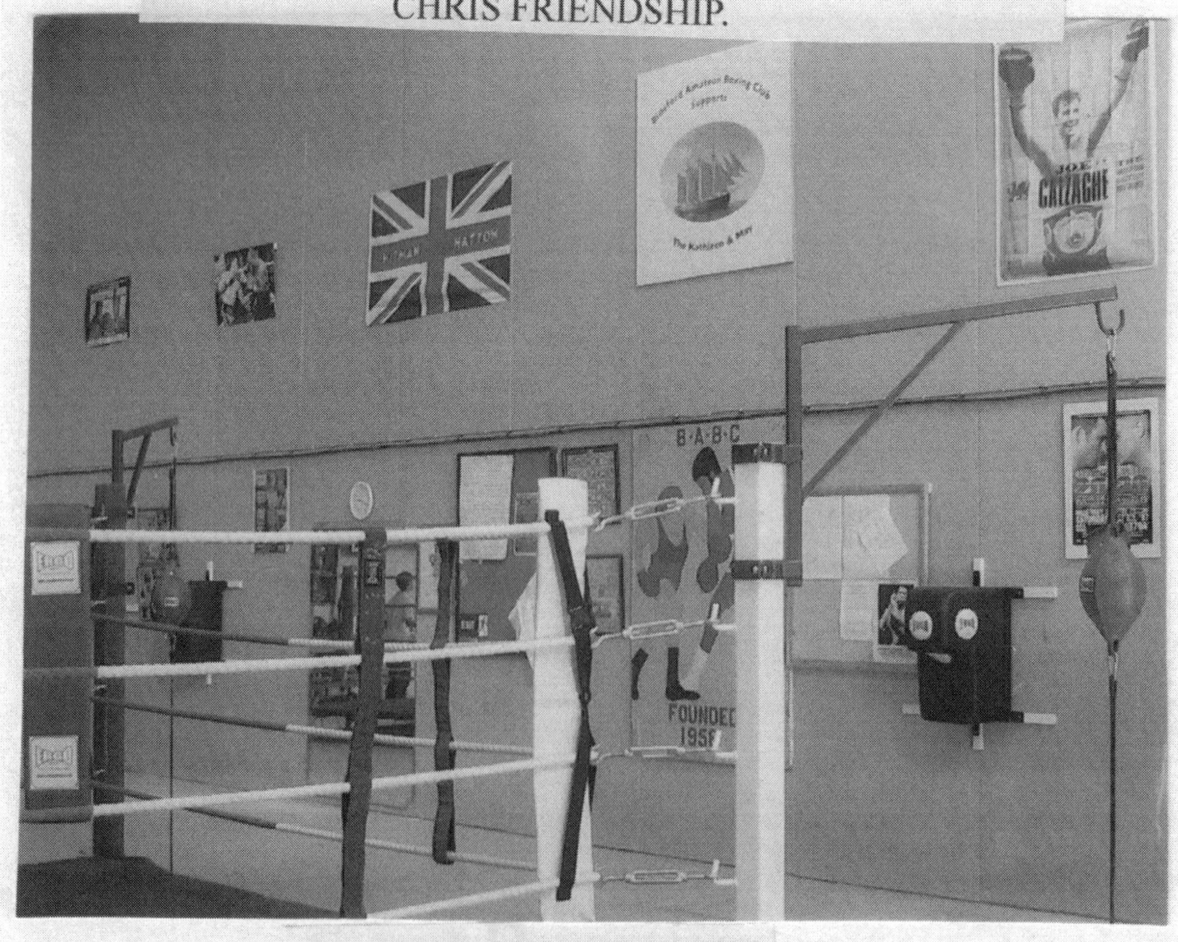

THE STEVE CLARKE GYM.

BIDEFORD ABC

MARK CARTER presents TROPHIES.

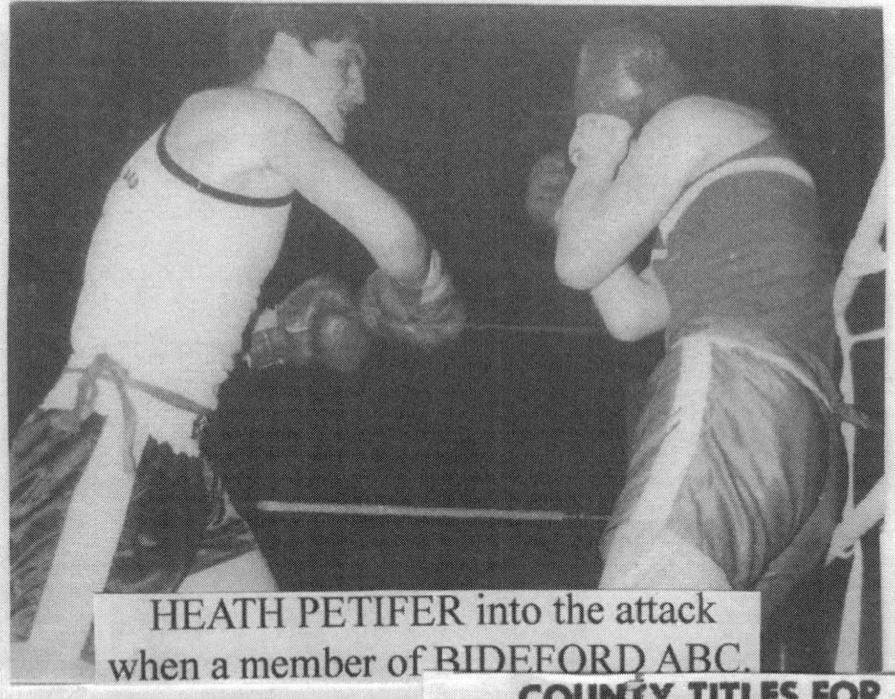

HEATH PETIFER into the attack when a member of BIDEFORD ABC.

TRIUMPHANT RETURN FOR DAVE

David Kersey, 29 year old Bideford Amateur Boxing Club member, made a triumphant return to the ring following a premature retirement eight years ago by forcing the retirement in the second round of his opponent, D Webber of Paignton, with a bad cut below the eye.

Earlier Heath Pettifer, of Bideford, had helped give the club's tournament staged at the Elizabethan Club, Westward Ho! an electrifying start when he took precisely 44 seconds to knock out F Hodge of Exmouth.

A well balanced programme of ten bouts which maintained interest throughout was clear evidence that the Bideford club is emerging successfully from its patch in the doldrums and is once more on the way to becoming a force in Westcountry boxing circles.

Eleven year old Sean Lydiate, of Bideford, lost his debut fight against the more experienced Craig Brooking of Riviera, by the slenderest of margins. Nigel Cox, also of Bideford, found the powerful punching of S Martin, of Paignton, too strong for him and had to take two compulsory counts of eight on his way to a points defeat and the referee stopped the bout after Bideford's Chris Green went down in the third against Barnstaple's Steve Cusack.

Tony Cloke, who completed the Bideford team, fully deserved his unanimous points decision against Riviera's Dave Bailey

Other results: I Gates (Combe Martin) beat D Watts (Paignton) on points; G Morrish (Riviera) beat D Dolby (Combe Martin) on points; S Farley (Combe Martin) beat Vince Jackson (Barnstaple), ko in 1min 19secs first round; and M Potter (Combe Martin) beat R Smith (Riviera) on points in a particularly fast and furious bout.

Local boxers successful

All three Bideford boxers in a Barnstaple Boxing Club tournament at the weekend stepped out of the ring as victors.

In the junior section Heath Pettifer won his bout against Yeovil's G Isaacs by a unanimous points decision.

The heavier punching of Dick Jones proved to be too much for his Barnstaple opponent V Jackson and the referee stopped the contest in the first round.

For Dick Kersey the only problems in his bout against D Savage, of Barnstaple, came in the second round when Savage started to put on the pressure, but Kersey overcame this to make it a clean sweep for the Bideford boxers.

COUNTY TITLES FOR THREE N DEVON BOXERS

THREE North Devon boxers won county titles when Holsworthy at the week-end played host to its first amateur boxing tournament in living memory.

Organised by Bideford Amateur Boxing Club in conjunction with Holsworthy Lions and Holsworthy Rotary Club the Devon novice championships consisted of a dozen bouts, including three supporting fights, featuring Bideford boxers.

Winners of county titles included 19-year-old Anthony Cloke of the Bideford club, who gained a majority points decision over C Bailey of Exeter in the light middleweight class. Anthony, who moved up a weight to compete, used his longer reach to out-jab his stocky opponent, but had to take some hard punishment in the second and third rounds before winning through.

Darren Todd of Barnstaple beat T Hutchings of Exminster in the lightweight final and Mike Potter of Combe Martin took the featherweight title in an action-packed last bout of the night against A Hill of Lymstone.

Results of the other finals were: welterweight, R Bowley (Exeter) beat A Haveran (Devonport); light heavy, S Summers (Exeter) beat R Jones (Exmouth); light welter, R Vincent (Ivybridge) beat T Jones (Riviera, Torquay).

In the supporting bouts 14-year-old Michael Higgens of Bideford won a split points decision in a particularly close bout with J Keown of Oxford YMCA and 14-year-old Heath Pettifer outpointed R Power of Wolvercote, Oxford.

Dick Jones of Bideford was also involved in a close battle with G Clarke of Wolvercote before narrowly losing his senior bout.

HOSTS TO COUNTY CHAMPIONSHIPS

Fourteen-year-old Bideford Amateur Boxing Club member Heath Pettifer hit form at the right time when he outpointed Paul Weller of the Sydenham Club at Bridgwater to record his first victory.

It was an opportune win for Heath, who will be boxing in a main supporting bout at the Elizabethan Club, Westward Ho! tomorrow night when the Bideford Club stage the Devon novice championships.

Heath boxed cleverly behind a left jab to keep out of trouble against the two-fisted hooks of an opponent who looked dangerous right up to the final bell.

Also taking part in supporting bouts tomorrow will be 11-year-old Thomas Fowler and 15-year-old Paul Estep of the Bideford club.

FIRST BOXING WINS FOR BIDEFORD BROTHERS

WITH eight out of 10 Bideford boxers recording victories and an attendance of more than 200 ensuring a good financial result, Bideford Amateur Boxing Club's combined dinner, boxing tournament and cabaret at Westward Ho! was an unqualified success.

Included among the Bideford wins was a family double for 14-year-old Paul Butler and his 12-year-old brother Andrew, who both recorded their first boxing victories in junior bouts. Unluckiest of the juniors was young Thomas Vowler, who struck his head after being bundled through the ropes and was unable to continue.

In the senior competition there was a decisive victory for Keith Owen, a former Bideford member now serving in the Royal Marines, who knocked out his opponent in the second round, while Dick Kersey continued his successful comeback with his sixth win since spending eight years out of the ring.

Anthony Cloak met his old adversary Lee Whyte of Newton Abbot and gained a points decision to hold the edge with two victories to Whyte's one.

Junior bouts: M Thomas (Honiton) bt T Vowler (Bideford) 2nd round; D Short (Bideford) bt P Dolan (St Austell) on pts; A Butler (Bideford) bt R Thorne (Honiton) on pts; P Butler (Bideford) bt M Joy (Combe Martin) on pts; K Evans (Honiton) bt R Cutler (Bideford) 1st round; H Pettifer (Bideford) bt M Doyle (Combe Martin) on pts.

Senior bouts: A Tithecott (Bideford) bt T Bearne (Newton Abbot) on pts; G Laing (Paignton) bt D Dolby (Combe Martin); D Kersey (Bideford) bt T Bulley (Torbay) on pts; K Owen (Bideford) bt D Watts (Paignton) 2nd round; P Garman (Honiton) bt A Warren (Torbay); A Cloak (Bideford) bt L Whyte (Newton Abbot) on pts.

HEATH is now a trainer at TORRINGTON POLICE ABC.

BIDEFORD AMATEUR BOXING CLUB

PRESENTS A

STAG NIGHT

DINNER BOXING CABARET

at the

ELIZABETHAN, WESTWARD HO!

on

WEDNESDAY, 3rd DECEMBER

DINNER

7.00 for 7.30 p.m.

SUIT OR DINNER JACKET ONLY

TICKETS £18.00

KNOCKOUT VALUE

Get your tickets early to avoid any disappointment

D. BROWNSON & D. KERSEY BID. 473386 – R. EDWARDS BID. 472178
P. VANSTONE BID. 475048 – M. BADCOCK BID. 477660
T. PRIDHAM & SON, 5 GRENVILLE STREET.

BIDEFORD

AMATEUR BOXING CLUB

PRESENTS

A GRAND BOXING TOURNAMENT

ON

SATURDAY 14TH MAY 1994

AT

Bideford

Pannier Market

KNOCKOUT VALUE

Admission :– £4·00 *OAP's and children under 14* £2.00

DOORS OPEN 6: 30

BOXING TO COMMENCE 7: 30

TWO BARS AND REFRESHMENTS AVAILABLE

Get Your tickets early to avoid any disappointment

THE GUEST OF HONOUR  ALAN MINTER

FORMER **-MIDDLEWEIGHT** **CHAMPION OF THE WORLD**

FROM

R Edwards Bid 472175 D Kersey Bid 473386 K Manley Bpie 22957

D Brownson Instow 860988 P Vangstone Bid 475048 M Badcock Bid 477660

AND

AT THE POLLYFIELD CENTRE, EAST THE WATER.

T.PRIDHAM & SON 5 GRENVILLE ST

BIDEFORD AMATEUR BOXING CLUB

PRESENTS

A GRAND BOXING TOURNAMENT

THE BIDEFORD PANNIER MARKET

SATURDAY 14th MAY 1994

A.B.A. OFFICIALS

Official Lucky Draw Programme No.

BIDEFORD AMATEUR BOXING CLUB

PRESENTS A

BIDEFORD SELECT TEAM v SHEFFIELD BOXING CENTRE

on SATURDAY, APRIL 24th, 1999
at BIDEFORD PANNIER MARKET

DOORS OPEN 6.30 p.m.
BOXING TO COMMENCE 7.30 p.m.

Admission £5.00
OAP's & children under14 £3.00

featuring

WILL JAMES - JOHN VANEMMENIS
STEVE BALLER - BRADLEY MUNDEN
TOMMY SIMPSON - BRIAN JURY

KNOCKOUT VALUE

BAR AND REFRESHMENTS AVAILABLE

Get your tickets early to avoid any disappointment from

DICK BROWNSON, DICK KERSEY BID. 473386 – P. VANSTONE BID. 475048
M. BADCOCK BID. 477660 and T. PRIDHAM & SON, 5 GRENVILLE STREET

BIDEFORD AMATEUR BOXING CLUB

PRESENTS A

BIDEFORD SELECT TEAM

v. BOXERS FROM

BRISTOL, SOMERSET, DORSET WILTSHIRE, HAMPSHIRE CORNWALL & DEVON

on SATURDAY, OCTOBER 30th 2004

at BIDEFORD PANNIER MARKET

DOORS OPEN 6.30 p.m.
BOXING TO
COMMENCE 7.30 p.m.

Admission £4.00
OAP's &
children under 14 £3.00

Featuring –

JOHN VAN EMMENIS - DAVE SHARKEY
TOMMY LANGFORD - JACK LANGFORD
BEN OWEN - SEAN CASSIDY-SEED
MATT VAN EMMENIS - NICK BOWES
NIC SUMMERS - STEVEN FOX
GARY ROBERTS

KNOCKOUT VALUE

BAR AND REFRESHMENTS AVAILABLE

Get your tickets early to avoid any disappointment from

DICK KERSEY, BIDEFORD 473386, DICK BROWNSON, KEITH OWEN
HEAVITREE ARMS, BIDEFORD, PATCH 'N' PARROT, BIDEFORD, LAMB INN, BIDEFORD

BIDEFORD AMATEUR BOXING CLUB

PRESENTS A

BIDEFORD SELECT TEAM

v. BOXERS FROM

SOMERSET, DORSET, WILTSHIRE, DEVON, HAMPSHIRE, CORNWALL

PLUS

JUNIOR ABA CHAMPIONSHIPS

Southern Division

on SATURDAY, 18th MARCH, 2006
at BIDEFORD PANNIER MARKET

DOORS OPEN 6.30 p.m.
BOXING TO
COMMENCE 7.30 p.m.

Admission £4.00
OAP's &
children under 14 £3.00

Featuring —

TOMMY LANGFORD
JACK LANGFORD
BEN MORRIS
MATT VAN EMMENIS
SEAN CASSIDY-SEED
JACK FRIENDSHIP

NICK BOWES
RAY PENFOLD
BEN OWEN
STEVE FOX
RICHARD GRIGG
KYLE DE-BANKS

KNOCKOUT VALUE

BAR AND REFRESHMENTS AVAILABLE

Get your tickets early to avoid disappointment from

DICK KERSEY (01237 424850), KEITH OWEN (07739 946097), JEFF FACEY (01237 420540)

or pay at the door on the night

BIDEFORD AMATEUR BOXING CLUB

PRESENTS A

BIDEFORD SELECT TEAM

v. BOXERS FROM

SOMERSET, DORSET DEVON, CORNWALL

on SATURDAY, 19th MAY, 2007

at BIDEFORD PANNIER MARKET

DOORS OPEN 6.30 p.m.
BOXING TO
COMMENCE 7.30 p.m.

Admission £5.00
OAP's &
children under 14 £3.00

Featuring —

LEE BARRY
DANIEL ASHMAN
JOSHUA MASON
RAYMOND PENFOLD
NICK BOWES
MATT VANEMMENIS

JACK LANGFORD
STEVEN FOX
THOMAS LANGFORD
KYLE DE-BANK
RICHARD GRIGG
BENJAMIN MORRIS

KNOCKOUT VALUE

BAR AND REFRESHMENTS AVAILABLE

Get your tickets early to avoid disappointment from

DICK KERSEY (01237 424850), KEITH OWEN (07739 946097), JEFF FACEY (01237 420540)

or pay at the door on the night

BIDEFORD
AMATEUR BOXING CLUB

ABA CHAMPIONSHIPS
OF THE
WESTERN COUNTIES
(Southern Division)
BOXERS FROM
CHANNEL ISLANDS
DEVON, CORNWALL
& DORSET
INCLUDING
Bideford Boxers
on SATURDAY, 29th MARCH 2008
at BIDEFORD PANNIER MARKET

DOORS OPEN 6.30 p.m.
BOXING TO
COMMENCE 7.30 p.m.

Admission £5.00
OAP's &
children under 14 £3.00

KNOCKOUT VALUE
BAR AND REFRESHMENTS AVAILABLE
Get your tickets early to avoid any disappointment from
DICK KERSEY (01237 424850), KEITH OWEN (07739 946097), JEFF FACEY (01237 420540)

BIDEFORD AMATEUR BOXING CLUB

NORTH DEVON BOXING EXTRAVAGANZA

BOXERS FROM

Bideford, Barnstaple, Combe Martin, South Molton, Tiverton & Ilfracombe

DEVON, CORNWALL AND DORSET

on SUNDAY, 28th SEPTEMBER 2008
at BIDEFORD PANNIER MARKET

DOORS OPEN 12 noon
BOXING TO COMMENCE 2.00 p.m.

Admission £5.00
OAP's & children under 14 £3.0(

KNOCKOUT VALUE

BAR AND REFRESHMENTS AVAILABLE

Get your tickets early to avoid any disappointment from

DICK KERSEY (01237 424850), RACHAEL LATTIMER (07825 502692), JEFF FACEY (07970 67190!

BIDEFORD AMATEUR BOXING CLUB

PRESENTS A

STAG NIGHT

DINNER BOXING CABARET

on

FRIDAY, 5th DECEMBER, 2008

at the

DURRANT HOUSE HOTEL, NORTHAM

BIDEFORD AMATEUR BOXING CLUB

PRESENTS A

GRAND BOXING TOURNAMENT

FEATURING THESE BIDEFORD BOXERS:

RICHARD GRIGGS
SOAN COYSH
BEN OWEN
KYLE ENGLAND
JAKE LANGDON
MATT VANEMMENIS

SAM KINSELLA
RAY PENFOLD
LEWIS CLARK
BILLY LEE
JOSH MASON
JAMES HILL-PERRIN

on SUNDAY, 11th OCTOBER 2009
at BIDEFORD PANNIER MARKET

DOORS OPEN 12.30 p.m.
BOXING TO
COMMENCE 2.00 p.m.

Admission £5.00
OAP's &
children under 14 £3.00

KNOCKOUT VALUE

BAR AND REFRESHMENTS AVAILABLE

Get your tickets early to avoid any disappointment from

DICK KERSEY (01237 424850), JEFF FACEY (07970 671909)

or pay at the door on the day

BIDEFORD
AMATEUR BOXING CLUB

PRESENTS A

SCHOOLBOY BOXING CHAMPIONSHIP

Western Counties Final

on

SUNDAY, 17th JANUARY, 2010

at

S.E.L. CLARKE

Clovelly Road Industrial Estate

DOORS OPEN 12.30 p.m.
BOXING TO
COMMENCE 1.00 p.m.

Admission £5.00
OAP's &
children under 14 £3.00

KNOCKOUT VALUE

BAR AND REFRESHMENTS AVAILABLE

Get your tickets early to avoid any disappointment from

DICK KERSEY (01237 424850), JEFF FACEY (07970 671909)

or pay at the door on the day

BIDEFORD AMATEUR BOXING CLUB

PRESENTS

SENIOR ENGLAND ABA QUARTER FINALS

WESTERN COUNTIES/LONDON

v

HOME COUNTIES & COMBINED SERVICES

plus Supporting Bouts - Bideford Boxers

on

SATURDAY, 17th APRIL, 2010

at

BIDEFORD PANNIER MARKET

DOORS OPEN 5.30 p.m BOXING TO COMMENCE 6.30 p.m. Admission £5.00

JACK LANGFORD
BEN OWEN
RAY PENFOLD
JAKE LANGDON
MATT VAN EMMENIS
SOANE COYSH
CHADE COYSH

JOSH MASON
KYLE ENGLAND
LEWIS CLARKE
JAMES HILL PERRIN
EMMA HOYLE
ROXANNE GUTTRIDGE

KNOCKOUT VALUE

BAR AND REFRESHMENTS AVAILABLE

Get your tickets early to avoid disappointment from

DICK KERSEY (01237 424850), JEFF FACEY (07970 671909)

PLEASE BOOK EARLY - LIMITED ENTRY

BIDEFORD
AMATEUR BOXING CLUB

PRESENTS A

GRAND BOXING TOURNAMENT

at the

POLLYFIELD CENTRE

on

SATURDAY, 18th FEBRUARY, 2012

Doors Open 6.30pm
BOXING COMMENCES 7.30pm

TICKETS £5.00

KNOCKOUT VALUE

Get your tickets early to avoid disappointment from

THE POLLYFIELD CENTRE

DICK KERSEY (01237 424850), JEFF FACEY (07970 671909)

BIDEFORD
AMATEUR BOXING CLUB

PRESENTS A

STAG
NIGHT

DINNER BOXING CABARET

at the

DURRANT HOUSE HOTEL, NORTHAM

on

FRIDAY, 23rd NOVEMBER, 2012

DINNER
7.00 for 7.30pm

SUIT OR DINNER JACKET ONLY

R.O.A.R.

TICKETS £30.00

KNOCKOUT VALUE

Get your tickets early to avoid disappointment from

DURRANT HOUSE HOTEL - 01237 472361

DICK KERSEY (01237 424850), JEFF FACEY (07970 671909)

Bideford Amateur Boxing Club
Presents

Grand Boxing Tournament

Bideford College

Saturday 26th April

Weigh in 6.30 pm Boxing starts 7.30

Entry Tickets only £5 Telephone

Dick Kersey 07841846552

Richard Grigg 07949770616

Jeff Facey 07970671909

Bideford Amateur Boxing Club

Proudly Presents

An Evening of Amateur Boxing

21st March 2015

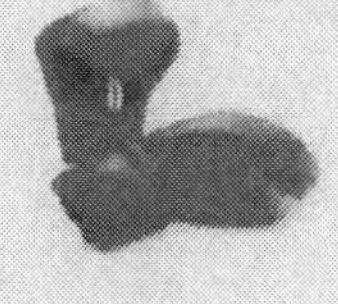

Alex Dovall

Jack Langford

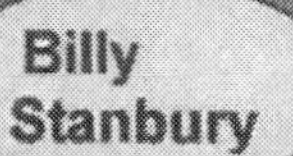

Billy Stanbury

Ebony Webber

Ben Owen

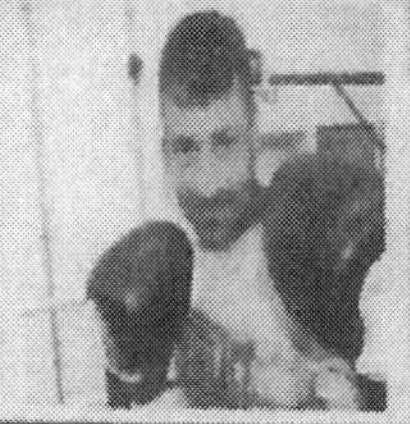

ANDY SHORT

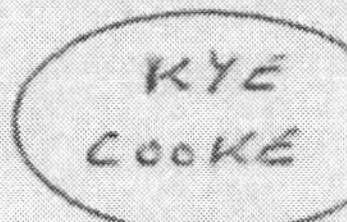

KYE COOKE

ALEX DOWNIE

Soane Coysh

FREDDIE WRIGHT

Bideford College

Tickets only £7

Doors open 6.30pm Boxing starts 7.30pm

Tickets - Tel: Dick Kersey 07841 846552, Richard Grigg 07949 770616, Jeff Facey 07970 671909 or on sale at Bideford College

Bar and Food available

Bideford Amateur Boxing Club
Thank you for your Support
and welcome Sponsors

Bideford Amateur Boxing Club

Proudly Presents

An Event of skills Boxing

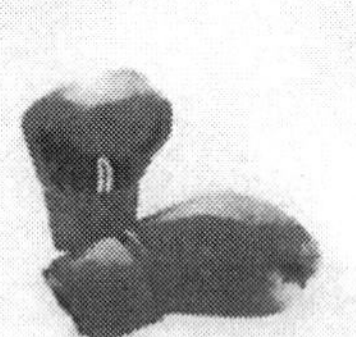

27th September 2015

Door open 1pm

Show Starts 2pm

Bideford, Barnstaple and Torrington Boxing Clubs
Together with other Devon Clubs are hosting a Fund Raising afternoon of Skills Bouts and Sparring Sessions in Aid of a North Devon Charity Appeal.

North Devon Children's Holiday Foundation.

The Charity started for the benefit and support of numerous children and families from North Devon

Raffle on the day

Bar and refreshments available

All Money raised will be given to North Devon Children's Holiday Foundation

Appledore Community Hall
(Royal British Legion Club)

Tickets - Appledore Community Hall
(Appledore Royal British Legion Club)

Tickets
Adult £5
Children £2.50

Bideford Amateur Boxing Club
Thank you for your Support
and welcome Sponsors

About the Club . . .

The Bideford and District Amateur Boxing Club came into operation on January 24th, 1958. It was formed primarily to provide the following activities for boys in the Torridge district, namely Gymnastics, Physical Training, Basket Ball, Football, and to learn the Art of Boxing. At the present time 63 boys have become members of the Club, which meets 3 times a week. Attendances vary, and on an average 20 to 30 boys attend on the main nights which are Monday and Friday. During the past week 75 boys were actively engaged in physical education. No boy is compelled to box, but does so at his own request. The Committee of this Club wholeheartedly devote their energies to the welfare of youth activities, but no organisation can exist without the support of parents, and if you have any young relatives who may be interested, please get in touch with any Committee Member.

During this present year our Boys have given a Physical Training Display, and a Junior Tournament.

Graham Fishleigh has graduated to Intermediate Class Boxing. R. Sherborne, has won the Devon County Heavyweight Championship.

I should like to thank all those members of the public who have assisted us in so many ways to provide our boys with an organisation they are all proud of. I am sure that you will agree that under the very active Presidency of Col. Birdwood and the rest of the Committee this Club deserves the support of each and every person.

H.P.P.

PANNIER MARKET, BIDEFORD

THE BIDEFORD AND DISTRICT AMATEUR YOUTH BOXING CLUB'S

President: Lt. Col. R. D. D. BIRDWOOD, M.C.

Third TOURNAMENT

THURSDAY, APRIL 30th, 1959

at 7.30 p.m.

Officials in Charge

O.I.C. J. GARDENER.

Referees: Messrs. PARSONS, RADFORD and MANSFIELD.

Judges: Messrs. HUXTABLE and POLLARD

Time Keeper: Mr. YEO.

M.C. Mr. MAYNE.

Hon. Sec.: H. P. PLANT, Esq., 13 Chudleigh Avenue, Bideford, E.

PROGRAMME - - - 6d.

PROGRAMME

OPEN CLASS

Bout No.

10 Stone 0 lb.

1 TERRY NICHOLAS, Exmouth, 6 Counties Champ. V Cpl. J. PHARE, R.E.M.E., I.S.B.A., Midlands County Champion, Army Representative

10 Stone 2 lb.

2 R. DAMERALL, Dockland Settlement, Former A.B.A. Junior Champion, 6 Counties Senior Champion V N. GILFEATHER, R.E.M.E., I.S.B.A., SCOTTISH INTERNATIONAL, Army Representative

Light Welter

3 Cpl. GEORGE GUY, R.E.M.E., Capt. England Golden Gloves and England International, Army Representative. V G. BOUSTED, Audley Park or JOHN TOOLEY Teignmouth

Light Welter

4 GRAHAM FINCH, Exeter 3 Counties or JOHN TOOLEY, Teignmouth. V Sgt. CHALMERS, R.E.M.E., Army Representative

Light Heavy

5 L/Cpl. COSH, Welsh Representative, R.E.M.E. Corps. Champion V CYRIL COWLING, Watchet, 6 Counties Champion.

11 Stone 2 lb.

6 P. HINE, S.W. District Corps Champion. V E. DANIELS, Dockland Settlement, 3 Counties Champion.

Light Middleweight

7 Cpl. NEWTON, R.A.F. Chivenor, Fighter Command Champion. V G. BRAY, Virginia House, 6 Counties Champion, A.B.A. 1 finalist.

INTERMEDIATE CLASS

Light Welter

8 G. ORR-MUNROE, London Representative R.E.M.E. V F. TOOLEY, Teignmouth.

INTERMEDIATE Continued—

9 Stone 12 lb.

9 R. WATERS, Dockland Settlement. V N. TWIGG, Belmus A.B.C. Essex

10 Stone 10 lb.

10 T. HARRIS, R.M. Commandos, Bideford Youth Boxing Club. V L/Cpl. MONKS R.E.M.E.

11 Stone

11 GRAHAM FISHLEIGH, Bideford. V ~~E. PRESCOTT~~, Barnstaple.

8 Stone 6 lbs.

12 P. KEARNS, Exeter or Cfn. LEWIS V C. BOVEY, Audley Park.

JUNIOR CLASS

13 RICHARD FISHLEIGH, Bideford V D. CLAREBULL, Exmouth.

14 ~~JOHN BLACKMORE~~, Bideford. V ~~ROGER BURRIDGE~~, Barnstaple

15 A SHERBORNE, Bideford. V F. HODGE, Exmouth

16 A. BROGAN, Bideford and Wellington College V T. WILLIAMS, Virginia House.

NOVICE CLASS

Heavy

17 R. COWAN, Dockland. V Cfn. BROOKS, R.E.M.E.

9 Stone

18 DAVID FOUND, Bideford. V P. JONES, Barnstaple.

Middle Weight

19 P. MAGRATTON, Dockland Settlement V Cfn. MILLER, R.E.M.E.

The Club wish to acknowledge the great assistance given by the Commanding Officer of No. 8 Training Battalion, R.E.M.E.

There will be an Interval for Refreshments obtainable in this Hall.

A LETTER FROM THE SECRETARY

Gentlemen,

This is the 5th Open Tournament to be held by our club. On this occasion I am sure I speak for all when I extend a hearty welcome to those Boxers who have not been to Bideford on a previous occasion and extend these greetings to the lads from all over Devon who faithfully support our efforts. I would also thank the Commanding Officer of No. 6. Btn. R.A.S.C. and Mr. Paul Howson of Robinsons of Bristol, also Flt. Lt. Rutter of the R.A.F.

It is not generally appreciated that if it were not for these gallant chaps appearing before you tonight, clubs such as ours would not be able to operate. They provide the class entertainment for your enjoyment, and as a result your support pays our rent.

I think we all appreciate the distance these boys travel after a tiring days work in order to appear on our show.

The Club is now in its 3rd year and has had a very successful season, the boys taking part in 85 contests and winning over half. We had one junior through to the Western Finals, viz. Larry Cudmoor and two 3 Counties Semi-Finalists, Eddie Prescott and Ron Sherbourne. When our youngsters have matured we shall have one of the finest sides in Devon. This ultimate goal can only be obtained by good support, which I am pleased to say we do enjoy, and the whole heartiest encouragement not only at the big open shows, but at the Novice and Junior Shows.

I would also like to thank all those people who assist us in many ways.

P. PLANT.

PANNIER MARKET, BIDEFORD

THE BIDEFORD & DISTRICT
AMATEUR YOUTH BOXING CLUB

President : Lt. Col. R. H. D. BIRDWOOD, M.C.

Fifth
TOURNAMENT

THURSDAY, 28th APRIL, 1960

at 7.30 p.m.

★

Tournament Matching and Club Secretary : P. PLANT,
Assisted by S. FISHLEIGH

A.B.A. Officials : J. A. MANSFIELD, B. POLLARD, J. MASON, C. H. PARSONS, R. PUNCHARD, J. GARDENER.

A.B.A. Officer in Charge : J. GARDENER,
Devon, Dorset and Cornwall A.B.A.

Timekeeper : T. YEO, Barnstaple.

M.C. : F. MAYNE, assisted by C. BRIGHT

Chairman : KEN WOODYATT.

PROGRAMME — SIXPENCE

PROGRAMME

OPEN

Bout 1. — Feather
R. DRAKELEY (R.A.S.C.—N.A.B.C. Champion 1956-57) v **B. HOGAN** (R.A.F.)

Bout 2. — L/Welter
J. KERR (West Scotland Champion 1955-56. R.A.S.C.) v **M. O'CONNOR** (Exmouth, A.B.A. Semi-Finalist)

Bout 3. — Welter
B. SLADE (London Federation Champion 56-57. Southern Command Champion 58-59 R.A.S.C.) v **D. DAMERELL** (Docklands, A.B.A. Semi-Finalist 6 Counties Champion.) or **K. JACKSON** (Torbay, A.B.A. Semi-finalist)

Bout 4. — Middle
J. EVANS (R.A.S.C. Champion 59-60. Army Rep. 59-60.) v **ERIC DANIELS** (A.B.A. Quarter Finalist Docklands. 6 Counties Champion.)

Bout 5. — Lt. Heavy
K. PALMER (R.A.S.C. Champion 58, 59, 60.) v **G. LAVIS** (Exmouth)

Bout 6. — Heavy
G. CHALLICE (Torbay) v **Sgt. LEWIS** (R.A.F.)

Bout 7. — Feather
R.A.S.C. (Selected) v **S.A.C. GROGAN** (R.A.F.)

Bout 8.
COLLINS R.A.S.C. or **B. MATHIAS** (Gt. Britain Youth Champion 55-56 R.A.S.C. Champion 57-58) v **D. DAMERELL** (Docklands, A.B.A. Semi-Finalist 6 Counties Champion.)

INTER

Bout 9. — Middle
T. MORGAN (R.A.F. or Bristol Rep.) v **E. PRESCOTT** (Bideford)

Bout 10. — Lt/Middle
E. C. TINGLE (R.A.S.C. Southern Command Finalist 1960. R.A.S.C. Champion 1960.) v **M. STEWART** (Bristol)

Bout 11. — Welter
R. MAY (R.A.S.C. and Sankeys) v **B. MOORE** (Virgina House)

Bout 12. — Feather
R.A.S.C. v **L. GILL** (Bristol)

Bout 13. — Lt/Welter
B. REID (R.A.S.C. and Camberwell) v **R. WATERS** (Docklands)

Bout 14. — Lightweight
BRADLEY (Bristol) v **P. JONES** (Barnstaple)

Bout 15.
GALLICHAMP (Exeter) v **L. TURNER** (Dockland.)

NOVICE

Bout 16. — L/Welter
NASH (Bristol) v **L. FISHLEIGH** (Bideford)

Bout 17. — Lightweight
B. DIMMOCK (Dockland Nov.) v **MAC HARRIS** (Bideford)

Bout 18. — L/Welter
TYTHCOTT (Barnstaple) v **O. FOUND** (Bideford)

Bout 19. — L/Welter
A. C. ROSE (R.A.F.) v **T. MILLS** (Exeter)

Reserves
G. HALLETT (Barnstaple) — **D. SHORT** (Barnstaple)

These Boxers all confirmed on 26/4/60. Subject to alteration.

A LETTER FROM THE CHAIRMAN

Ladies and Gentlemen.

It is with great pleasure that my committee welcome you to our Sixth Open Tournament, and it is our sincere hope that you will witness tonight, the class of boxing that you have enjoyed seeing on the occasions of our Five previous Tournaments.

Since our previous tournament we have unfortunately lost the services, as secretary, of Peter Plant, who owing to pressure of work has handed over to Stan Fishleigh as Tournament Secretary and to Bobbie Beckerley as Club Secretary. With such a fine combination as this I am sure our Club will continue to foster the sporting instinct for the Youth of our town.

We continue our search for suitable club premises of our own and in this connection we would appreciate the co-operation of our followers and all members of the public.

Our major item of expense is still in providing and maintaining the standard of prizes for the competitors of our tournament and although our local tradesmen and sportsmen continue to support us, any further help would be greatly appreciated.

The Ladies Committee of our Club continue to be responsible for the entire catering arrangements at our Tournament and for their outstanding efforts we say "Thank you ladies."

I would finally like to thank, publicly, the Management Committee for their unfailing and continued support. I am sure that under the continued Presidency of such an outstanding sportsman and leading personality as Councillor Lieut. Col. Birdwood, M.C., who has captained our ship since we first set sail nearly four years ago, we shall continue to provide Bideford with a first class Amateur Boxing Club.

KENNETH WOODYATT,
Chairman.

PANNIER MARKET, BIDEFORD

THE BIDEFORD & DISTRICT
AMATEUR YOUTH BOXING CLUB

President : Lt. Col. R. D D. BIRDWOOD, M.C.

Sixth
TOURNAMENT

THURSDAY 6th OCTOBER 1960

at 7.30 p.m.

★

Officials in Charge

Referees : Messrs. POLLARD, MANSFIELD and RADFORD
Judges : Messrs. GARDNER, PUNCHARD and ECKLEY
Timekeeper : Mr. T. YEO
M.Cs. : Messrs. F. MAYNE and C. BRIGHT
Tournament Secretary :
Mr. S. FISHLEIGH, "Furzeball," Alverdiscott, Bideford
Club Secretary :
Mr. R. BECKERLEY, 48 Barton Tors, Bideford

PROGRAMME — SIXPENCE

PROGRAMME

OPEN CLASS

Bout No.			
		Light Welter	
1	**D. DAMERAL** (Dockland) Former 3 Counties Champion, Schoolboy and Junior Champion	V	**Lce.-Cpl. N. GILFEATHER** (Scottish A.B.A. Welterweight Champion) R.E.M.E.
		Light Welter	
2	**J. TOOLEY** (Teignmouth) 6 Counties Light Welterweight Champion	V	**Dvr. COLLINS** R.A.S.C.
		Light Middle	
3	**R. COOKSLEY** Dockland	V	**J. MONAGHAN** R.A.S.C., I.S.B.A. Champion 1959-60
		Middle	
4	**E. DANIEL** Dockland. 6 Western Counties Champion	V	**Pt. McMILLAN** National Coal Board Champion 1959-60
		Bantam	
5	**H. CLATWORTHY** Teignmouth. Former Western Counties Flyweight Champion	V	**Dvr. J. MALLON** R.A.S.C. British Army Representative. Flyweight Champion
		Heavy	
6	**P. COPE** Kingsbridge. 3 Counties Heavyweight Champion	V	**J. WEIGHT** Virgina House. Former Plymouth City Police Force

INTERMEDIATE CLASS

		Light Middle	
7	**G. HALLETT** Barnstaple A.B.C.	V	**J. M. GIBBON** R.A.F. Mountbatten

INTERMEDIATE Continued—

		Feather	
8	**L. TURNER** Dockland	V	**Pte. VEYSI** R.A.S.C. Or Selected Opponent
		Light Middle	
9	**A. GALLAGHER** Teignmouth	V	**B. MOORE** Virginia House
		Light Middle	
10	**G. FISHLEIGH** Bideford	V	**M. LAINE** Virginia House
		Light Welter	
11	**R. WATERS** Dockland	V	**Dvr. MAY** R.A.S.C.
		Light Welter	
12	**G. TURNER** Dockland	V	**M. DIXON** Kingsbridge

NOVICE CLASS

		Light	
13	**L. HARRIS** Bideford A.B.C.	V	**J. DANN** Mayflower
14	**D. COOPER** Dockland Settlement	V	**Pte. JAMEISON** R.A.S.C. Yeovil
		Light Welter	
15	**L. FISHLEIGH** Bideford A.B.C.	V	**D. G. WILLIAMSON** R.A.F. Mountbatten
16	**D. GANDER** Dockland	V	**Dvr. REID** R.A.S.C.
		Light Middle	
17	**LESLIE JONES** Dockland	V	**Pte. FERNS** R.A.S.C.

The Club wish to acknowledge the great assistance given by the Commanding Officers of No. 8 Training Battalion, R.E.M.E., and 6th Training Battalion, Yeovil.

There will be an Interval for Refreshments obtainable in this Hall

A Letter from the Secretary

Ladies and Gentlemen,

For our Twelfth Open Tournament, the Bideford Amateur Youth Boxing Club welcome boxers from Midlands Clubs to oppose Devon boxers, and we sincerely hope their visit will be most enjoyable.

We thank all boxers present tonight for so readily accepting the invitation to appear on our programme and for their full co-operation, without which a tournament would not be possible.

We also thank Secretaries and Trainers of clubs represented this evening with a special mention to Mr. Ron. Bennett who undertook the task of arranging this selected Midland team, the officials, the Holiday Centre and all others for their co-operation in arranging this tournament.

It is a great pleasure to our Tournament Secretary to be able to invite Amateur boxers from so far afield, but he gives the credit to you, our supporters, for making this financially possible. If you will continue to give us good support he will be delighted to invite new names in Amateur boxing for your future entertainment especially now that he has made good connections throughout the country.

Last season's achievement of producing an A.B.A. semi-finalist and a National Schoolboys Champion has increased the keenness in our club, our boxing strength has increased in the junior section and they are very promising young boxers who will become excellent successors to our present seniors in seasons to come and maintain the successes which they have achieved. In the championships our boxers will strive for the highest honours.

Our President Lt.-Col. R. D. D. Birdwood, M.C. and the Committee wish you a most enjoyable evening and will look forward to seeing you again in March.

B. BECKERLEY,
Club Secretary.

HOLIDAY CENTRE, WESTWARD HO!

THE BIDEFORD AND DISTRICT
AMATEUR YOUTH BOXING CLUB

President: Lt.-Col. R. D. D. BIRDWOOD, M.C.

Twelfth
TOURNAMENT

Saturday, 23rd November, 1963

at 7-30 p.m.

Officials in Charge:

Official in Charge: A. MASON.
Clerk of Scales: K. WOODYATT.
M.O's. Asst.: L. EITELBERG.
Referees: J. COOTE, B. POLLARD.
Judges: J. .ADFORD, C. BRIGHT, K. WOODYATT, A. MASON, L. ITELBERG, R. PUNCHARD, D. COLLINGWOOD.
Timekeeper: T. YEO.
M.C's.: F. MAYNE, C. BRIGHT

Tournament Secretary:
Mr. S. FISHLEIGH, Watertown, Landcross, Bideford
Phone: Bideford 1059

Club Secretary:
Mr. B. BECKERLEY, 48, Barton Tors, Bideford.

PROGRAMME - - - SIXPENCE

A. H. Johns, Printer, Bideford, Devon.

DEVON REPRESENTATIVE TEAM v MIDLANDS CLUBS

OPEN

Bout	RED CORNER		GREEN CORNER
	Featherweight	3 x 3 min. Rounds	
1.	**D. THOMPSON** Torbay ABC (D.D.C. Finalist 1963)	v	**P. TAYLOR** Wednesfield ABC (Former Wembley Semi-Finalist)
	Lightweight	3 x 3 min. Rounds	
2.	**B. COTTAR** Mayflower ABC (Six Counties Champion 1962)	v	**T. WIMBLEDON** Swindon ABC
	Welterweight	3 x 3 min. Rounds	
3.	**J. THOMAS** St. Budeaux ABC (Western Counties Contender)	v	**J. WILBREY** Wednesfield ABC (Former Wembley Finalist)
	Heavyweight	3 x 3 min. Rounds	
4.	**A. BROGAN** Bideford ABC (Irish International 1963 Selected Eire v W. Germany & Scotland)	v	**P. DIMMICK** Mayflower ABC (D.D.C. Finalist 1963)
	Light Heavyweight	3 x 3 min. Rounds	
5.	**H. LIGHTFOOT** Devonport ABC (D.D.C. Finalist 1963)	v	**C. TRANTER** Warley ABC (Midlands Leading Lt. Heavy)
	Middleweight	3 x 3 min. Rounds	
6.	**G. FISHLEIGH** Bideford ABC (D.D.C. Finalist 1963)	v	**V. BAKER** Mitchell & Butlers ABC (Midlands Contender)
	Welterweight	3 x 3 min. Rounds	
7.	**M. DIXON** Kingsbridge ABC (D.D.C. Finalist 1963)	v	**R. TAYLOR** Mitchell & Butlers ABC (Midlands Finalist v W. Counties 1963)

INTERMEDIATE

Bout	RED CORNER		GREEN CORNER
	Lightweight	3 x 2 min. Rounds	
8.	**K. WILSON** Mayflower ABC	v	**N. BROWN** Ladywood ABC
	Featherweight	3 x 2 min. Rounds	
9.	**S. PHILLIPS** Barnstaple ABC	v	**B. FRANKLYN** Mitchell & Butlers ABC
	Bantamweight	3 x 2 min. Rounds	
10.	**D. TALL** Mayflower ABC	v	**Sgt. HALL** or **T. BURKE** R. Sigs. Swindon ABC

NOVICE

Bout	RED CORNER		GREEN CORNER
	Middleweight	3 x 2 min. Rounds	
11.	**T. SMITH** Bideford ABC	v	**A. WHITE** Austin Motors ABC

JUNIOR

3 x 1½ min. Rounds

Bout	RED CORNER		GREEN CORNER
12.	**R. ELLIS** Bideford ABC	v	**T. MORGAN** Mayflower ABC
13.	**J. SMALE** Appledore ABC	v	**T. SWIFT** Mayflower ABC

SPECIAL JUNIOR CONTEST (2 of England's best Juniors)

2 x 2 min. Rounds 1 x 1½ min. Round

Bout	RED CORNER		GREEN CORNER
14.	**A. BROOKING** Torquay ABC	v	**K. McDOWELL** Devonport ABC

SPECIAL PAPERWEIGHT BOUT

Bout	RED CORNER		GREEN CORNER
15.	**YOUNG BROWN** Bideford ABC	v	**TINY SMALE** Appledore ABC

THERE WILL BE AN INTERVAL FOR REFRESHMENTS OBTAINABLE ON THE PREMISES

PANNIER MARKET, BIDEFORD

THE BIDEFORD & DISTRICT
AMATEUR YOUTH BOXING CLUB

President: Lt. Col. R. D. D. BIRDWOOD, M.C.

Ninth
TOURNAMENT

Wednesday, 28th March, 1962

at 7.30 p.m.

Officials in Charge:

Official in Charge:	J. MANSFIELD	
Clerk of Scales:	A. MASON	
Referees and Judges:	J. RADFORD	B. POLLARD
	A. COLLINGWOOD	
Timekeeper:	T. YEO	
M.C.s:	Mr. F. MAYNE	Mr. C. BRIGHT

Tournament Secretary:
Mr. S. FISHLEIGH, Watertown, Landcross, Bideford
Phone Bideford 1059

Club Secretary:
Mr. B. BECKERLEY, 48, Barton Tors, Bideford

PROGRAMME—SIXPENCE

PROGRAMME

OPEN CLASS

Bout			
	Lightweight 3 x 2 min. Rounds		
1	D. THOMPSON Torbay A.B.C. Three Counties Featherweight Champion 1962	v.	B. COTTAR Mayflower A.B.C. Three Counties Lightweight Champion 1962
	Bantamweight 3 x 3 min. Rounds		
2	J. ISAAC Barnstaple A.B.C. Junior A.B.A. Champ. 1961	v.	R. BROAD Mayflower A.B.C. Six Counties Champion 1962
	Light Heavyweight 3 x 3 min. Rounds		
3	A. BROGAN Bideford A.B.C. Three Counties Champion	v.	M. COLEMAN Virginia House Western Counties Contender

SPECIAL CONTEST

Bout			
	Middleweight 3 x 3 min. Rounds		
4	G. FISHLEIGH Bideford A.B.C. Three Counties Finalist	v.	A. ENSOR Barnstaple

INTERMEDIATE CLASS

Bout			
	Heavyweight 3 x 3 min. Rounds		
5	J. MASON Exeter A.B.C.	v.	A. MURRAY Virginia House & R.A. Regt.
	Welterweight 3 x 2 min. Rounds		
6	D. STACEY Torbay A.B.C.	v.	A. SKINNER Virginia House A.B.C.
	Middleweight 3 x 2 min. Rounds		
7	E. PRISCOTT Bideford A.B.C.	v.	C. TURNER Exmouth A.B.C.

NOVICE CLASS

Bout			
	Bantamweight 3 x 2 min. Rounds		
8	R. BURRIDGE Barnstaple A.B.C.	v.	T. STONEMAN Torbay A.B.C.
	Middleweight 3 x 2 min. Rounds		
9	S. CRANER Appledore A.B.C.	v.	D. JARVIS Kingsbridge A.B.C.
	Bantamweight 3 x 2 min. Rounds		
10	T. SPILLER Bideford A.B.C.	v.	B. WILSHIRE Northbrook School
	Light Welterweight 3 x 2 min. Rounds		
11	B. DALTON Dockland A.B.C.	v.	A. THORNE Northbrook School

JUNIOR CLASS

2 x 2 min. and 1 x 1½ min. Rounds

Bout			
12	C. MARREN Virginia House A.B.C.	v.	D. JACKSON Torbay A.B.C.
13	R. BARTER Appledore A.B.C.	v.	R. BONNER Northbrook School
14	G. REEVES Exeter A.B.C.	v.	D. SAUNDERS Northbrook School
15	R. DRAYTON Bideford A.B.C.	v.	M. ELLIS Barnstaple A.B.C.

NO DECISION CONTEST

S. BROWN Bideford A.B.C.	v.	A. DRAYTON Bideford A.B.C.

RESERVES

G. KROLL (Exeter), D. WILLIAMS (Barnstaple), A. McDONALD (Barnstaple).

HOLIDAY CENTRE, WESTWARD HO!

THE BIDEFORD & DISTRICT
AMATEUR YOUTH BOXING CLUB

President : Lt.-Col. R. D. D. BIRDWOOD, M.C.

Fourteenth

TOURNAMENT

Saturday, 6th November, 1965

at 7.30 p.m.

Officials :

Official in Charge :	K. WOODYATT
Clerk of Scales :	A. MASON
Referees :	B. POLLARD, J. COOTE
Judges :	K. WOODYATT, A. MASON, H. EITELBERG, C. BRIGHT, W. WOOD, B. MIDDLEMISS
Timekeeper :	Mr. WINKLE
M.C. :	Mr. F. MAYNE

Tournament Secretary :
Mr. S. FISHLEIGH, Watertown, Landcross, Bideford
Phone Bideford 3059

Club Secretary :
Mr. B. BECKERLEY, 48, Barton Tors, Bideford

PROGRAMME — SIXPENCE

A Letter from the Secretary

Ladies and Gentlemen,

A year ago in this hall the first Amateur Boxing International in the South West of England was held between England and Poland. The President and Committee of this club realised it was a great undertaking but never-the-less we applied for it on behalf of you, our supporters ; we always aim for a high standard and an international for a town as big as ours is surely reaching high.

You will realise, as did the Committee, that this venture would be the most expensive ever undertaken by this club and my Committee would never have taken the risk without having absolute confidence in you, our supporters. We regret it was necessary to increase our admission prices considerably for the occasion, but you still filled this hall as you have always done and it seems you enjoyed the evening which gives us the greatest pleasure. You may like to know that this club managed to pay the bill, if only just, due entirely to your generous support. The President and Committee sincerely thank you all and are most grateful.

We have pleasure in presenting boxers from Devon and Nottingham for your entertainment this evening as they meet in sporting rivalry for an inter-county match, and we are sure the standard of boxing will be to your liking. We welcome our visitors and hope they will enjoy their short visit to our county and we trust the Devon boxers will find the same enjoyment when they visit Nottingham for the return match early in 1966.

Our Tournament Secretary organised a visit of eight Devon boxers to Eire in September and the appreciation of the audience gives every reason to expect another invitation in the future. The Devon boxers recorded two wins for the evening against a very strong Irish team, but we believe the journey, by air from Exeter to Dublin, then 80 miles from Dublin by mini-bus to the venue of the tournament, handed out greater punishment to the Devon boys than anything else. We congratulate the boxers concerned for a grand performance against these odds.

We take this opportunity to thank all the boxers, trainers, their clubs, the officials and the Management of the Holiday Centre for the part they play in making this evening possible. We thank especially Mr. Alan Smith, Secretary, Nottingham A.B.A. and our own Mr. Stan Fishleigh for the effort and time they have given to provide the bill we shall see tonight.

The President and Committee wish you all a very enjoyable evening, a pleasant journey home and hope to see you again at our next tournament.

Yours faithfully,

B. BECKERLEY.

GAZETTE PRINTING SERVICE, BIDEFORD, TEL. 2815

DEVON A.B.A. v. NOTTINGHAM A.B.A.

ALL CONTESTS 3 ROUNDS 3 MINUTES EACH ROUND

Bout

Heavyweight
1 D. CHALLICE (Torbay A.B.C.) v. J. COATES (Notts A.B.A.)

Light Heavyweight
2 E. PRESCOTT (Bideford A.B.C.) v. P. GARFOOT (Notts A.B.A.)

Middle
3 A. TYRELL (Exeter A.B.C) v. J. SMITH (Notts A.B.A.)

Middle
4 A. ENSOR (Barnstaple A.B.C.) v. M. BROWN (Notts A.B.A.)

Light Middle
5 J. BURKE (Ilfracombe A.B.C.) v. P. LANE (Notts A.B.A.)

Welter
6 W. CHOULES (Exeter A.B.C.) v. R. POLAK (Notts A.B.A.)

Light Welter
7 A. BROOKING (Torbay A.B.C.) v. T. BEARDSLEY (Notts A.B.A.)

Feather
8 J. ISAAC (Barnstaple A.B.C.) v. G. SHIELDS (Notts A.B.A.)

Bantam
9 D. TALL (Mayflower A.B.C.) v. D. POLAK (Notts A.B.A.)

	1	2	3	4	5	6	7	8	9	10	Result
Notts											Bouts
Devon											Bouts

FULL SUPPORTING CONTESTS

JUNIOR CONTESTS

2 x 2 MINUTE ROUNDS, 1 1½ MINUTE ROUND

Bout

10 R. KENWOOD (Barnstaple A.B.C.) v. T. ANDERTON (Notts A.B.A.)

11 T. MORGAN (Mayflower A.B.C.) v. G. NORRISH (Notts A.B.A.)

12 S. BROWN (Bideford A.B.C.) v. W. GILES (Mayflower A.B.C.)

SENIOR CONTESTS

3 x 2 MINUTE ROUNDS

Light Welter
13 R. ELLIS (Bideford A.B.C.) v. J. DANN (Mayflower A.B.C.)

Lightweight
14 S. PHILLIPS (Barnstaple A.B.C.) v. B. WOOD (Mayflower A.B.C.)

SPECIAL CONTEST

3 x 3 MINUTE ROUNDS

Light Heavyweight
15 D. LEWIS (Watchet A.B.C.) (Six Counties Champion, 1965) v. G. GUNN (Redruth A.B.C.) (Devon, Dorset and Cornwall Champion, 1965)

By kind permission of MR. ALAN SMITH.

THE KINGSLEY LEISURE CLUB

Proudly Present

on 19th January 1979 at 7 pm.

A BOXING TOURNAMENT

organised by

BIDEFORD AMATEUR BOXING CLUB

featuring DEVON A. B. A.

under A. B. A. rules

SUPPORTING **CABARET**

Guest of honour HOWARD WINSTONE. M.B.E.
former featherweight CHAMPION OF THE WORLD.

SOUVENIR PROGRAMME.

RED CORNER		BLUE CORNER
1. Junior Bout 2x1½mins, 1x2mins.		
D.ASPLIN Riviera	V	C.DAWSON Exmouth
2. Junior Bout 3x1½mins.		
C.PROUSE Bideford	V	A.N.OTHER
3. Junior Bout 2x1½mins, 1x2mins.		
R.ARNOLD Bideford	V	P.JONES Exmouth
4. Junior Bout 2x1½mins, 1x2mins.		
D.PIPER Bideford	V	P.KINGSBURY Exmouth
5. Junior Bout 2x1½mins, 1x2mins.		
R.DAVIS Bideford	V	J.RICKARD Exmouth
6. Junior Bout 2x1½mins, 1x2mins.		
K.OWEN Bideford	V	C.LEAK Exmouth
7. Junior Bout 3x1½mins.		
P.HALLET Barnstaple	V	T.BURGESS Lympstone
8. Junior Bout 3x1½mins.		
S.HUXTABLE Barnstaple	V	C.NORRIS Exmouth
9. Junior Bout 2x1½mins, 1x2mins.		
P.SULLIVAN Mayflower	V	T.JONES Riviera

ELLIS TROPHIES
F. C. & K.M.ELLIS

RED CORNER		BLUE CORNER
10. Welter Weight 3x2mins.		
D.KENDALL Riviera	V	S.VENNER Plymouth Mayflower
11. Light Welterweight 3x2mins.		
S.BROWN Barnstaple	V	B.SWATTON Plymouth Mayflower
12. Light Welterweight 3x2mins.		
C.BROWN Barnstaple	V	H.HARDY Riviera
13. Featherweight 3x2mins.		
D.THOMAS Barnstaple	V	V.HERD Exeter
14. Light Middleweight 3x2mins.		
S.BATES Exmouth	V	M.SMALE Plymouth Mayflower
15. Flyweight 3x2mins.		
V.EDGECOMBE Riviera	V	A.HAGGAR Exeter

This programme is subject to alteration.

OFFICIALS

Official in Charge	A.FRENCH
Referee	V.CHRISTIAN
Judges	G.BEACHAM. N.PARSONS J.HEAL. R.PHILLIPS M.BATESON. W.BRASSINGTON
Clerk of Scales	V.CHRISTIAN
Timekeeper	J.WOODLEY
Medical Officers assistant/Recorder	L.WETHERALL
Medical Officer	DR.RICHARDSON

Bideford ABC

OFFICIAL PROGRAMME
1987-88 SEASON

Support your local

AMATEUR

BOXING CLUB

SCHOOLS & JUNIORS

J. STEVENSON Bideford	v	?. HOOPER Penzance-Falmouth
R. YOUNG Plymouth Mayflower	v	C. TEMPLETON Penzance-Falmouth
T. HARNETT Bideford	v	?. DILLING Lympstone
L. MACDONALD Bideford	v	?. NEWTON Plymouth Mayflower
D. POUND Bideford	v	?. WOODWARD Lympstone
M. NEWTON/M. BRANCH Bideford	v	I. POORE Penzance-Falmouth

SENIORS

Light-Weight

T. DOWLING Bideford	v	F. TOUHY R.A.F. Chivenor

Light-Welter Weight

B. PENFOLD Penzance-Falmouth	v	C. BRYNE R.A.F. Chivenor

Welter Weight

S. HAYWARD Bideford	v	C. HUNKIN Penzance-Falmouth

Light-Welter Weight

L. PETERS R.A.F. Chivenor	v	M. CLEMO St. Austell

Light-Heavy Weight

C. GREEN Bideford	v	S. RUTHERS R.A.F. Chivenor

Light-Middle Weight

A. TITHECOTT Bideford	v	I. POORE Penzance-Falmouth

BIDEFORD AMATEUR BOXING CLUB

PRESENTS

A GRAND BOXING TOURNAMENT

Official Programme

for

1994 - 1995 Season

A.B.A. OFFICIALS

JUNIOR

1) **J. VINCENT** PLYMOUTH MAYFLOWER V **D. BURNARD** LAUNCESTON

LIGHT-WEIGHT

2) **A. PIPER** BIDEFORD V **N. BEARN** KINGSTEIGNTON

LIGHT-WEIGHT

3) **S. JAMES** BARNSTAPLE V **R. PETHERICK** DAWLISH

FEATHER-WEIGHT

4) **D. CHARNOCK** LAUNCESTON V **P. WESTLAKE** PLYMOUTH MAYFLOWER

LIGHT MIDDLE-WEIGHT

5) **S. WHITFIELD** TEIGNMOUTH V **S. WESTLAKE** PLYMOUTH MAYFLOWER

MIDDLE-WEIGHT

6) **J. SHORT** BIDEFORD V **R. MANN** TORBAY

LIGHT HEAVY-WEIGHT

7) **M. HICKEY** BIDEFORD V **B. WHITE** APOLLO

HEAVY-WEIGHT

8) **D. KEENOR** BARNSTAPLE V **J. MILLS** DEVONPORT

LIGHT MIDDLE-WEIGHT

9) **K. OWEN** BIDEFORD V **S. BUCKINGHAM** LAUNCESTON

BIDEFORD AMATEUR BOXING CLUB

PRESENTS A

GRAND BOXING TOURNAMENT

on SATURDAY, APRIL 24th, 1999
at BIDEFORD PANNIER MARKET

PROGRAMME
50p

PROGRAMME

RED		BLUE
CARL ELKINS BARNSTAPLE	v	**M. SLINGSBY** SHEFFIELD
JAMIE WESTON TORBAY	v	**DWAYNE HILL** SHEFFIELD
B. JURY BIDEFORD	v	**LUKE MOUSLEY** DEVONPORT
BRINLEY BENNELLICK BIDEFORD	v	**P. CHEWIN** SAXON
C. PARMENTER DEVONPORT	v	**D. BEAVIS** SHEFFIELD
BRETT BENNELLICK BIDEFORD	v	**L. RILEY** PLYMOUTH MAYFLOWER
D. ROBINSON TORBAY	v	**J. SMITH** SYDENHAM
B. MARSHALL DEVONPORT	v	**J. FEWKES** SHEFFIELD
BEN BENNELLICK BIDEFORD	v	**GAVIN BROOKS** PLYMOUTH MAYFLOWER
S. BALLER BIDEFORD	v	**A. REZALUDSKI** PLYMOUTH MAYFLOWER
JOHN VANEMMENIS BIDEFORD	v	**MARCUS CARROL** PAIGNTON
P. HARDCASTLE DEVONPORT	v	**T. VYSNIAUSKAS** SHEFFIELD
M. GORGIO TORBAY	v	**D. COLLIER** SYDENHAM
C. MATHEWS APPOLLO	v	**S. FRANCIS** SHEFFIELD

BIDEFORD AMATEUR BOXING CLUB

PRESENTS A

BIDEFORD SELECT TEAM
V
SHEFFIELD BOXING CENTRE

on SATURDAY, APRIL 22nd, 2000
at BIDEFORD PANNIER MARKET

DOORS OPEN 6.30 p.m.
BOXING TO COMMENCE 7.30 p.m.

Admission £4.00
OAP's & children under14 £3.00

featuring

WILL JAMES - JOHN VANEMMENIS
DAVE SHARKEY - JULIAN BRAY
DEAN COOK

KNOCKOUT VALUE

BAR AND REFRESHMENTS AVAILABLE

Get your tickets early to avoid any disappointment from

DICK BROWNSON BID. 425833 – DICK KERSEY BID. 473386
PHIL VANSTONE BID. 475048 – MICK BADCOCK BID. 477660

PROGRAMME

BRINLEY BENNELLICK BIDEFORD	**Junior Under 15** v 3 x $1^1/_2$	**WILL PERKINS** MINEHEAD
BEN DOOLEY BARNSTAPLE	**Junior Under 15** v 3 x $1^1/_2$	**AMER QUYYAN** SHEFFIELD
DEAN COOK BIDEFORD	**Junior Class A** v 3 x 2	**DAN KENNEDY** LEONIS
BILLY BANKS WATCHET	**Junior Under 15** v 3 x $1^1/_2$	**BOB MARSDEN** SHEFFIELD
BEN BENNELLICK BIDEFORD	**Junior Under 15** v 3 x $1^1/_2$	**TYRONE RIDDLE** SYDENHAM
GAVIN BROOKS MAYFLOWER	**Junior Under 15** v 3 x $1^1/_2$	**JOHN FEWKES** SHEFFIELD
BILLY BENNELLICK BIDEFORD	**Junior Class A** v 3 x 2	**NUNO ANDRADE** LEONIS
BILLY BANKS WATCHET	**Junior Under 15** v 3 x $1^1/_2$	**BOB MARSDEN** SHEFFIELD
STEVE BALLER BIDEFORD	**Junior Class A** v 3 x 2	**STEVE SUTTON** SYDENHAM
BRADLEY MUNDEN BIDEFORD	**Junior Class A** v 3 x 2	**S.P.**
TOMMY SIMPSON BIDEFORD	**Junior Class A** v 3 x 2	**CAR CARE** MAYFLOWER
CHRIS BWYE BARNSTAPLE	**Junior Class A** v 3 x 2	**LES BULPIN** LEONIS
JOHN VANEMMENIS BIDEFORD	**Junior Class B** v 3 x 2	**LES BARNES** BOURNEMOUTH
JOE MAGRATH LEONIS	**Senior** v 3 x 2	**GLEN BROWN** POOLE
WILL JAMES BIDEFORD	**Light Welter** v 3 x 2	**DAVID ENTWHISTLE** WATCHET
TONY BROWN LEONIS	**Light Middle** v 3 x 2	**REGAN DENTON** SHEFFIELD
MARK JOSLIN BARNSTAPLE	**Light Middle** v 3 x 2	**STEVE SHENTON** SHEFFIELD
KEITH OWEN BIDEFORD	**Light Middle** v 3 x 2	**MARK PLUNKETT** POOLE

BIDEFORD
AMATEUR BOXING CLUB

PRESENTS A

GRAND BOXING TOURNAMENT

on SATURDAY, 28th OCTOBER, 2000
at BIDEFORD PANNIER MARKET

PROGRAMME
50p

PROGRAMME

RED		BLUE
B. BENNILICK BIDEFORD	v	**M. SLINGSBY** SHEFFIELD
B. JURY BARNSTAPLE	v	**M. SAUNDERS** KING ALFRED
J. THOMPSON TORBAY	v	**R. HILL** SHEFFIELD
T. RIDDLE KING ALFRED	v	**A. QUYYAM** SHEFFIELD
S. ANGUS LAUNCESTON	v	**C. WILD** SHEFFIELD
R. BOARDMAN KING ALFRED	v	**J. WOODHOUSE** SHEFFIELD
A. PIPER BIDEFORD	v	**L. NORTHAM** LAUNCESTON
W. WELLER DEVONPORT	v	**J. IBBOTSON** SHEFFIELD
BEN ZARCHARKIW PHOENIX	v	**J. FEWKES** SHEFFIELD
K. BAILEY TORBAY	v	**I. KHAN** SHEFFIELD
TREVOR WAYBORN BIDEFORD	v	**NICK ALLEN** BRIDPORT
NICK KENDALL APOLLO	v	**MARTIN ELKINS** BARNSTAPLE

SOUTHERN DIV. NOVICE CHAMPIONSHIPS

Light-weight Class A

DAVE SHARILEY BIDEFORD	v **3x2 Rounds**	**SIMON KINGDOM** DEVONPORT

Light-Welterweight Class B

JOHN VANEMMENIS BIDEFORD	v **4x2 Rounds**	**TOBY FROLIC** DEVONPORT

Middle-weight Class A

MARC BLANC BARNSTAPLE	v **3x2 Rounds**	**MARK STEVENS** TRURO

BIDEFORD AMATEUR BOXING CLUB

PRESENTS A

GRAND BOXING TOURNAMENT

on SATURDAY, 20th OCTOBER, 2001
at BIDEFORD PANNIER MARKET

PROGRAMME
50p

PROGRAMME

RED		BLUE
Preliminary Bouts for		
Novice Championships		
TOMMY LANGFORD BIDEFORD	v	**CODY McGUIRE** PLY / MAYFLOWER
SAM STEVENS BIDEFORD	v	**A. CHURCHWOOD** W.B.B.
CHRIS A'LEE BIDEFORD	v	**SEAN GLYN** PHEONIX
JIMMY BRIGGS BARNSTAPLE	v	**DEAN NILS** SYDNHAM
CARL ELKINS BIDEFORD	v	**LIAM POWER** PAIGNTON
BILLY PEACH BIDEFORD	v	**MATHEW SMITH** PLY / MAYFLOWER
JACOB EGGLETON BIDEFORD	v	**CRAIG FREEWIN** W.B.B.
SEAN O'BRIAN SYDNHAM	v	**S. COOMBES** PLY / MAYFLOWER
BEN BENNILICK BIDEFORD	v	**D. ROBINSON** TORBAY
JOHN VANEMMINES BIDEFORD	v	**J. HICKS** YEOVIL / RECKSFORD
MATT ACRES BIDEFORD	v	**DOUG GEARING** TORBAY
SOUTHERN DIVISION NOVICE CHAMPIONSHIPS		
J. RUSSEL DEVONPORT	v WELTERWEIGHT	**J. STANLEY** POOLE
L. JONES DEVONPORT	v LIGHT MIDDLEWEIGHT	**V. SLUMAN** EXETER

Winner of Preliminary Bouts

BIDEFORD AMATEUR BOXING CLUB

PRESENTS A

GRAND BOXING TOURNAMENT

on SATURDAY, 19th OCTOBER, 2002
at BIDEFORD PANNIER MARKET

Relax and enjoy a drink at THE OLD COACH INN after the boxing

PROGRAMME
50p

PROGRAMME

LIAM POWERS APPOLLO v **SCOTT SELDON** EXETER
SCHOOLBOY

CHRIS A'LEE BIDEFORD v **M. WREY** W.B.B.
SCHOOLBOY

GARY TURNER BARNSTAPLE v **SHANE EASTON** DEVONPORT
JUNIOR

BILLY PEACH BIDEFORD v **JOHN HOBBS** BARNSTAPLE
JUNIOR

JOHN VANEMMINES BIDEFORD v **DES O'CONNER** DEVONPORT
LT. WELTER

JODY BRAY BIDEFORD v **P. HACKMAN** BARNSTAPLE
LT. HEAVY

LUKE WAYNE APPOLLO v **JOHN IBBOTSON** SHEEFFIELD
LT. HEAVY

GARY ROBERTS BIDEFORD v **NICKY WEIGHT** PLY / MAYFLOWER
SCHOOLBOY

AARON SELDON EXETER v **LEE PEART** DEVONPORT
SCHOOLBOY

L. ACKERS SHEFFIELD v **MATTHEW MITCHELL** PLY/MAYFLOWER
SCHOOLBOY

LEE ROBINSON TITANS v **BEN PARSONAGE** PLY/MAYFLOWER
JUNIOR

TOMMY LANGFORD BIDEFORD v **MATTHEW DENSHAM** EXETER
SCHOOLBOY

J. STANELY BARNSTAPLE v **J. WAINWRIGHT** SHEFFIELD
JUNIOR

ANGELO CROW PLY/MAYFLOWER v **LEWIS BROWNING** EXETER
SCHOOLBOY

BIDEFORD AMATEUR BOXING CLUB

PRESENTS A

GRAND BOXING TOURNAMENT

on SATURDAY, 25th OCTOBER, 2003
at BIDEFORD PANNIER MARKET

PROGRAMME
50p

PROGRAMME

Preliminaries – Class A

64-69 Kg	**ANTHONY WHITE**	PORTLAND
	BEN SMITH	POOLE
	RICKY UNDERWOOD	BODMIN
	v	
69-75 Kg	**ANDREW McGIVERN**	PORTLAND
	TOBY CREBER	TORBAY
	MARK TAYLOR	MAYFLOWER
	v	
75-81 Kg	**GORDON CHARLES**	BRIDPORT
	CRAIG BRACHER	TRURO
	DAVID NOTTLE	BODMIN
	JEREMY LANGFORD	PAIGNTON
	MARK COADE	DEVONPORT
	SCOT ROUTLEDGE	TORBAY

W.C.A.B.A. SOUTHERN AREA NOVICE CHAMPIONSHIPS

Class A

81-91 Kg **JOSEPH HARVEY** WEYMOUTH v **TERRY HINES** CAMB/RED

Class B

60-64 Kg **JAMES STANLEY** POOLE v **TREVELYAN CONYON** APOLLO

69-75 Kg **JOHN ORCHARD** POOLE v **PAUL CROKE** DEVONPORT

Supporting Bouts

BEN OWEN BIDEFORD v **MATTHEW MITCHEL** PILGRIMS

JACK LANGFORD BIDEFORD v **MATT BRADBURY** DEVONPORT

TOMMY LANGFORD BIDEFORD v **CODY McGUIRE** PILGRIMS

BILLY PEACH BIDEFORD v **MATTHEW SMITH** PILGRIMS

JOHN VANEMMINES BIDEFORD v **ROBIN FEARNLEY** TRURO

BIDEFORD
AMATEUR BOXING CLUB

PRESENTS A

GRAND BOXING TOURNAMENT

on SATURDAY, 17th APRIL, 2004
at BIDEFORD PANNIER MARKET
10th Anniversary

THANK YOU FOR YOUR SUPPORT

PROGRAMME
50p

PROGRAMME

1.	**NICK BOWES** BIDEFORD	v (Kid Gloves)	**ASHTON DONOVAN** BIDEFORD
2.	**BEN OWENS** BIDEFORD	v	**JASON BROOKER** STURMINSTER NEWTON
3.	**JIMMY CONNORS** BROAD PLAINS	v	**JASON BROOKER** HASTINGS
4.	**STEVE FOX** BIDEFORD	v	**J. LUTON** TAUNTON
5.	**BEN CHAPPLE** BARNSTAPLE	v	**J. ASHMEAD** BROAD PLAINS
6.	**MATT VANEMMINES** BIDEFORD	v	**CLAUD DELANGE** STURMINSTER NEWTON
7.	**JACK LANGFORD** BIDEFORD	v	**MATHEW MITCHEL** PILGRIMS
8.	**GARY ROBERTS** BIDEFORD	v	**CHARLIE BOSWORTH** CAMBORNE/REDRUTH
9.	**JAMIE SPATE** APPOLLO	v	**LUKE CHAPMAN** HASTINGS
10.	**LEE ROBINSON** TITANS	v	**BEN PARSONAGE** PILGRIMS
11.	**TOM LANGFORD** BIDEFORD	v	**CONROY GAYNOR** HASTINGS

Junior A.B.A. Western Counties Final

12.	**DANNY BUTLER** BROAD PLAINS	v	**NICK CURTIS** CAMBORNE/REDRUTH

13.	**G. SMITH** PILGRIMS	v	**D. BUCHANNON** HASTINGS
14.	**BILLY PEACH** BIDEFORD	v	**K. MARSHALL** W.B.B. KINGSTEIGNTON
15.	**DES O'CONNOR** DEVONPORT	v (4 x 2 Rds)	**BARRY BUCHANNON** HASTINGS
16.	**SIMON SMITH** BIDEFORD	v	**CURTIS BETTERIDGE** W.B.B. KINGSTEIGNTON
17.	**PAUL CROKE** DEVONPORT	v	**ADAM HANIVER** HASTINGS

BIDEFORD AMATEUR BOXING CLUB

PRESENTS A

GRAND BOXING TOURNAMENT

on SATURDAY, 30th OCTOBER, 2004
at BIDEFORD PANNIER MARKET

THANK YOU FOR YOUR SUPPORT

PROGRAMME
50p

PROGRAMME

1.	**RAY PENFOLD** BIDEFORD	v	**ALEX KELSALL** SPUR / LYMPSTONE
2.	**NICK BOWES** BIDEFORD	v	**SHAUN HUGHES** STURMINSTER / NEWTON
3.	**BEN CHAPPEL** BARNSTAPLE	v	**GLEN DELANGE** STURMINSTER / NEWTON
4.	**BEN OWEN** BIDEFORD	v	**DEAN GARDENER** KING ALFRED
5.	**MATT VANEMMINES** BIDEFORD	v	**CLAUD DELANGE** STURMINSTER / NEWTON
6.	**JIMMY RANDEL** BARNSTAPLE	v	**TRYSTEN KELSALL** SPUR / LYMPSTONE
7.	**JACK LANGFORD** BIDEFORD	v	**MATTHEW MITCHELL** PILGRIMS
8.	**CARL WINDSOR** BARNSTAPLE	v	**RICKY CROSS** KING ALFRED
9.	**GARY ROBERTS** BIDEFORD	v	**MICHAEL DONAHOUGH** STURMINSTER / NEWTON
10.	**TOM LANGFORD** BIDEFORD	v	**LEWIS BROWNING** EXETER
11.	**CODY McGUIRE** PILGRIMS	v	**TOM KNIGHT** LYMPSTONE
12.	**LEE MAYNE** EXETER	v	**ADAM PIERCE** PILGRIMS
13.	**BILLY PEACH** BARNSTAPLE	v	**ROBBIN GAMMON** CAMBORNE / REDRUTH
14.	**JOHN VANEMMINES** BIDEFORD	v	**DESSIE O'CONNOR** DEVONPORT

BIDEFORD
AMATEUR BOXING CLUB

PRESENTS A

GRAND BOXING TOURNAMENT

on SATURDAY, 16th APRIL, 2005
at BIDEFORD PANNIER MARKET

THANK YOU FOR YOUR SUPPORT

PROGRAMME
50p

PROGRAMME

RAY PENFOLD BIDEFORD	v	**ADAM WINFIELD** STURMINSTER / NEWTON
NICK BOWES BIDEFORD	v	**RYAN MORRIS** KING ALFREDS
NICCO FAASSEN BARNSTAPLE	v	**JOE OSGOOD** KING ALFREDS
BEN OWEN BIDEFORD	v	**BARRY DANN** PILGRIMS
T. HAMMET BARNSTAPLE	v	**JAMIE QUIN** PILGRIMS
JACK LANGFORD BIDEFORD	v	**GLEN DELANGE** STURMINSTER / NEWTON
GARY ROBERTS BIDEFORD	v	**MIKE DONAHOUGH** STURMINSTER / NEWTON
DAN SQUIRES BARNSTAPLE	v	**SCOTT GREY** KING ALFREDS
BEN MORRISH BIDEFORD	v	**DANNY NEIL** NEWTON ABBOT
JAMIE CREEK BARNSTAPLE	v	**LUKE LAURIE** PILGRIMS
JOHN LUTLEY DEVONPORT	v	**A. PIERCE** PILGRIMS
RICHARD GRIGGS BIDEFORD	v	**J. PRESTON** DEVONPORT

BIDEFORD
AMATEUR BOXING CLUB

PRESENTS A

STAG NIGHT

DINNER BOXING CABARET

Special Guest

SCOTT DANN

British Middleweight Champion

PROGRAMME

Red Corner		Blue Corner
NICK BOWES BIDEFORD	v	**JOSH BEST** BLANDFORD
RAY PENFOLD BIDEFORD	v	**ADAM WINFORD** STURMINSTER NEWTON
MATT VANEMMINES BIDEFORD	v	**SEAN HUGHES** BLANDFORD
BEN OWEN BIDEFORD	v	**TRYSTEN KELSO-SPUR** LYMPSTONE
JACK LANGFORD BIDEFORD	v	**DANNY BENHAM** BLANDFORD
GARY ROBERTS BIDEFORD	v	**DANNY RIGG** STURMINSTER NEWTON
SEAN CASSIDY-SEAD BIDEFORD	v	**LUKE MOUSLEY** DEVONPORT
KYLE DE-BANKS BIDEFORD	v	**SAM BEARD** BARNSTAPLE
BEN MORRISH BIDEFORD	v	**SCOTT ROSE** STURMINSTER NEWTON
JAMIE CREEK BARNSTAPLE	v	**STEVE WILSON** PILGRIMS
RICHARD GRIGG BIDEFORD	v	**TOM KNIGHT** LYMPSTONE
JOHN VANEMMINES BIDEFORD	v	**BEN MORRISH** PILGRIMS

BIDEFORD
AMATEUR BOXING CLUB

PRESENTS A

STAG NIGHT

DINNER BOXING CABARET

on

FRIDAY, 1st DECEMBER, 2006

at the

DURRANT HOUSE HOTEL, NORTHAM

PROGRAMME

Red Corner		Blue Corner
SKILLS BOUT		
JOSH MASON	v	**MICHAEL COMPTON**
BIDEFORD		STURMINSTER / NEWTON
DANIEL ASHMAN	v	**LEE GREEN**
BIDEFORD		EXMOUTH
MATT VANEMMINES	v	**GEORGE BEVERAGE**
BIDEFORD		BARNSTAPLE
RAY PENFOLD	v	**ADAM WINFIELD**
BIDEFORD		STURMINSTER / NEWTON
BEN OWEN	v	**MATT MITCHELL**
BIDEFORD		PILGRIMS
JACK LANGFORD	v	**DANNY BENHAM**
BIDEFORD		BLANDFORD
JOE KERNER	v	**L. COUTS**
BARNSTAPLE		PILGRIMS
STEVE GALLIENNE	v	**SEAN HOPTE**
BIDEFORD		STURMINSTER / NEWTON
ADAM VANEMMINES	v	**RYAN BROWNING**
BIDEFORD		EXETER
KYLE DE-BANKS	v	**MARTIN MYLTON**
BIDEFORD		LYMPSTONE
RICHARD GRIGG	v	**J. SKINNER**
BIDEFORD		EXMOUTH
TOMMY LANGFORD	v	**DEAN MILLS**
BIDEFORD		SYDENHAM

BIDEFORD AMATEUR BOXING CLUB

PRESENTS A

GRAND BOXING TOURNAMENT

on SATURDAY, 19th MAY, 2007 at BIDEFORD PANNIER MARKET

THANK YOU FOR YOUR SUPPORT

PROGRAMME £1.00

PROGRAMME

BARRY LEE BIDEFORD	v	**JAZZ KELMAN** DEVONPORT
DANIEL ASHMAN BIDEFORD	v	**JACK TAYLOR** BARNSTAPLE
JOSH MASON BIDEFORD	v	**CONNOR WEBB** DEVONPORT
NICK BOWES BIDEFORD	v	**BEN ROOK** APOLLO
MATT VANEMMENIS BIDEFORD	v	**GEORGE BEVERAGE** BARNSTAPLE
RAY PENFOLD BIDEFORD	v	**CAMERON LYNCH** BLANDFORD
JULIAN McALISTER BIDEFORD	v	**BILLY MOUSELY** DEVONPORT
TOMMY HAMMET BARNSTAPLE	v	**ADAM LAWES** BLANDFORD

STEVE FOX BIDEFORD	v	**TOBIN FOOTE** DEVONPORT
MATT MITCHELL PILGRIMS	v	**DANNY BENHAM** BLANDFORD
JACK LANGFORD BIDEFORD	v	**GLEN DELANOE** STURMINSTER / NEWTON
SOANE COYSH BIDEFORD	v	**JORDAN PLATT** LAUNCESTON
BEN MORRISH BIDEFORD	v	**BYRYN HEYWOOD** BARNSTAPLE
KYLE DE BANKS BIDEFORD	v	**DAVE WELSH** PILGRIMS
RICHARD GRIGGS BIDEFORD	v	**JAMIE SPENCER** PLYMOUTH/MAYFLOWER

BIDEFORD AMATEUR BOXING CLUB

PRESENTS

ABA CHAMPIONSHIPS OF THE WESTERN COUNTIES

(Southern Division)

on SATURDAY, 29th MARCH, 2008
at BIDEFORD PANNIER MARKET

THANK YOU FOR YOUR SUPPORT

PROGRAMME
£1.00

PROGRAMME

Red Corner		Blue Corner
	3 x 2	
JACK LANGFORD BIDEFORD	v	**RICKY PIPE** GOSPORT
Southern Division Final – (64kg-69kg)		
FAHEEM KHAN KINGSTEIGNTON	v 4 x 2	**RICKY UNDERWOOD** BODMIN
Southern Division Final – (67kg-75kg)		
LUKE WAYNE APPOLLO	v 4 x 2	**TONY COLES** CAMBORNE / REDRUTH
	3 x 2	
SOAME COYSH BIDEFORD	v	**DALE PALMER** BARNSTAPLE
	3 x 2	
WILL DEACON BIDEFORD	v	**KEITH JEANS** LYMPSTONE
	3 x 2	
CHADE COYSH BIDEFORD	v	**RICHARD INGLE** CAMBORNE / REDRUTH
	3 x 2	
STEVE FIDDY BIDEFORD	v	**JONATHAN COX** WELLS
	3 x 2	
KYLE DE-BANKS BIDEFORD	v	**ROSS CHARD** LAUNCESTON

Red Corner		Blue Corner
	3 x $1^{1/2}$	
DANIEL ASHMAN BIDEFORD	v	**JACK TAYLOR** BARNSTAPLE
	3 x $1^{1/2}$	
JOSH MASON BIDEFORD	v	**ZACK PATCHING** BODMIN
	3 x $1^{1/2}$	
RAY PENFOLD BIDEFORD	v	**LEWIS BREMNER** WELLS
	3 x 2	
MATT VANEMMENIS BIDEFORD	v	**CARL CONNOR** LYMPSTONE
	3 x 2	
BEN OWEN BIDEFORD	v	**BRANDON PAULS** NEWQUAY
	3 x 2	
STEVE FOX BIDEFORD	v	**LUKE WILLIS** GOSPORT
Southern Division Final – (57kg-60kg)		
JAMIE SPEIGHT APPOLLO	v 4 x 2	**BEN ZACHARKIW** PILGRIMS
Southern Division Final – (60kg-64kg)		
JAMIE EDDY DEVONPORT	v 4 x 2	**TOM WATSON** BOURNEMOUTH

BIDEFORD
AMATEUR BOXING CLUB

PRESENTS A

NORTH DEVON BOXING EXTRAVAGANZA

on SUNDAY, 28th SEPTEMBER, 2008
at BIDEFORD PANNIER MARKET

THANK YOU FOR YOUR SUPPORT

PROGRAMME
£1.00

PROGRAMME

Red Corner		Blue Corner
LEWIS CLARK BIDEFORD	v	**COREY WESTBROOKE** TIVERTON
DAN HEARSAY COMBE MARTIN	v	**KAI AVERY** TIVVY S. MOLTON
JAKE ENGLAND BIDEFORD	v	**SAM PERKINS** TIVERTON
BILLY LEE BIDEFORD	v	**BILLY WATSON** STURMINSTER / NEWTON
CALLUM DOVELL COMBE MARTIN	v	**TOYGA KEKELLI** TIVERTON
EDDIE SHIELS TIVVY S. MOLTON	v	**SCOTT HOSEA** TIVERTON
MATT VANEMMENIS BIDEFORD	v	**DANNY WATERS** ILFRACOMBE
DAVE QUINN BIDEFORD	v	**RYAN FISHER** BODMIN
RAY PENFOLD BIDEFORD	v	**CHRIS ADAWAY** MAYFLOWER
JAKE LANGDON BIDEFORD	v	**DANNY WILSON** MINEHEAD
BEN OWEN BIDEFORD	v	**FION OMERA** STURMINSTER / NEWTON

Red Corner		Blue Corner
	LIGHT WELTERWEIGHT	
CHADE COYSH BIDEFORD	v	**KIEREN WELSH** TORBAY
	WELTERWEIGHT	
TOMMY HERD COMBE MARTIN	v	**KEITH JEANS** LYMPSTONE
	HEAVYWEIGHT	
STEVE FIDDY BIDEFORD	v	**ROB GUPPY** TIVERTON
	LIGHT WELTERWEIGHT	
GOANE COYSH BIDEFORD	v	**ROSS BURT** MAYFLOWER
	HEAVYWEIGHT	
VALENTINE BUMBLE COMBE MARTIN	v	**NEIL HERBERT** MAYFLOWER
	WELTERWEIGHT	
TOMMY LANGFORD BIDEFORD	v	**MICHAEL JEWELL** TORBAY

BIDEFORD AMATEUR BOXING CLUB

PRESENTS A

STAG NIGHT

DINNER BOXING CABARET

on

FRIDAY, 5th DECEMBER, 2008

at the

DURRANT HOUSE HOTEL, NORTHAM

PROGRAMME

LEWIS CLARK BIDEFORD	v	**JOE OGIJEWICZ** BARNSTAPLE
SAM KINSELLA BIDEFORD	v	**KIER McKINNON** BARNSTAPLE
JAKE LANGDON BIDEFORD	v	**CALLUM HARPER** WATCHET
JASON HORRELL BIDEFORD	v	**STEVE EDWARDS** BARNSTAPLE
BEN OWEN BIDEFORD	v	**TOBIN FOOTE** DEVONPORT
JACK LANGFORD BIDEFORD	v	**HOWARD HART** MAYFLOWER
CHADE COYSH BIDEFORD	v	**KIERAN WELSH** TORBAY
STEVE FIDDY BIDEFORD	v	**DEAN McNALLY** NEWQUAY
JOE DAVIS COMBE MARTIN	v	**KMIL TUZIMEK** TORBAY
LEE COUTS PILGRIMS	v	**DARREN HULL** BARNSTAPLE
KYLE DEBANKS BIDEFORD	v	**MATT SPOONER** DEVONPORT
RICHARD GRIGGS BIDEFORD	v	**JUSTIN HICKS** STURMINSTER / NEWTON

BIDEFORD AMATEUR BOXING CLUB

PRESENTS A

GRAND BOXING TOURNAMENT

on SATURDAY, 28th MARCH, 2009
at BIDEFORD PANNIER MARKET

THANK YOU FOR YOUR SUPPORT

PROGRAMME
£1.00

PROGRAMME

Red Corner		Blue Corner
LEWIS CLARK BIDEFORD	v	**JACK NAPTON** TIVERTON
ISHTAR WHITT BIDEFORD	v	**SIMON KNOWLES** PENHILL
STEVEN CLARK STURMINSTER / NEWTON	v	**THOMAS POWER** TAUNTON
JAKE ENGLAND BIDEFORD	v	**CALLUM DUVELL** COMBE MARTIN
HARRY SUGARS BARNSTAPLE	v	**COREY WESTBROOK** TIVERTON
DAN ASHMAN BIDEFORD	v	**PAUL AUGUSIYNIK** TAUNTON
RAY PENFOLD BIDEFORD	v	**LOUIS TRINDER** PENHILL
SAM KINSELLA BIDEFORD	v	**SCOTT HOSEA** TIVERTON
KYLE ENGLAND BIDEFORD	v	**ALEX STEEL** VICTORY
JAKE LANGDON BIDEFORD	v	**FRED NICHOL** PENHILL
JASON HORRELL BIDEFORD	v	**KIERON JORDON** YEOVIL
JACK LANGFORD BIDEFORD	v	**RYAN HART** MAYFLOWER
CHADE COYSH BIDEFORD	v	**KIERAN WALSH** TORBAY
VALANTIN BUMBEL COMBE MARTIN	v	**NEIL HERBERT** MAYFLOWER
JENS KLINGENSEIN COMBE MARTIN	v	**JOSE CAMPUSANO** YEOVIL
STEVE FIDDY BIDEFORD	v	**MARK COOPER** TAUNTON

BIDEFORD
AMATEUR BOXING CLUB

PRESENTS A

GRAND BOXING TOURNAMENT

on SAUNDAY, 11th OCTOBER, 2009
at BIDEFORD PANNIER MARKET

THANK YOU FOR YOUR SUPPORT

PROGRAMME
£1.00

PROGRAMME

Red Corner		Blue Corner
JAMES HILL-PERRIN BIDEFORD	v	**JAKE KNOWLES** PENHILL
LEWIS CLARKE BIDEFORD	v	**SAM PARKIN** TIVERTON
JOSH MASON BIDEFORD	v	**SHANE HAYWOOD** STURMINSTER / NEWTON
KIA AVERY TIVERTON	v	**JACK KNAPTON** TIVERTON
DAN ASHMAN BIDEFORD	v	**JAMES RICHARDS** PENHILL
SAM KINSELLA BIDEFORD	v	**COLTON VINCENT** PILGRIMS
ROSS DANN MAYFLOWER	v	**LOUIS TRINDER** PENHILL
MATT VANEMMINES BIDEFORD	v	**LLOYD ROBERTS** YEOVIL
RAY PENFOLD BIDEFORD	v	**CHRIS ADAWAY** PLYMOUTH / MAYFLOWER
BEN OWEN BIDEFORD	v	**CHRIS ADAMS** STURMINSTER / NEWTON
JAKE LANGDON BIDEFORD	v	**JAY GAAL** EXETER
TOM ALLUM BARNSTAPLE	v	**DARREN PARKER** PILGRIMS
CHADE COYSH BIDEFORD	v	**KIERAN WALSH** TORBAY
TONY NARDIELLO YEOVIL	v	**FAHEEM KHAN** EXETER
SOAN COYSH BIDEFORD	v	**JAMES DAVIE** TORBAY
STEVE FIDDY BIDEFORD	v	**PETER RICHARDS** PENHILL

BIDEFORD AMATEUR BOXING CLUB

PRESENTS A

STAG NIGHT

DINNER BOXING CABARET

on

FRIDAY, 27th NOVEMBER, 2009

at the

DURRANT HOUSE HOTEL, NORTHAM

PROGRAMME

JAMES HILL-PERRIN BIDEFORD	v	**JOSH HARTLY** TORBAY
LEWIS CLARK BIDEFORD	v	**SAM PARKIN** TIVERTON
JOSH MASON BIDEFORD	v	**ROSS DANN** MAYFLOWER
DAN ASHMAN BIDEFORD	v	**DANIAL RUDDLE** BLANDFORD
RAY PENFOLD BIDEFORD	v	**SHANE HAYWOOD** STURMINSTER / NEWTON
KYLE ENGLAND BIDEFORD	v	**BRADLEY RICHARDS** COMBE MARTIN
MATT VANEMMINES BIDEFORD	v	**MARCUS HODSON** LAUNCESTON
BEN OWEN BIDEFORD	v	**CHRIS ADAMS** STURMINSTER / NEWTON
BROOK HAWKINS BARNSTAPLE	v	**PETER NURDIN** BLANDFORD
CHADE COYSH BIDEFORD	v	**KIERON WALSH** TORBAY
JACK LANGFORD BIDEFORD	v	**DANNY CARR** PILGRIMS

BIDEFORD
AMATEUR BOXING CLUB

PRESENTS

SENIOR ENGLAND
ABA
QUARTER FINALS

on SATURDAY, 17th APRIL, 2010
at BIDEFORD PANNIER MARKET

THANK YOU FOR YOUR SUPPORT

PROGRAMME
£1.00

PROGRAMME

Red Corner		Blue Corner
LEWIS CLARKE (BIDEFORD)	v	**ALEX PRENTICE** (NEWQUAY)
KYLE ENGLAND (BIDEFORD)	v	**HERBIE COOPER** (SYDENHAM)

CHAMPIONSHIPS

Red Corner		Blue Corner
LIGHT FLY,U 48Kg		
SHAUN HUSSAIN (WEST HAM)	v	**BENJAMIN FOWL** (HODDESDON)
FLY, U 51Kg		
BRADLEY WATSON (AMALGAMATED)	v	**ADAM WHITFIELD** (ARMY)
BANTAM, U 54Kg		
VICTOR JENNINGS (LYNN)	v	**JAMES ALLEN** (ARMY)
FEATHER, U 57Kg		
MARTIN WARD (REPTON)	v	**AARON DOWNES** (ARMY)
LIGHT, U 60Kg		
MARLON MELLISH (TIMES)	v	**MARTIN STEAD** (ARMY)
LIGHT WELTER, U 63.5Kg		
JOE HUGHES (MALMESBURY)	v	**STEVE TURNER** (ARMY)
WELTER, U 67Kg		
DUDLEY O'SHAUGHNESSY (WEST HAM)	v	**DAVEY DOCHERTY** (BUSHEY)
LIGHT MIDDLE, U 71Kg		
TOM BAKER (WESTHAM)	v	**SHANE SADLER** (ARMY)
MIDDLE, U 75Kg		
KIRK GARVEY (EARLSFIELD)	v	**NIKI GITTUS** (ARMY)
LIGHT HEAVY, U 81Kg		
CHARLIE DUFFIELD (WESTHAM)	v	**GREG WELLING** (NAVY)
CRUISER, U 86Kg		
DEION JUMAHV (DALE YOUTH)		**MOHAMME JORAAT** (CHESHUNT)
HEAVY, U 91Kg		
WADI CAMACHO (PEACOCK)	v	**EMMANUEL IZONRITEI** (ARMY)

Red Corner		Blue Corner
ASHLEY KNOWLES (BIDEFORD)	v	**ANTONY COLLINS** (SYDENHAM)
JAKE LANGDON (BIDEFORD)	v	**CONNER RILEY** (NEWQUAY)

BIDEFORD
AMATEUR BOXING CLUB

PRESENTS A

STAG NIGHT

DINNER BOXING CABARET

on

FRIDAY, 26th NOVEMBER, 2010

at the

DURRANT HOUSE HOTEL, NORTHAM

PROGRAMME

MATT VANEMMINES BIDEFORD	v	**KYLE COCKRAM** DOWNEND
JACOB GRATTON BIDEFORD	v	**DANNIEL RUFFLE** LLANTWIT MAJOR
WILL DEACON BIDEFORD	v	**SCOTT COUCH** PILGRIMS
JAMES MELVIN HALL GREEN	v	**GARETH SMITH** PILGRIMS
BEN OWEN BIDEFORD	v	**CRAIG CHARNOCK** LAUNCESTON
JAKE LANGDON BIDEFORD	v	**JACK BELLINGHAM** PILGRIMS
RICKY DYMOND BIDEFORD	v	**JAKE DEMMERY** DOWNEND
JAMES HILL-PERRIN BIDEFORD	v	**TOM RENNIE** ILFRACOMBE
CHARLIE CHANEY HALL GREEN	v	**JACOB DURRANT** PAIGNTON
JAMES HATCH BIDEFORD	v	**TAI ROSENSTIEN** PILGRIMS
KYLE ENGLAND BIDEFORD	v	**BRAD BUGDAKE** DEVONPORT
RAY PENFOLD BIDEFORD	v	**ROSS DANN** PILGRIMS

BIDEFORD
AMATEUR BOXING CLUB

PRESENTS

WESTERN COUNTIES JUNIOR ABA FINALS

PLUS SUPPORTING BOUTS

on SATURDAY, 26th MARCH, 2011
at S.E.L. CLARKE,
CLOVELLY ROAD INDUSTRIAL ESTATE

THANK YOU FOR YOUR SUPPORT

PROGRAMME
£1.00

PROGRAMME

CLASS 4 - 3 X 2 MINUTE ROUNDS

Red Corner		Blue Corner
JOE OGIJEWICZ (BARNSTAPLE)	v 46k	**LEWIS STACEY** (TITANS)
KRISTIAN SPRANGLE (MAYFLOWER)	v 52k	**BILLY HEARLE** (DOWNEND)
TYRONE TICKER (HINKES STURMINSTER)	v 54k	**CALLUM O'CONNELL** (BROADPLAIN)
NATHAN MACKIN (APOLLO)	v 57k	**JAKE SMITH** (PADDY JOHNS)
TOBY OSMOND (WEYMOUTH)	v 63k	**LEWIS TRINDER** (PENHILL)
BILLY STANBURY (COMBE MARTIN)	v 66k	**THOMAS McDONAGH** (WALCOTT)
DAN RUDDLE (BLANDFORD)	v 70k	**CHRIS BOWERS** (PENHILL)
AARON EDWARDS (TIVERTON)	v 75k	**PAWEL AUGUSTYNIK** (TAUNTON)
RICKY DIAMOND (BIDEFORD)	v	**JORDAN LANE** (TIVERTON)
JAKE HATCH (BIDEFORD)	v	**HENRY SWAIN** (BARNSTAPLE)

CLASS 5 - 3 X 2 MINUTE ROUNDS

Red Corner		Blue Corner
RAY PENFOLD (BIDEFORD)	v 57k	**ABDINWAHB ABDULLAHI** (PADDY JOHNS)
REECE McCAVOY (POOLE)	v 60k	**TYLER CARTER** (BAKER STREET)
JOE PREECE (TORBAY)	v 63k	**CONNOR WELLS** (WALCOTT)
DYLAN COURTNEY (CAMBORNE)	v 66k	**JAKE HEAL** (SYNWELL)
DARREN HATCH (BIDEFORD)	v	**KYLE SIMPSON** (PILGRIMS)

CLASS 6 - 4 X 2 MINUTE ROUNDS

Red Corner		Blue Corner
KYLE ENGLAND (BIDEFORD)	v 54k	**COREY SMITHERMAN** (TROWBRIDGE)
CHRIS ADAWAY (MAYFLOWER)	v 57k	**RYAN WHEELER** (TROWBRIDGE)
CLAUDE DE LANGE (PORTLAND)	v 60k	**KANE STEWART** (PADDY JOHNS)
KIER McKINNON (BIDEFORD)	v 67k	**FREDDIE NICHOL** (PENHILL)

BIDEFORD AMATEUR BOXING CLUB

PRESENTS A

STAG NIGHT

DINNER BOXING CABARET

on

FRIDAY, 25th NOVEMBER, 2011

at the

DURRANT HOUSE HOTEL, NORTHAM

PROGRAMME

MAX JOHNSON BIDEFORD	v	**ROBBIE SQUIRES** BARNSTAPLE
ALFIE KING BIDEFORD	v	**FRANKY KILLORAN** BRACKNELL
BILLY BUTLER BIDEFORD	v	**ASHTON KIRBY** SALTASH
LEWIS CLARK BIDEFORD	v	**HARRY SUGARS** BARNSTAPLE
RICKEY DYMOND BIDEFORD	v	**JOE SIMPSON** PILGRIMS
JAKE HATCH BIDEFORD	v	**SHANNON WILLEY** EXETER
MATT VANEMMINES BIDEFORD	v	**CORA HOLDEN** MAYFLOWER
BEN OWEN BIDEFORD	v	**RYAN FISHER** BODMIN
CHADE COYSH BIDEFORD	v	**KYLE SIMPSON** PILGRIMS
TOM ALLEN BARNSTAPLE	v	**JACK TAYLOR** COMBE MARTIN
SOANE COYSH BIDEFORD	v	**DARREN TOWNLEY** PILGRIMS
TOM LANGFORD BIDEFORD & HALL GREEN	v	**WESLEY SMITH** LAUNCESTON

BIDEFORD AMATEUR BOXING CLUB

PRESENTS A

GRAND BOXING TOURNAMENT

on

SATURDAY, 18th FEBRUARY, 2012

at the

POLLYFIELD CENTRE

PROGRAMME

AIDEN VITALI	v	**TOM UPSHALL**
BIDEFORD		STURMINSTER NEWTON
ALFIE KING	v	**TOBY DURRANT**
BIDEFORD		PAIGNTON
CHEYE SAUNDERS	v	**JOHN ROGERS**
BIDEFORD		BLANDFORD
JAMES HILL-PERRIN	v	**LEWIS STACEY**
BIDEFORD		TITANS
BILLY PARSONS	v	**JACK KONDAK**
BIDEFORD		POOL
DAN DAVIS	v	**JAKE VARLEY**
BIDEFORD		APOLLO
LEWIS CLARK	v	**KAI AVERY**
BIDEFORD		BARNSTAPLE

BILLY BUTLER	v	**BEN JACKSON**
BIDEFORD		PAIGNTON
RICKY DIAMOND	v	**HARRY SUGARS**
BIDEFORD		BARNSTAPLE
BEN OWEN	v	**RAYNOR MASON**
BIDEFORD		POOLE
JAKE HATCH	v	**ANTHONY TUCKER**
BIDEFORD		EXETER
MATT VANEMMINES	v	**LIAM SPEAR**
BIDEFORD		KINGS
ROBBIE PALMER	v	**MARCUS HODGSON**
BIDEFORD		LAUNCESTON
JAKE LANGDON	v	**CHRIS ADAMS**
BIDEFORD		STURMINSTER NEWTON

BIDEFORD
AMATEUR BOXING CLUB

PRESENTS A

GRAND BOXING TOURNAMENT

on

SATURDAY, 24th March, 2012

at the

BIDEFORD PANNIER MARKET

PROGRAMME

JUNIOR ABA 2012 BOX-OFF TO FINALS

COREY WESTBROOK TIVERTON
TYLER BARWOOD PAIGNTON
RICKY DYMOND BIDEFORD
KIERON CLEWETT DORCHESTER

LEWIS CLARKE BIDEFORD
JOE SIMPSON PILGRIMS
JAMES MILLAR MAYFLOWER
LUKE ALDER PORTLAND
JAMIE GOSNEY DORCHESTER
SAM DAVIS BLANDFORD

AIDEN VITALI BIDEFORD	v	**TIM POOK** SALTASH
RYAN GUMMLY BIDEFORD	v	**SAM COPELAND** DEVONPORT
MAX JOHNSON BIDEFORD	v	**BEAU- DEAN PRICE** BLANDFORD
BILLY BUTLER BIDEFORD	v	**KIA AVERY** BARNSTAPLE
BEN SHORT BIDEFORD	v	**BART JANUS** DOWNEND
JAMES HILL PERRIN BIDEFORD	v	**TOBY DURRANT** PAIGNTON
ALFIE KING BIDEFORD	v	**LEWIS STACEY** TITANS
CHEYE SAUNDERS BIDEFORD	v	**RYAN BROMAGE** KING ALFREDS
BILLY PARSONS BIDEFORD	v	**BRADLEY CAMPBELL** BARNSTAPLE
KYLE ENGLAND BIDEFORD	v	**KYLE COCKRAM** DOWNEND
JAKE HATCH BIDEFORD	v	**NATHAN GARGETT** DEVONPORT
MATT VANEMMINES BIDEFORD	v	**LIAM SPEAR** KINGS
SOANE COYSH BIDEFORD	v	**NICO FAASSON** BARNSTAPLE
ROBBIE PALMER BIDEFORD	v	**LLOYD BARWOOD** PAIGNTON
BEN OWEN BIDEFORD	v	**CHRIS BROAD** EXETER

BIDEFORD
AMATEUR BOXING CLUB

PRESENTS A

GRAND BOXING TOURNAMENT

on

SATURDAY, 16th March, 2013

at the

POLLYFIELD CENTRE

PROGRAMME

CHARLIE COYSH	**v**	**ALFIE MALLAFRE**
BIDEFORD A.B.C.		PILGRIMS A.B.C.
	Kid Gloves 3x1	
KYLE COOK	**v**	**JACK MCCLELLAN**
BIDEFORD A.B.C.		DEVONPORT POLICE A.B.C.
	School Boy 3x1.5	
RYAN GUMBLEY	**v**	**HARRISON SANSON**
BIDEFORD A.B.C.		HAMILTON GREENS A.B.C.
	Junior 3x2	
BILLY PARSONS	**v**	**RYA COLES**
BIDEFORD A.B.C.		BODMIN A.B.C.
	Junior 3x2	
BRANDON MADDOCK	**v**	**ZAK JORDAN**
BARNSTAPLE A.B.C.		DEVONPORT POLICE A.B.C
	Junior 4x2	
RICKEY DYMOND	**v**	**JACK STRINGER**
BIDEFORD A.B.C.		GOLD RING A.B.C.
	Junior 4x2	
RAY PENFOLD	**v**	**TYLER BARWOOD**
BIDEFORD A.B.C.		PAIGNTON A.B.C.
	Senior Featherweight 4x2	
FREDDY BAZELL	**v**	**WILL ELLICOTT**
BIDEFORD A.B.C.		TAMAR A.B.C.
	Senior Light/Middleweight 3x2	
CHADE COYSH	**v**	**RYAN HIBBERD**
BIDEFORD A.B.C.		PILGRIMS A.B.C.
	Senior Light/Middleweight 3x2	
BEN OWEN	**v**	**HOWARD HART**
BIDEFORD A.B.C.		PLYMOUTH/MAYFLOWER A.B.C.
	Senior Welterweight	
JAMIE CREEK	**v**	**DAVID ASHTON**
BIDEFORD A.B.C.		HAMILTON GREEN A.B.C
	V. Senior Heavyweight 4x2	
SOANE COYSH	**v**	**KYLE GARGETT**
BIDEFORD A.B.C.		PILGRIMS A.B.C.
	V. Senior Lightweight	
KYLE DE.BANK	**v**	**CORTNY RICHARDS**
BIDEFORD & ROYAL NAVY A.B.C.		CARLS BOXING STABLE A.B.C.
	V. Senior Heavyweight	

BIDEFORD
AMATEUR BOXING CLUB

PRESENTS A

GRAND BOXING TOURNAMENT

on

SATURDAY, 11th May, 2013

at the

PANNIER MARKET

PROGRAMME

BAILEY RATCLIFF COMBE MARTIN	v	**CONNER MERSON** PORTLAND
CHARLIE COYSH BIDEFORD	v	**MARK MEDDON** BODMIN
ZAK JONES TIVERTON	v	**OWEN PIRRET** DOWNEND
KYLE COOK BIDEFORD	v	**ARRON ROBISON** LYMPSTONE
ADE SMITH JONES TORRINGTON POLICE	v	**ROBERT LATHAN WILLOWS** TORPOINT RAME PENINSULA
CHEYE SAUNDERS BIDEFORD	v	**TOBIAS HACKER** DOWNEND
JOSEPH TARRANT TORRINGTON POLICE	v	**BRANDON MADDOCK** BARNSTAPLE
COREY WESTBROOK TIVERTON	v	**BEN DEMMERY** DOWNEND
BILLY PARSONS BIDEFORD	v	**JORDON JONES** BARNSTAPLE
BEN OWEN BIDEFORD	v	**DAN DAWS** YEOVIL
RAY PENFOLD BIDEFORD	v	**KYLE GARGATE** PILGRIMS
SOANE COYSH BIDEFORD	v	**CRISTIAN SPANGLE** PLYMOUTH MAYFLOWER
JAMIE CREEK BIDEFORD	v	**MATT LESLIE** DOWNEND

BIDEFORD AMATEUR BOXING CLUB

PRESENTS A

STAG NIGHT

DINNER BOXING CABARET

on

FRIDAY, 22nd NOVEMBER, 2013

at the

DURRANT HOUSE HOTEL, NORTHAM

PROGRAMME

CHARLEY COYSH	**v**	**TAZ TURNER**
BIDEFORD		TORBAY
	Schoolboy	
LEWIS MALE	**v**	**JAMIE KENT**
COMBE MARTIN		PLYMOUTH MAYFLOWER
	Junior	
TYLER THAKE	**v**	**KARL GREATOREX**
BIDEFORD		TORBAY
	Schoolboy	
KYE COOK	**v**	**ALEX LEOWY**
BIDEFORD		TORBAY
	Schoolboy	
RYAN GUMBLEY	**v**	**JACOB CROOT**
BIDEFORD		DOWNEND
	Junior	
BEN OWEN	**v**	**RAYNOR MASON**
BIDEFORD		PLYMOUTH MAYFLOWER
	Light Welter Weight 3x2	
ALEX JONES	**v**	**LIAM LAIRD**
TIVERTON		BARNSTAPLE
	Light Welter Weight 3x2	
RICKY DYMOND	**v**	**HARRY SUGARS**
BIDEFORD		BARNSTAPLE
	Welter Weight 4x2	
JACK LANGFORD	**v**	**DYLAN COURTNEY**
BIDEFORD		CAMBORNE/REDRUTH
	Middle Weight 3x3	

BIDEFORD AMATEUR BOXING CLUB

PRESENTS

An Evening of Amateur Boxing Including Junior ABA Championship Bouts

SATURDAY 26 APRIL 2014

BIDEFORD COLLEGE

Thank you for your support

Programme 50P

PROGRAMME

Red Corner		Blue Corner	
Jacob Stevenson Bideford	v	Brad Richmond Hamilton Green	Skills Bout 3 x 1 min
Ethan Wells Bideford	v	Callum Broadley Combe Martin	Skills Bout 3 x 1 min
~~Tyler Thake Bideford~~	~~v~~	~~Oskar Wekwest Hamilton Green~~	~~School boy 3 x 1.5 min~~
Robbie Moore Torrington	v	Callan Bryant Tiverton	Junior 3 x 2 min
Jake Christie Bideford	v	Sam Williams Paignton	Junior 3 x 2 min
Kane Wildman Cambourne	v	Brandon Stacey Devonport	JABA 52kg Class A 3 x 2 min
Ryan Gumbley Bideford	v	Curtis Hill Devonport	Youth 3 x 2 min
Billy Butler Torrington	v	Sam Williams Paignton	Youth 3 x 2 min

Red Corner		Blue Corner	
Jake Carr Wessex	v	Flin Elworthy Barnstaple	JABA 75kg Class A 3 x 2 min
Sam Ingram Cambourne	v	Sam Copeland Mayflower	JABA 63kg Class B 3 x 2 min
Andrew Wheeler Lympstone	v	Rob Squire Barnstaple	JABA 81kg Class B 3 x 2 min
Lewis Clarke Bideford	v	Jordan Ruth Plymton	Senior Welter wt 3 x2 min
Ricky Dymond Bideford	v	Harry Sugars Barnstaple	Senior Middle wt 3 x3 min
Brad Riggs Tiverton	v	Jake Abraham Paignton	Senior Welter wt 4 x 2 min
Billy Stanbury Bideford	v	Stephen Mitchell St Agnes	Senior Lt Heavy wt 3 x 2 min
Ben Read Torrington	v	Rob Wrey Barnstaple	Senior Lt Heavy wt 3 x 2 min
Ben Owen Bideford	v	Dean Dodge Yeovil	Senior Lt Welter wt 3 x 2 min

BIDEFORD AMATEUR BOXING CLUB

PRESENTS

3 Course Dinner

An Evening of

Amateur Boxing

Entertainment

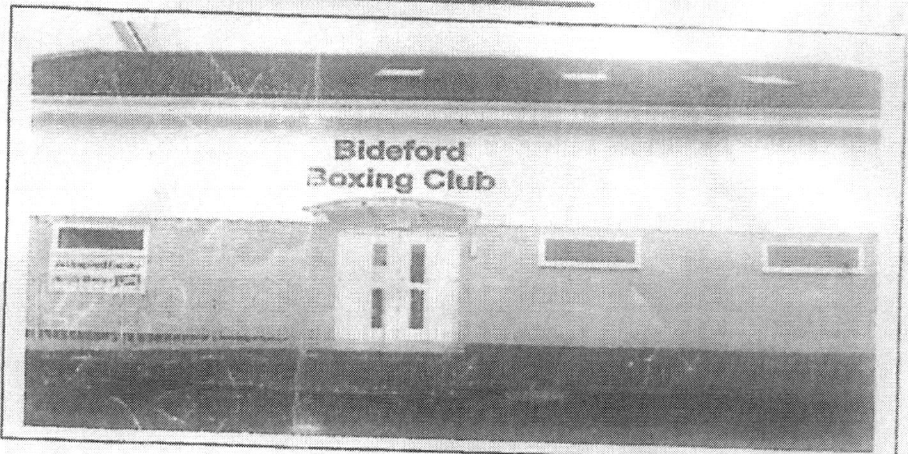

Friday 14 November 2014

The Durrant House Hotel

Thank you for your support

Programme Free

	Red Corner		Blue Corner	
1.	Jacob Stevenson Bideford	v	Ethan Wells Bideford	Skills Bout 3 x 1 min
2.	Bayley Ratcliffe Bideford	v	Jake Hooper Barnstaple	Junior 3 x 2 min
3.	Tyler Thake Bideford	v	Tayler Barbar Tamar	Junior 3 x 2 min
4.	Robbie Moore Torrington	v	James Parker CWMGoors Wales	Junior 3 x 2 min
5.	Aiden Vitali Bideford	v	Tristan Williams CWMGoors Wales	Junior 3 x 2 min
6.	Zack Jones Tiverton	v	William Hughes Bagian Bulldogs Wales	Junior 3 x 2 min
7.	Ryan Gumbley Bideford	v	Brandon Maddock Barnstaple	Youth 3 x 2 min
8.	Shane Medlen Paignton	v	Thomas Gillheaney Bagian Bulldogs Wales	Youth 3 x 3 min
9.	Andy Short Bideford	v	Laurence Carter Exeter	Senior 3 X 2 min
10.	Ben Owen Bideford	v	Morgan Macintosh Bagian Bulldogs Wales	Senior 3 x 3 min
11	Alex Dovell Bideford	v	Rhys Hill CWMGoors Wales	Senior 3 x 2 min
12.	Billy Stanbury Bideford	v	William Gillheaney Bagian Bulldogs Wales	Senior 3 x 2 min
13.	Jack Langford Bideford	v	Aaron Bird Bagian Bulldogs Wales	Senior 3 x3 min

BIDEFORD AMATEUR BOXING CLUB

PRESENTS

An Evening of Amateur Boxing Including Elite Championship Bouts

Sponsored by handf Finance London

SATURDAY 21 March 2015

BIDEFORD COLLEGE

Thank you for your support

Programme
50P

PROGRAMME

Red Corner		Blue Corner	
Freddie White Bideford	v	George Lock Torrington	Skills Bout 3 x 1 min
Jacob Stevenson Bideford	v	Ned Pettifer Torrington	Skills Bout 3 x 1 min
Bayley Radcliffe Bideford	v	Buddy Holly Barton Hill	Junior 3 x 2 min
Callum Cunningham Bideford	v	Jake Hooper Barnstaple	Junior 3 x 2 min
Josh Short Bideford	v	Jack Evans Intense	Junior 3 x 2 min
George Parker Bideford	v	Josh Cunningham Devonport	Youth 3 x 2 min
Aiden Vitali Bideford	v	Nick Forrest Barnstaple	Youth 3 x 2 min
Danny Smith Tamar	v	Dylan Courtney Cambourne	Senior Champ Lt Heavy wt 3 x 3 min
Andy Short RNLI	v	Mark Morrey Postman	Senior super Hv wt 3 X 2 min
Billy Parsons Bideford	v	Jack Marks Exeter	Senior Middle wt 3 x 2 min
Alex Downie Bideford	v	Joe Golding Ilfracombe	Senior Lt Heavy wt 3 x 2 min
Alex Dovall Bideford	v	Colum Siddens Weymouth	Senior Middle wt 3 x 2 min
Liam Laird Barnstaple	v	Tom Frame Jersey	Senior Champ Lt Welter 3 x3 min
Matt Vanemminis Bideford	v	Alex Jones Tiverton	Senior Welter wt 3 x3 min
Ben Owen Bideford	v	Ryan Hibbert Devonport	Senior Welter wt 3x 3 min
Billy Stanbury Bideford	v	Storm Lock Weymouth	Senior Lt Heavy wt 3 x 3min

SUPPORTERS

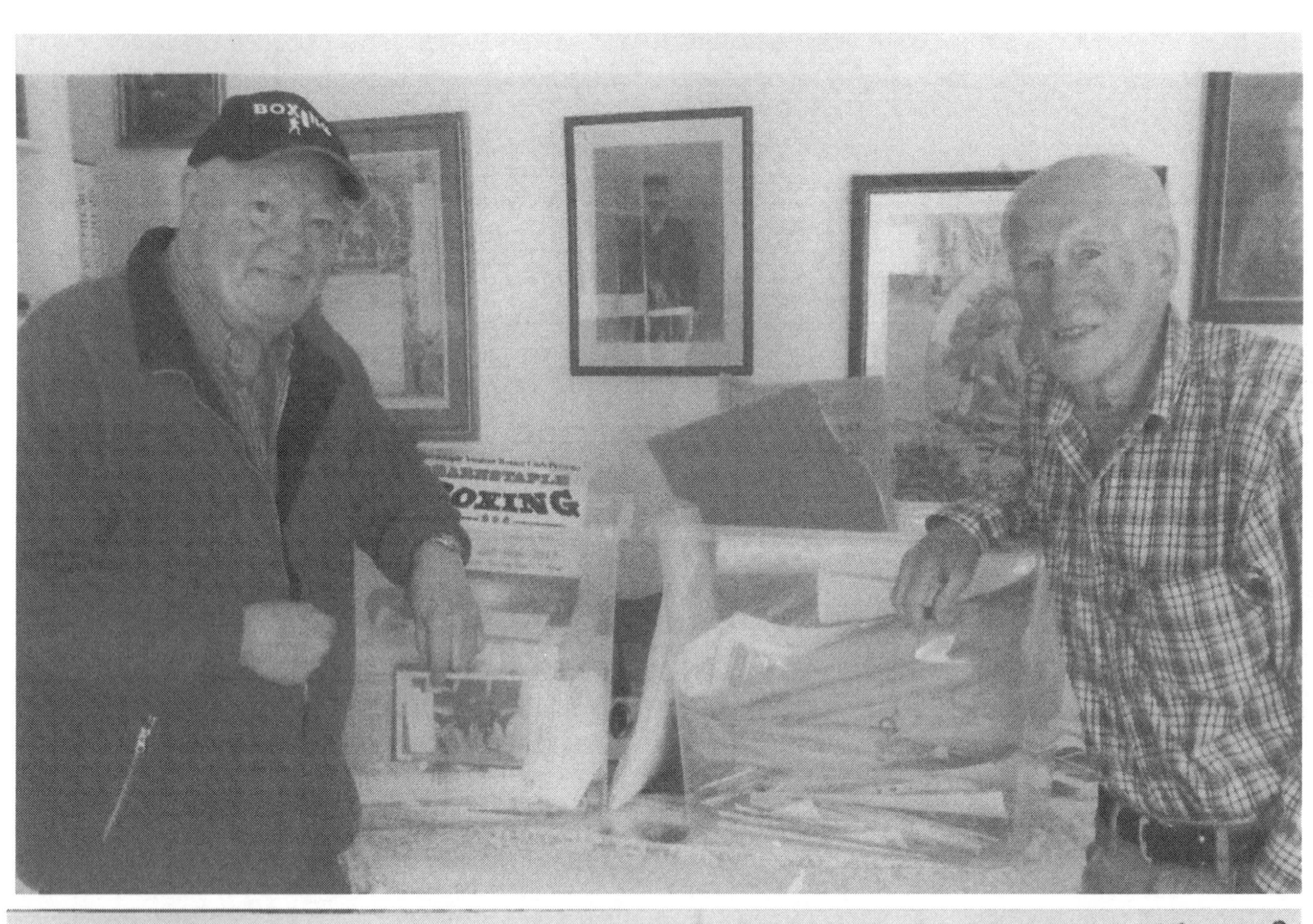

DB with veteran boxer, SAMMY WREY view the amount of research for Volume..2 before the 'sorting out' began.

TONY RUTHERFORD

Too much cannot be written in praise of this gentleman's contribution to and continued support of BIDEFORD ABC. He has been approached on numerous occasions to accept the position of PRESIDENT of the CLUB but continues to prefer a background seat.

TONY RUTHERFORD and SAMMY WREY
...getting ready for action !

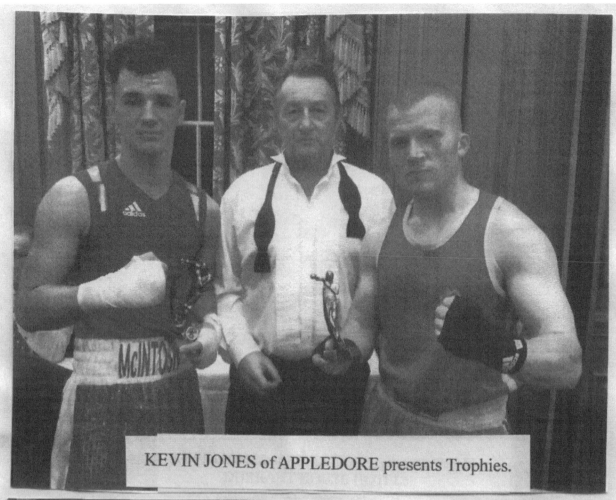

KEVIN JONES of APPLEDORE presents Trophies.

KEVIN JONES, SAMMY WREY and GUESTS, DB with camera.
The TONY RUTHERFORD 'TABLE.'

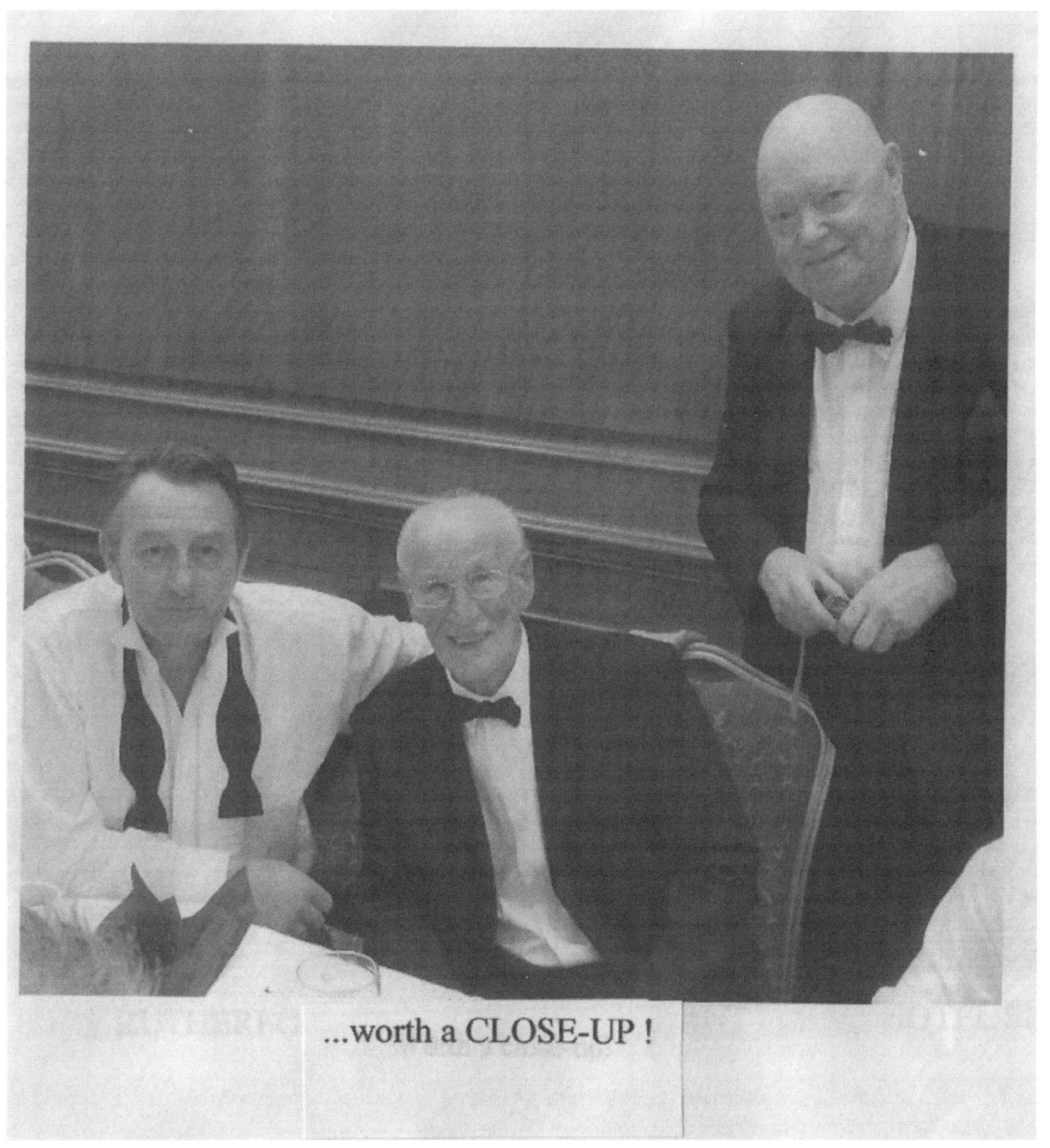

...worth a CLOSE-UP !

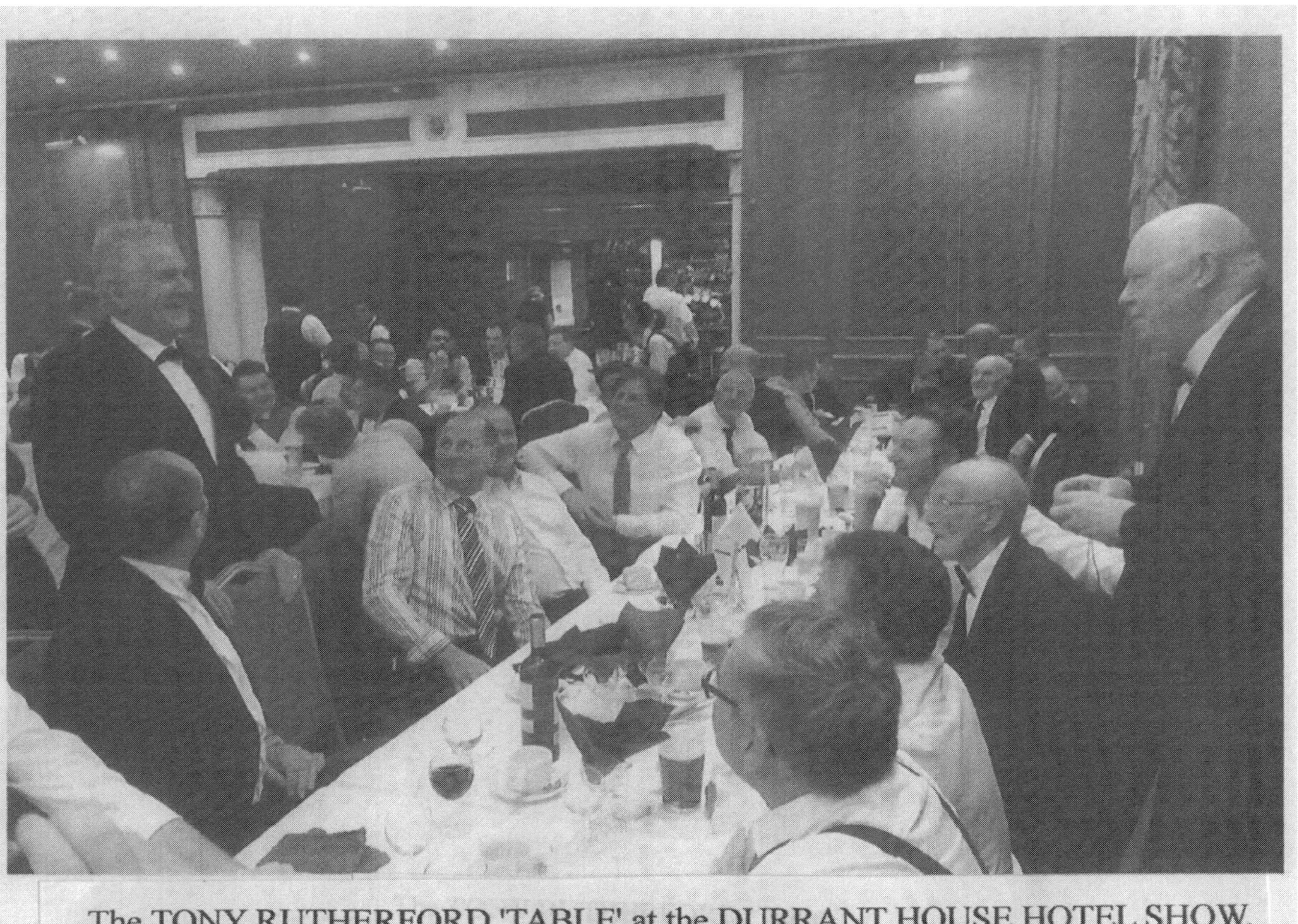

The TONY RUTHERFORD 'TABLE' at the DURRANT HOUSE HOTEL SHOW.
DB looks on.

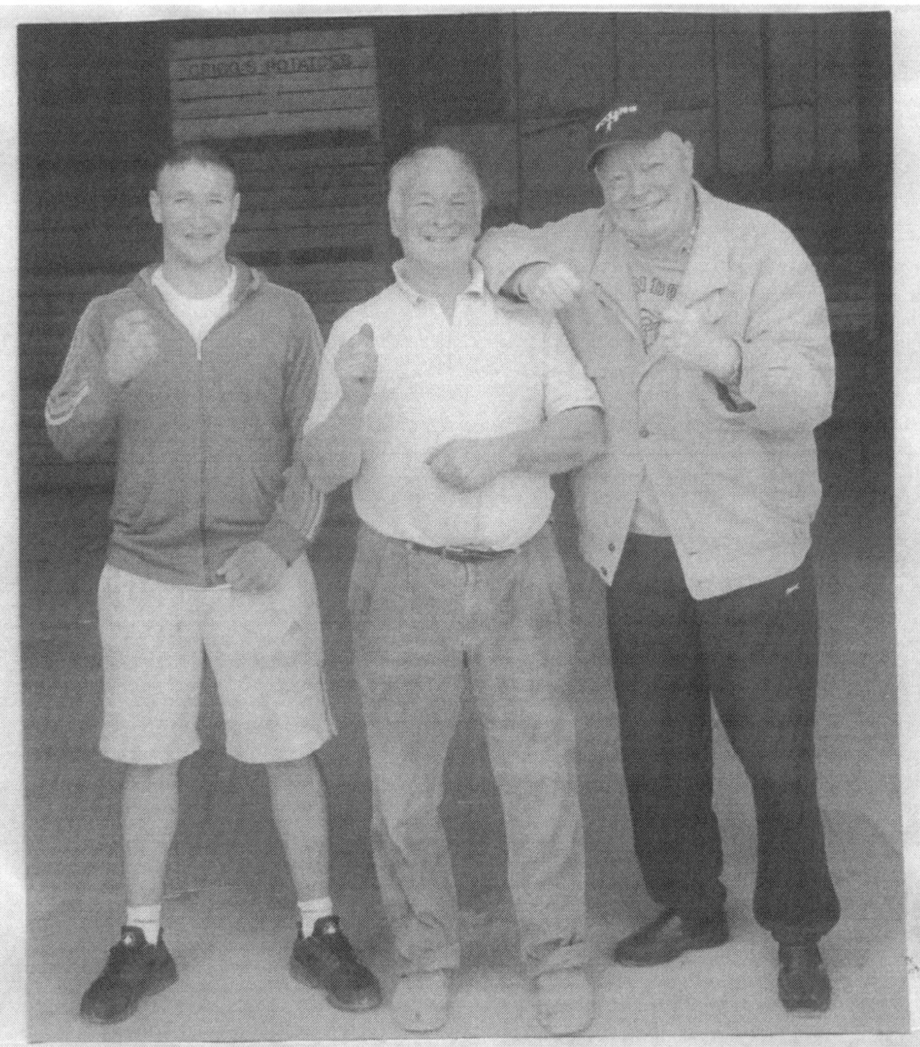

RICHARD GRIGG, father DAVID and DB outside one of the BARNS used as a GYM for a year before moving into POLLYFIELD.

DAVID GRIGG from EASTLEIGH is as much known for his son RICHARD being one of the most talented boxers to represent BIDEFORD ABC in recent years and who now passes on his knowledge and expertise as Trainer/Coach at the CLUB, as he is for GROWING his EXCELLENT POTATOES.
When we vacated the STEVE CLARKE GYM a year was spent in using a FARM BARN as a gym, kindly put at the CLUB'S disposal by DAVID. I could often visualise the old time Cornish World Champ, BOB FITZSIMMONS turning up for a workout, he would not have found conditions so different from his early life and times!
It was a great experience for everyone connected with the Club and we cannot thank DAVID enough for his generosity.

He continues to be a GREAT SUPPORTER of BIDEFORD ABC.

One thing we had when training in the BARNS was PLENTY of SPACE and LOADS of FRESH AIR !

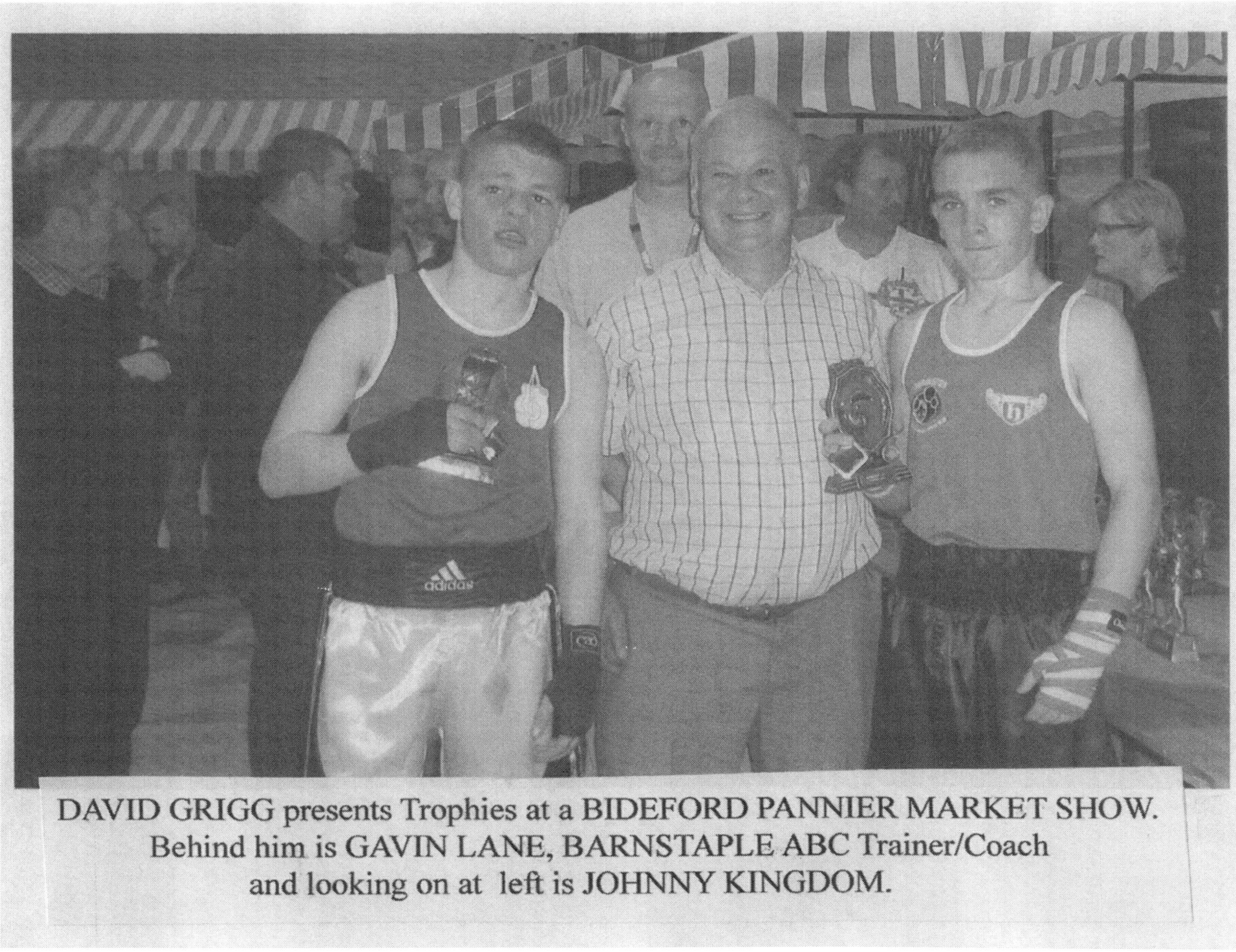

DAVID GRIGG presents Trophies at a BIDEFORD PANNIER MARKET SHOW.
Behind him is GAVIN LANE, BARNSTAPLE ABC Trainer/Coach
and looking on at left is JOHNNY KINGDOM.

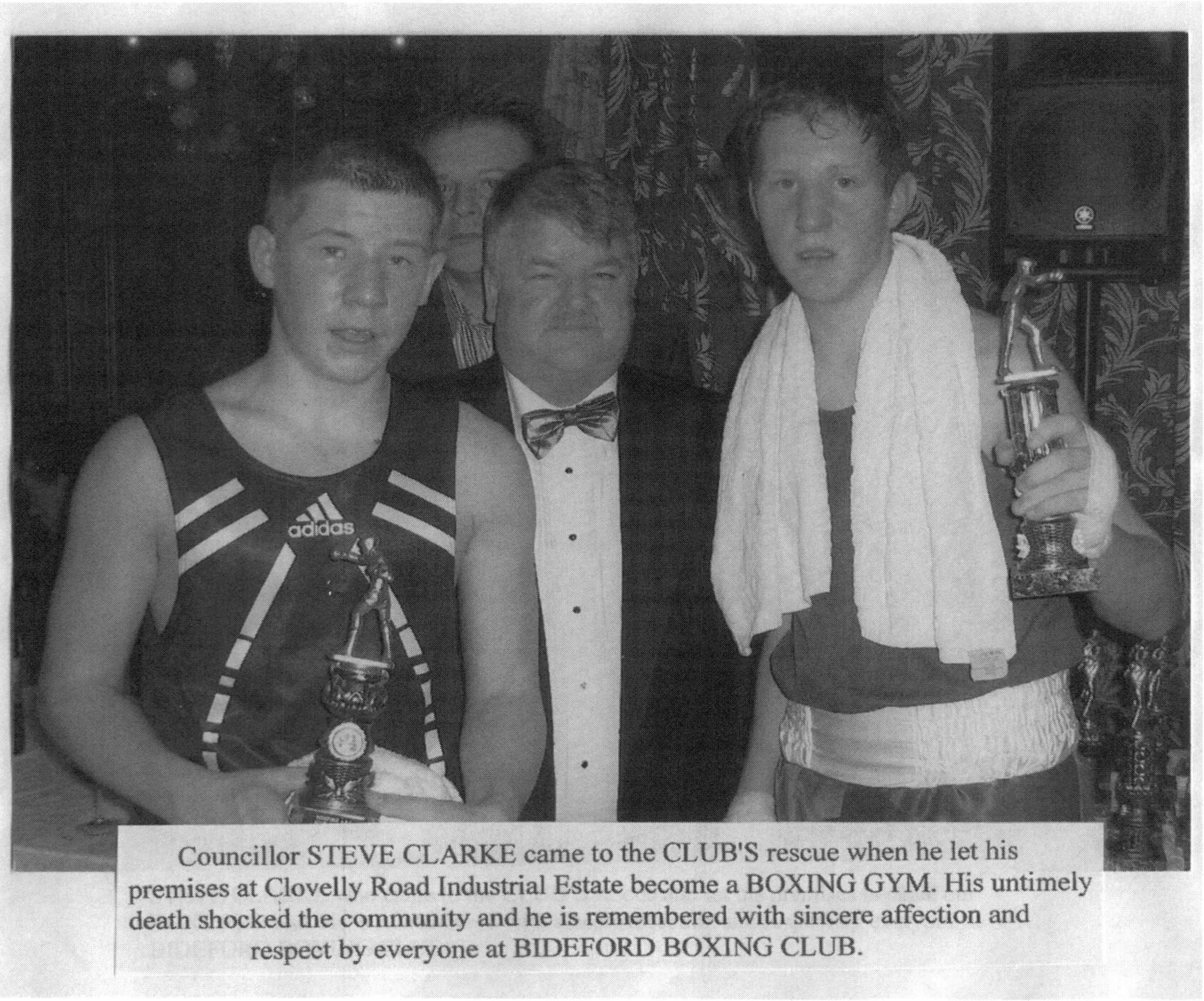

Councillor STEVE CLARKE came to the CLUB'S rescue when he let his premises at Clovelly Road Industrial Estate become a BOXING GYM. His untimely death shocked the community and he is remembered with sincere affection and respect by everyone at BIDEFORD BOXING CLUB.

By KATHRYN SMITH
ksmith@c-dm.co.uk

HOPES of creating a boxing centre of excellence in Bideford have taken another step forward.

Young boxers in the town are celebrating after securing a new place to train.

The Bideford Amateur Boxing Club urgently needed a new home after its previous tenancy ran out a few weeks ago.

The club had made a number of public appeals for help.

Last month Bideford businessman, Steve Clarke, offered members the use of a couple of industrial units at Clovelly Road Industrial Estate.

The plans to change the units into a gym and storage were approved by Torridge District Council and the club is already making full use of them.

The club says its ultimate aim is still to secure permanent premises at the Pollyfield Centre in East-the-Water, but has given special thanks to Mr Clarke for providing a new base.

The club's development officer, Jeff Facey, said: "Bideford Amateur Boxing Club (BABC) would like to thank everybody concerned for supporting this new and exciting phase that will endorse the continuous improvement plan of BABC.

"A special thanks is given to Steve Clarke, owner of the unit and the Kathleen & May, for providing the unit. Of course, BABC's ultimate aim is to secure permanent premises at the Pollyfield Centre, East the Water, Bideford."

Mr Facey said the club will mark its official opening with an open day this Sunday from 12 to 4pm.

He said: "Anyone who would like to discuss, and see the new facilities available to existing and potential new members, are welcome and encouraged to attend."

Mr Facey added: "The new boxing club is situated on the Clovelly Road Industrial Estate and is in close proximity to other fitness facilities. Therefore, parents and guardians of young people who wish to take up boxing in a safe environment also have the opportunity to attend their own fitness programmes at the same time.

"The new facilities will now enable BABC to promote and secure new working relationships with local schools, the police and other boxing clubs nationally, perhaps leading to a centre of excellence for talented boxers from the South West of England."

Torridge District Council planning officers had recommended that the application was granted but it was referred to the plans committee as owner Steve Clarke is also a town and district councillor, and Mr Facey's partner is an officer at the authority.

The club boasts more than 80 young members, some who have gone forward to box for England.

■ NEW HOME: Boxers Tommy Langford (in grey) and Richard Grigg spar in front of coach Christopher Friendship, and chief coach Bob Ellis at the club's new premises. Picture: Mike Southon 0908-53_05

SAVED by the BELL !

..or more to the point..by STEVE CLARKE !!

Councillor STEVE CLARKE, O.B.E.,

JILL CAMPBELL and BIDEFORD PROFESSIONAL BOXER, TOMMY LANGFORD with the TOM POW MEMORIAL PLATE.

The TOM POW MEMORIAL PLATE donated to the CLUB by JILL CAMPBELL, TOM'S DAUGHTER.

BILLY CAMPBELL presenting trophies at a Bideford Pannier Market Show.

DAVID POWE, VERONICA POWE, DB, TOMMY LANGFORD, JILL CAMPBELL, BILLY CAMPBELL.

It's great that present day members of the POWE family support local boxing. Their sporting relatives from another era would be proud of them.

DB, JILL CAMPBELL, DICK KERSEY.

DAVID POWE presenting trophies at the Durrant House Hotel...

JOHNNY KINGDOM…TOMMY LANGFORD…DAVID POWE

DECEMBER 6th 2006.

BIDEFORD Amateur Boxing Club's dinner tournament at the Durrant House Hotel attracted a capacity audience of 250.

Local young boxers put on a fine display against visiting opponents from neighbouring Barnstaple and from Exmouth, Plymouth and Sturminster Newton, winning five bouts and losing four.

Fight of the night was an all-action encounter between Richard Grigg of Bideford and John Smith of Exmouth, with Grigg stopping his opponent in the second round.

Bideford national schoolboys champion Tommy Langford was too good for his Exmouth opponent Tommy Shaw and also stopped him in the second. His brother Jack also seemed to have done enough against heavier opponent Danny Benham and there was disappointment when a majority decision went against him.

Brothers Adam and Matt Vanemmenis also had differing outcomes, with Adam stopping M Beeling of Sturminster in the second, but Matt losing a close contest with George Groves of Barnstaple on points.

In his first bout Daniel Ashman stopped Lee Green from Exmouth in the second and Ray Penfold turned the odds in his favour with a unanimous decision over Adam Winfield of Sturminster, each having won one in previous encounters.

Ben Owen lost a good bout with Matt Mitchell of Plymouth club Pilgrims and Steve Gallienne lost on points to Shaun Hopte of Sturminster.

The evening was marked by a special presentation to Dr Mike Cracknell on his retirement after more than 30 years as the Bideford club's medical officer.

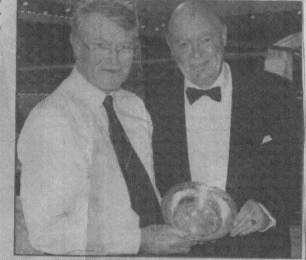

● **AWARD for Dr Cracknell from Bideford ABC chairman Dick Brownson** *(Pic Brian Saunders)*

■ **FOND FAREWELL: Dr Mike Cracknell took up his usual seat as ringside doctor for the final time on Saturday night.**

■ **Dr Cracknell has been an indispensable member of the behind-the-scenes team needed to hold an amateur boxing show for the past 32 years.**

■ **But he is now retiring from Bideford Medical Centre – although he won't become a stranger at future boxing tournaments, and will help successor Dr Yuk Chan ease into his new ringside role.**

■ **Dr Cracknell said: "I have always done the Bideford shows and the Barnstaple ones when needed.**

■ **"I was delighted when the club came back to the Pannier Market – I think it is a fantastic venue for boxing."** 06039503

DOCTOR MIKE CRACKNELL.

THE COMMITTEE CAN NEVER THANK DOCTOR MIKE ENOUGH FOR HIS CONTRIBUTION TO THE SMOOTH RUNNING AND SUCCESS ACHIEVED DURING HIS 32 YEARS OF SERVICE TO THE BOXING CLUB.

DOCTOR CHAN.

...WHO TOOK OVER FROM DOCTOR MIKE CRACKNELL AND IS AT PRESENT MEDICAL OFFICER FOR THE CLUB.

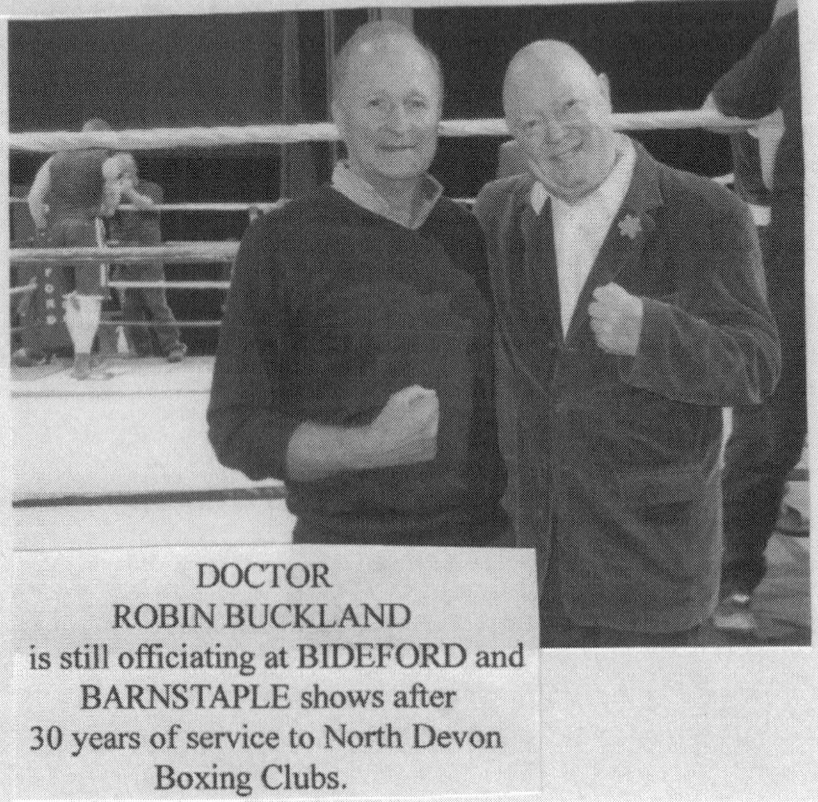

DOCTOR
ROBIN BUCKLAND
is still officiating at BIDEFORD and BARNSTAPLE shows after 30 years of service to North Devon Boxing Clubs.

NORTH DEVON

Gazette

5 June, 2013

▲ Local news legend: Geoff Staddon.

Our Geoff retires after 47 years at the *Gazette*

THE *North Devon Gazette's* Geoff Staddon retired on Friday after a remarkable 47-year career at the newspaper.

It was two months before England won the World Cup and four years before man landed on the moon that the 16-year-old grammar school leaver was offered a job on the old *Bideford Gazette*.

Then produced at the former offices in Grenville Street, the *Gazette* was still a broadsheet – Torridge's paid-for newspaper.

It was the time of hot metal, a time when the clickety-clack of the typewriter and the haze of cigarette smoke was the stuff of newsrooms.

During his long-service to Bideford and the wider North Devon community Geoff has turned countless stones on local democracy, reported stories of human endeavour and tragedy, and told incredible tales of triumph over adversity.

In later years, he turned his attentions to sports reporting, covering everything from football to model yacht racing.

Long-serving Bideford councillor and local historian Peter Christie said Geoff's reports were always worth reading and could be relied on for their accuracy and fairness.

He said: "Geoff was always willing to put councillors on the spot in the nicest possible way. His questions were always searching but never leading and you could always be sure his reports were fair and accurate.

"If you saw a report with the name Geoff Staddon on it you knew it was one that was worth reading."

Geoff bows out this week as one of the longest serving reporters in North Devon.

Gazette editor Andy Keeble said: "You really couldn't wish for a better colleague than Geoff.

"His reputation for accuracy and honesty was second to none and will be sorely missed by everyone at the *Gazette* – not least for his quick wit, friendly manner and calm persona, even during turbulent times on the newsdesk."

GEOFF STADDON gave BIDEFORD BOXING CLUB tremendous support over his 47 years with the GAZETTE. The CLUB COMMITTEE and BOXERS wish him a LONG and HAPPY RETIREMENT.

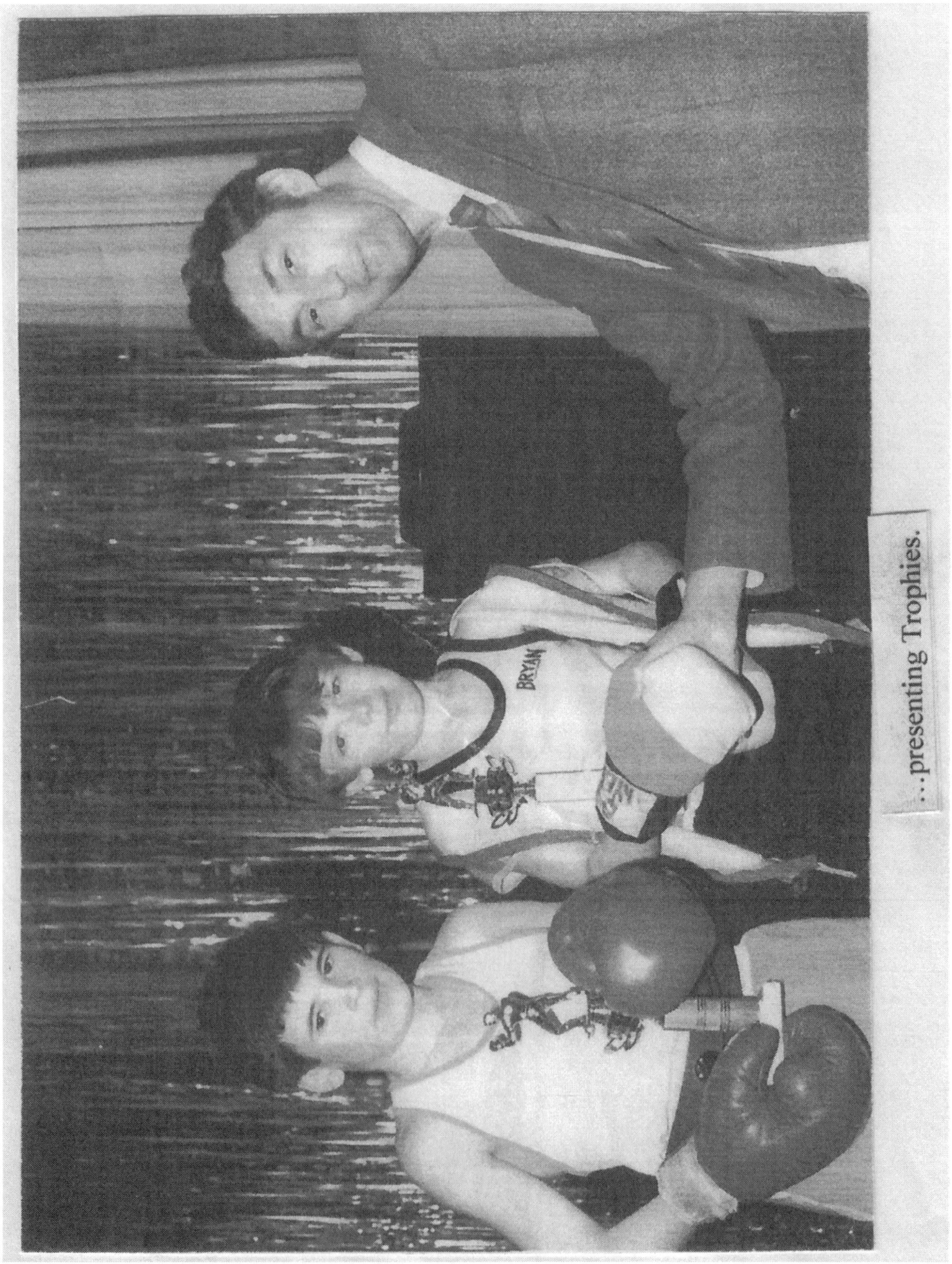

...presenting Trophies.

Councillors ANDREW EASTMAN and NOEL DEAKES with GUESTS
at a
BIDEFORD PANNIER MARKET SHOW.

BIDEFORD PANNIER MARKET BOXING SHOW,
'TOP TABLE.'

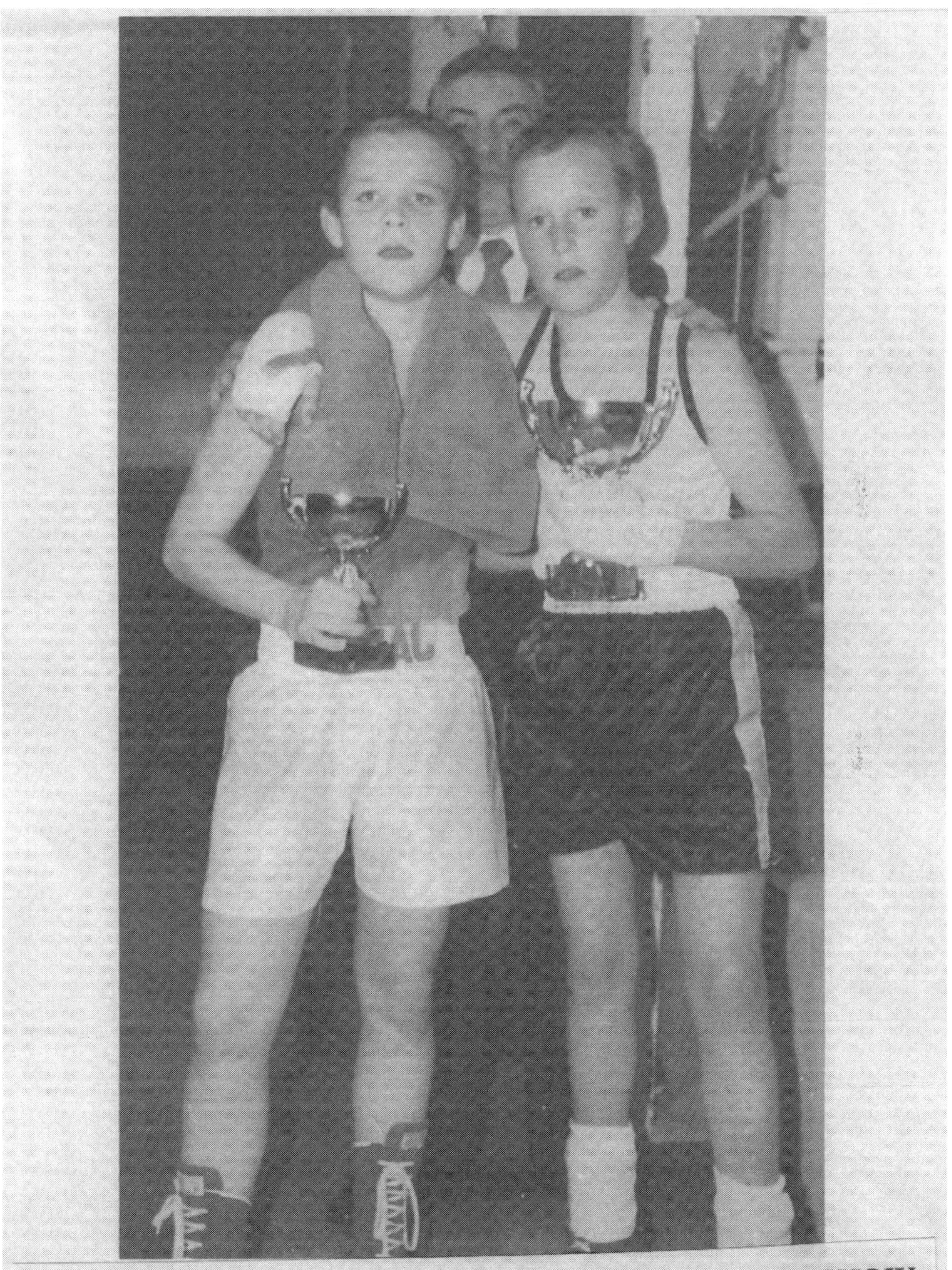

Presenting Trophies at a BIDEFORD PANNIER MARKET SHOW.

Councillor NOEL DEAKES presents Trophies.
CHRIS A'LEE of BIDEFORD ABC in the black shorts.

Thursday, August 2, 2001

Star at boxing club fun day

A MEMBER of top pop band EMF has pledged his support to an event which aims to raise money for a children's charity.

Derry Brownson, who plays keyboards and samplers with the band which topped the charts in the early 1990s, will be joining boxers and officials from Bideford Amateur Boxing Club at the Family Fun Day in aid of CLIC (Cancer and Leukaemia in Childhood) on Sunday August 19.

EMF reformed recently with a tour to support the release of their 'Greatest Hits' album *Epsom Mad Funkers*.

Now Derry will join his father Dick Brownson and others from the boxing club at the event which is being held in memory of David Barrett, a manager at Appledore Shipbuilders until his untimely death in September last year. The Fun Day has been organised by Appledore AFC and will be held at the football club's ground.

Malcolm Boswell, one of the organisers of the event, paid tribute to Mr Barrett, a lifetime Tottenham Hotspur FC fan.

"He coached football at Appledore and the Devon Boys Club and then went on to manage the Jewson South West League. We felt it was a fitting tribute to him to arrange this Fun Day and to send the money raised to one of his favourite charities."

A number of diverse events will take place on the day, including football matches for veterans, competitions and auctions of rugby and football memorabilia.

☎ Information from Appledore AFC on 01237-477099.

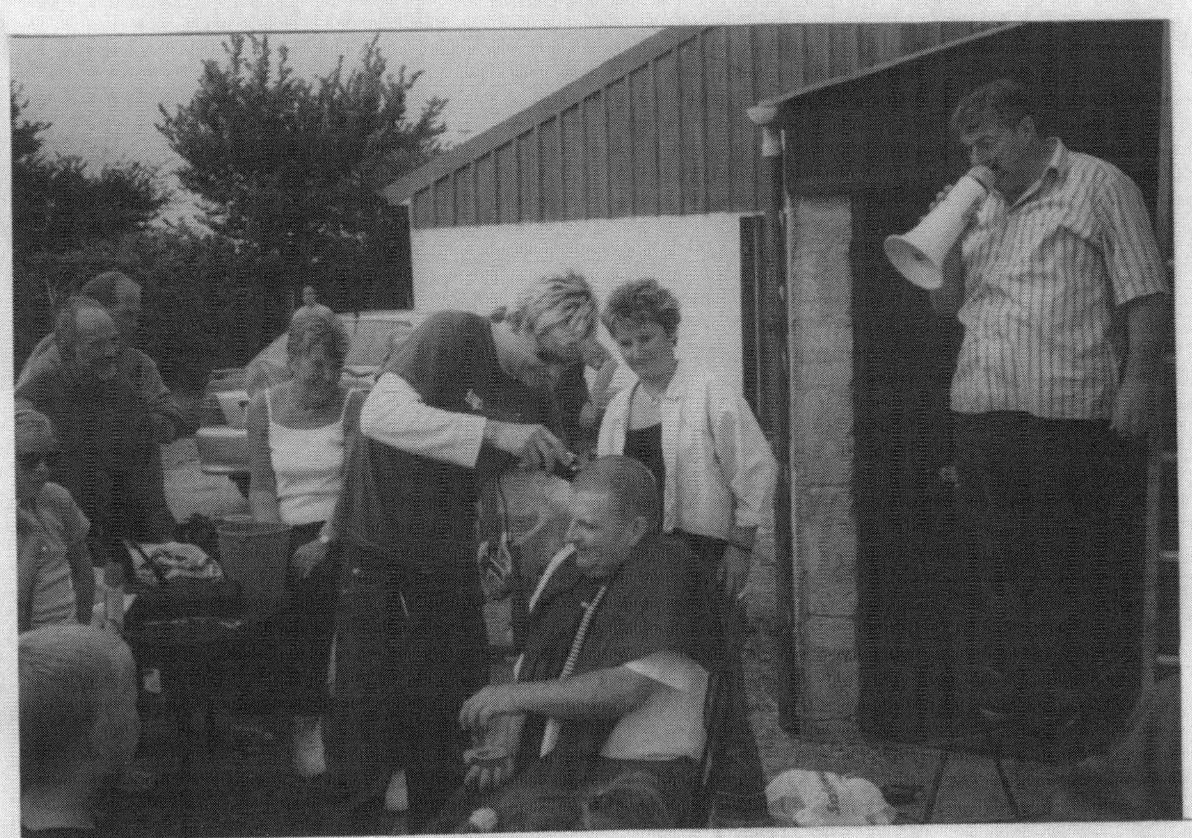

KENNY MAY, a Great Sport, has his head shaved by DERRY BROWNSON.
A fund raising gesture for the Charity CLIC.
Councillor ANDREW EASTMAN keeps a watchful eye on proceedings !

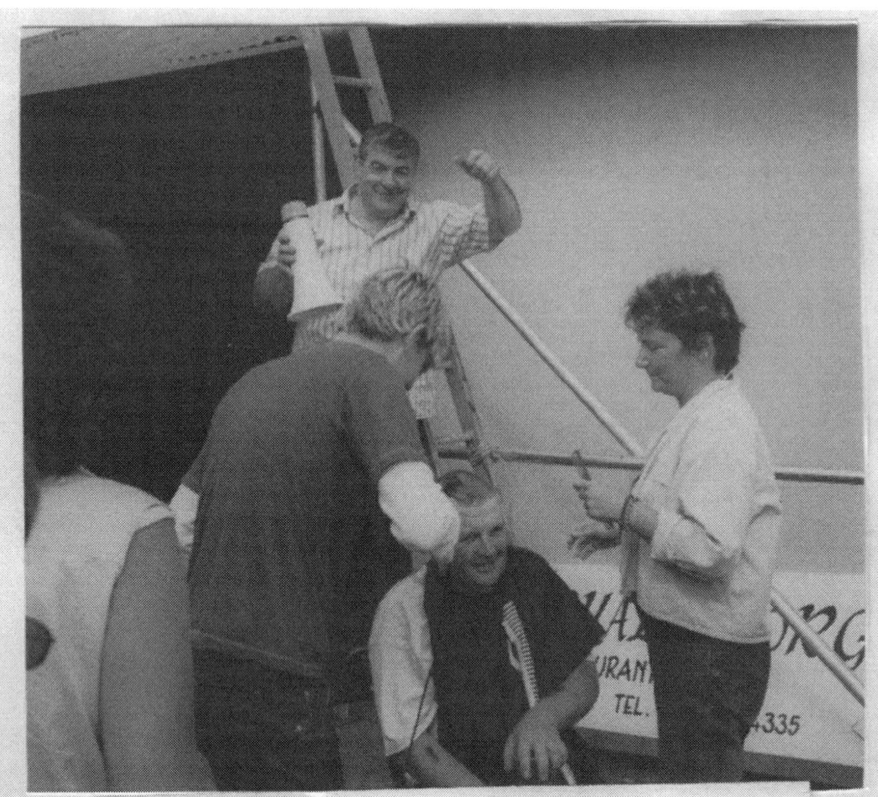

DERRY BROWNSON

Councillor ANDREW EASTMAN spurs DERRY on.

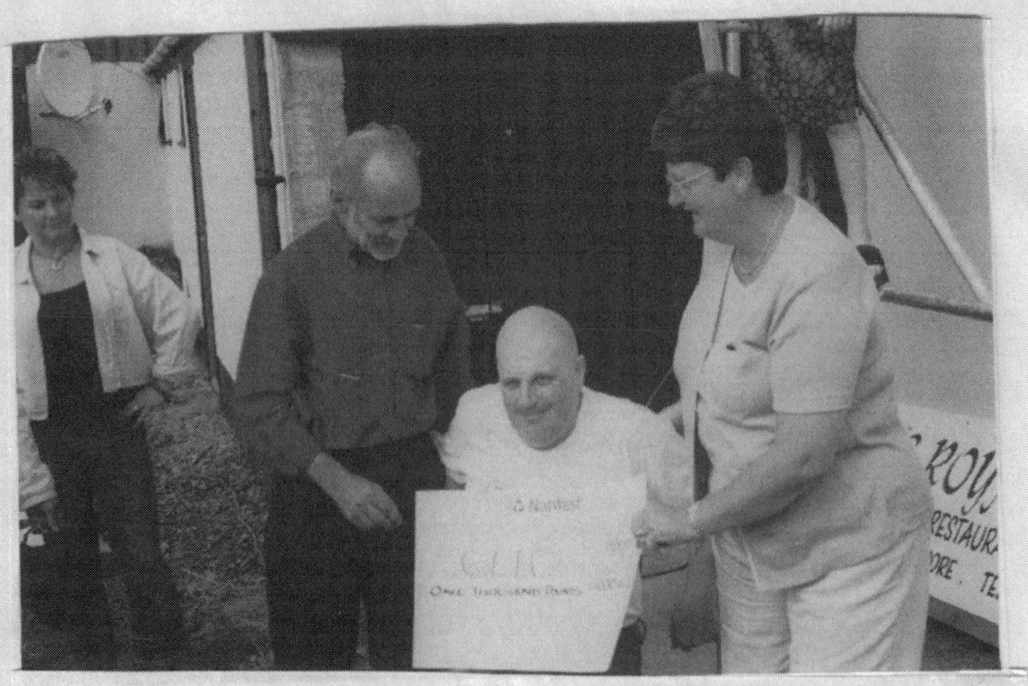

HEAD SHAVED ! A GREAT CHARITABLE GESTURE...UNBELIEVABLE !

C.L.I.C. Stand...'TOP of the WORLD !'

DERRY BROWNSON with DICK KERSEY who organised the boxing exhibition by BIDEFORD ABC.

A very enjoyable afternoon and all for an excellent cause.

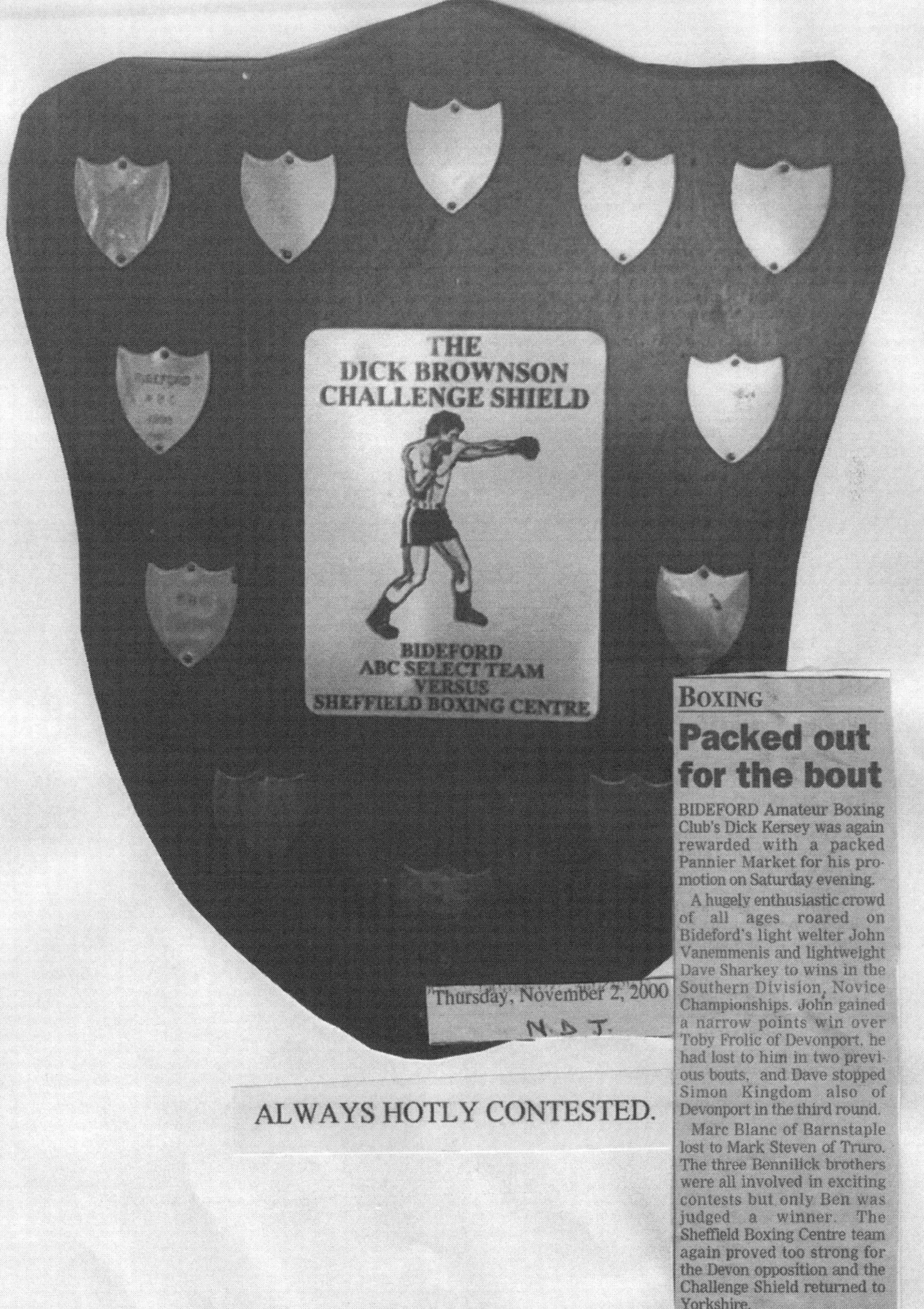

BOXING

Packed out for the bout

BIDEFORD Amateur Boxing Club's Dick Kersey was again rewarded with a packed Pannier Market for his promotion on Saturday evening.

A hugely enthusiastic crowd of all ages roared on Bideford's light welter John Vanemmenis and lightweight Dave Sharkey to wins in the Southern Division, Novice Championships. John gained a narrow points win over Toby Frolic of Devonport, he had lost to him in two previous bouts, and Dave stopped Simon Kingdom also of Devonport in the third round.

Marc Blanc of Barnstaple lost to Mark Steven of Truro. The three Bennilick brothers were all involved in exciting contests but only Ben was judged a winner. The Sheffield Boxing Centre team again proved too strong for the Devon opposition and the Challenge Shield returned to Yorkshire.

Thursday, November 2, 2000
N.D.J.

ALWAYS HOTLY CONTESTED.

Outside the NEW INN, BIDEFORD where the CLUB always met.

Sheffield boxers train in Bideford

BIDEFORD ABC and colleagues from Barnstaple treated boxers from Sheffield to a training weekend away from the city.

Sheffield Burn Greave ABC were successful in obtaining funding for a training weekend away and chose to visit Bideford.

They started by joining the Bideford boxers for an evening of training at their new premises on the Clovelly Road industrial estate. Then came two mornings of training with boxers from Bideford and Barnstaple and more training at Westward Ho! in the afternoons.

Bideford club spokesman Jeff Facey said the Bideford and Barnstaple boxers had benefited from the different training methods and styles of their Sheffield counterparts, while Sheffield were impressed with the technique that local boxers had attained.

"The weekend was a win-win situation for Bideford, Barnstaple and Sheffield. Respective trainers were eager to impart their knowledge and experience to all boxers who attended. Local boxers gained further skills and training experience from the visiting club and Sheffield also gained valuable skills from the nationally successful clubs of Bideford and Barnstaple," he said. "Bideford welcome back their Sheffield counterparts and friends and may try to obtain funding for a return visit."

Sheffield trainer Phil Wood said the visit had "exceeded expectations."

BURNGREAVE ABC FORMED 2007

TRAINERS PHIL WOOD, PETE KITSON, CHRIS KITSON

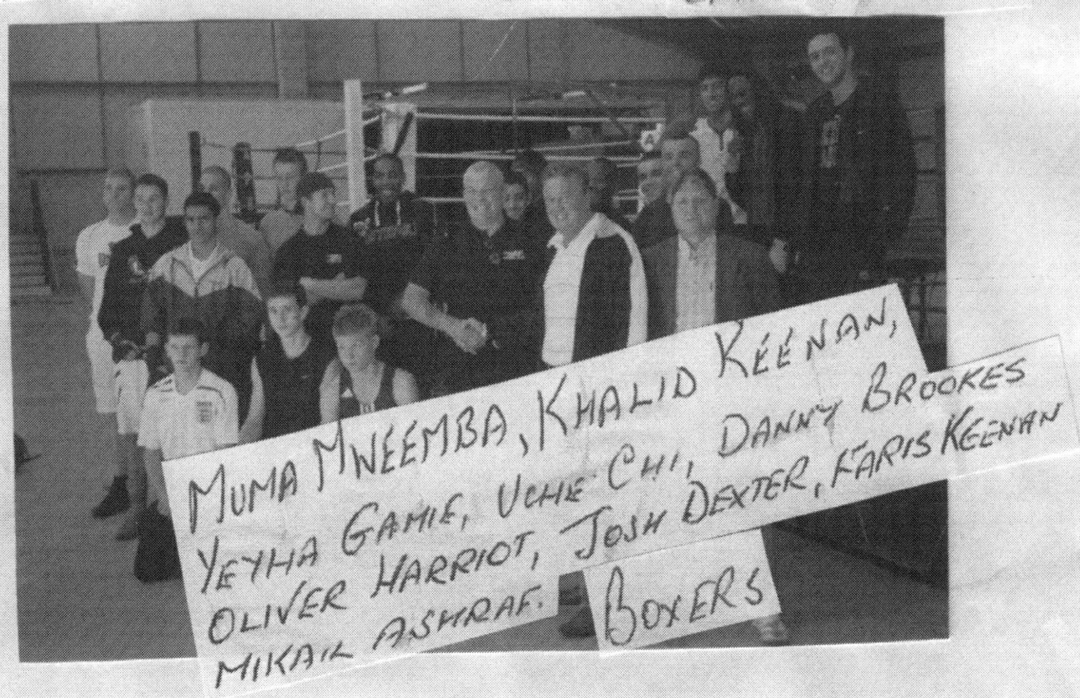

MUMA MWEEMBA, KHALID KEENAN,
YEYHA GAMIE, UCHE CHI, DANNY BROOKES
OLIVER HARRIOT, JOSH DEXTER, FARIS KEENAN
MIKAIL ASHRAF.
BOXERS

A GREAT MANY BOXERS from SHEFFIELD stayed with DICK KERSEY and his mother VIOLET. Also at INSTOW with DICK and NIKKI BROWNSON. Many had never seen the sea before and rushed from the house, vaulted the sea wall, landing straight into the high tide !

SOME OF THE SHEFFIELD BOXING TEAM.

DB hands the SHIELD to BIDEFORD BOXING CLUB TRAINER, CLIVE WHITMORE, for onward transmission to the winners SHEFFIELD BOXING CENTRE.

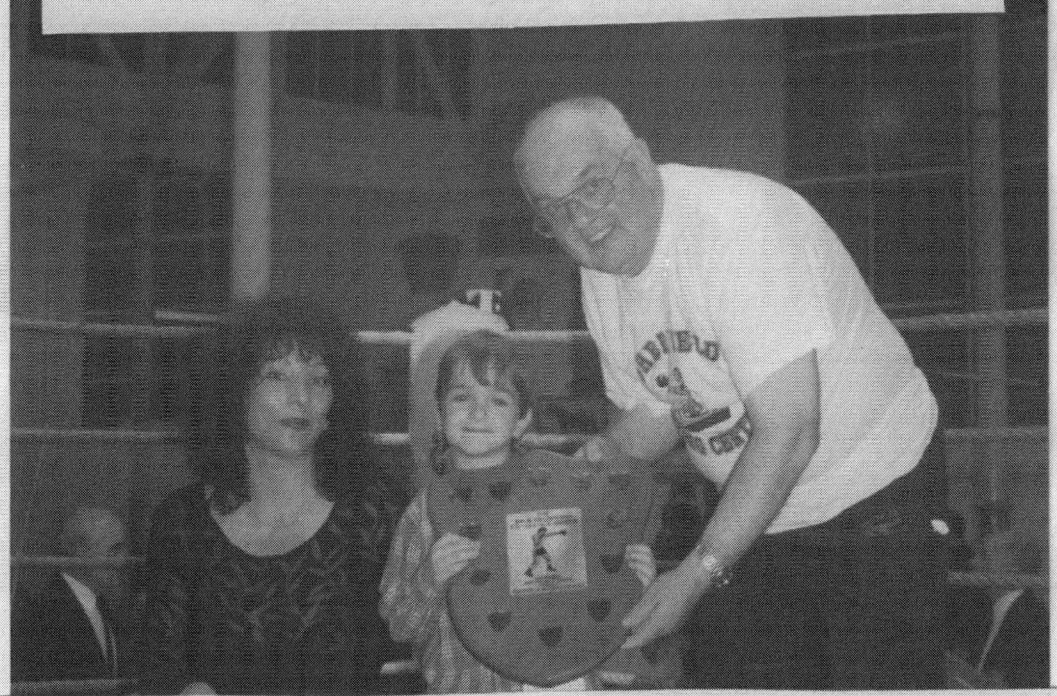

NIKKI BROWNSON presents the SHIELD to the winning SHEFFIELD trainer and young fan.

GLYN RHODES, SHEFFIELD BOXING SUPREMO with DB at INSTOW.

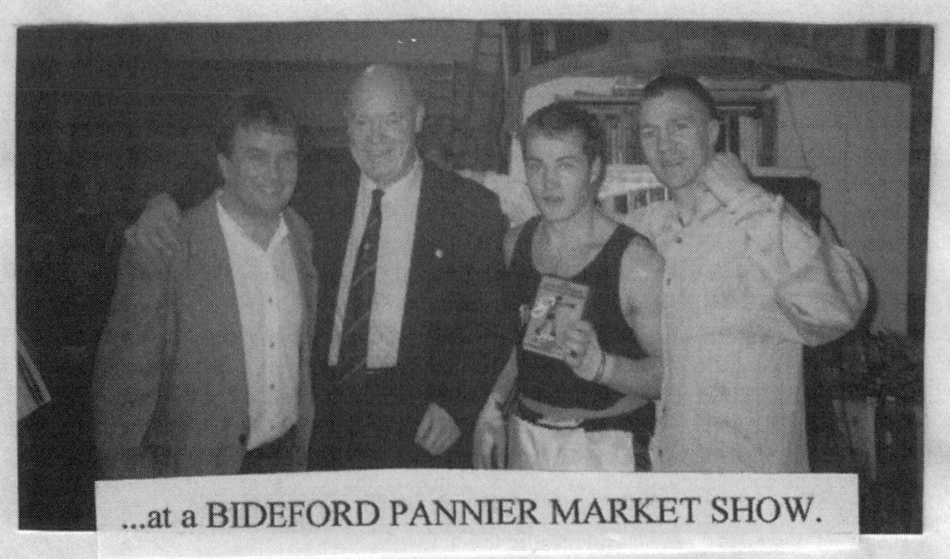

...at a BIDEFORD PANNIER MARKET SHOW.

ONE OF the big names in British boxing is in Bideford on Saturday for what promises to be a big night of sport.

Herrol "Bomber" Graham, the former British, Commonwealth and European middleweight champion will be the guest of honour at Bideford Boxing Club's show in the Pannier Market.

A team of boxers from his home town of Sheffield are on the bill, along with nine Bideford fighters and five from Barnstaple.

And Bideford coach and match-maker Ken Manley can hardly contain his enthusiasm about the evening.

"No-one has withdrawn yet," he said this week, "and we look certain to have a full card. It should be a great night's boxing."

HEROL GRAHAM was a regular visitor to INSTOW and BIDEFORD BOXING CLUB. The SHEFFIELD BOXERS received expert advice from him and GLYN RHODES.
All of them were training with PROFESSIONALS years before it became the normal arrangement in most gyms.
Never-the-less, NORTH DEVON boxers always gave them hard bouts.

N. D. J.

Thursday, March 28, 2002

■ BRIGHT FUTURE: Bideford Boxing Club's youngsters have new equipment to help them make the grade thanks to the generosity of a local boxing family. The three sons of the late Cyril Bright - a founder member of the club who died last year - donated the gear in memory of their father, who became a judge after he retired from the amateur ring.

■ And one of them, Kevin - pictured her in the centre - was at the club on Wednesday to present it to (L to R): Dick Kersey, Jodie Bray, John Van Emmenis, Chris Evans, Clive Whitmore, Keith Owen and, in front, Chris A'Lee and Tommy Langford.

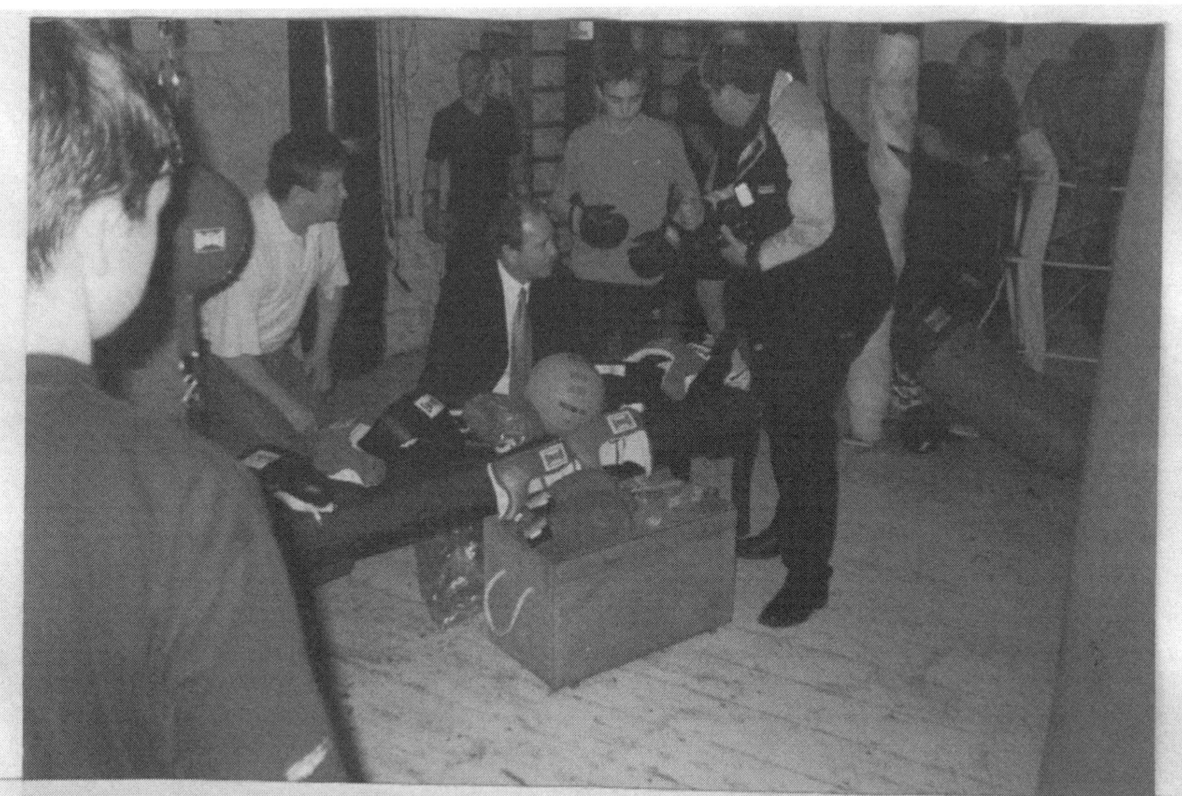

CYRIL BRIGHT was a FOUNDER MEMBER of BIDEFORD BOXING CLUB. This boxing equipment was donated to the Club in his memory by his three sons. KEVIN continues to support all the Club shows and is seen in these photographs in the boxing gym with the equipment,surrounded by boxers.

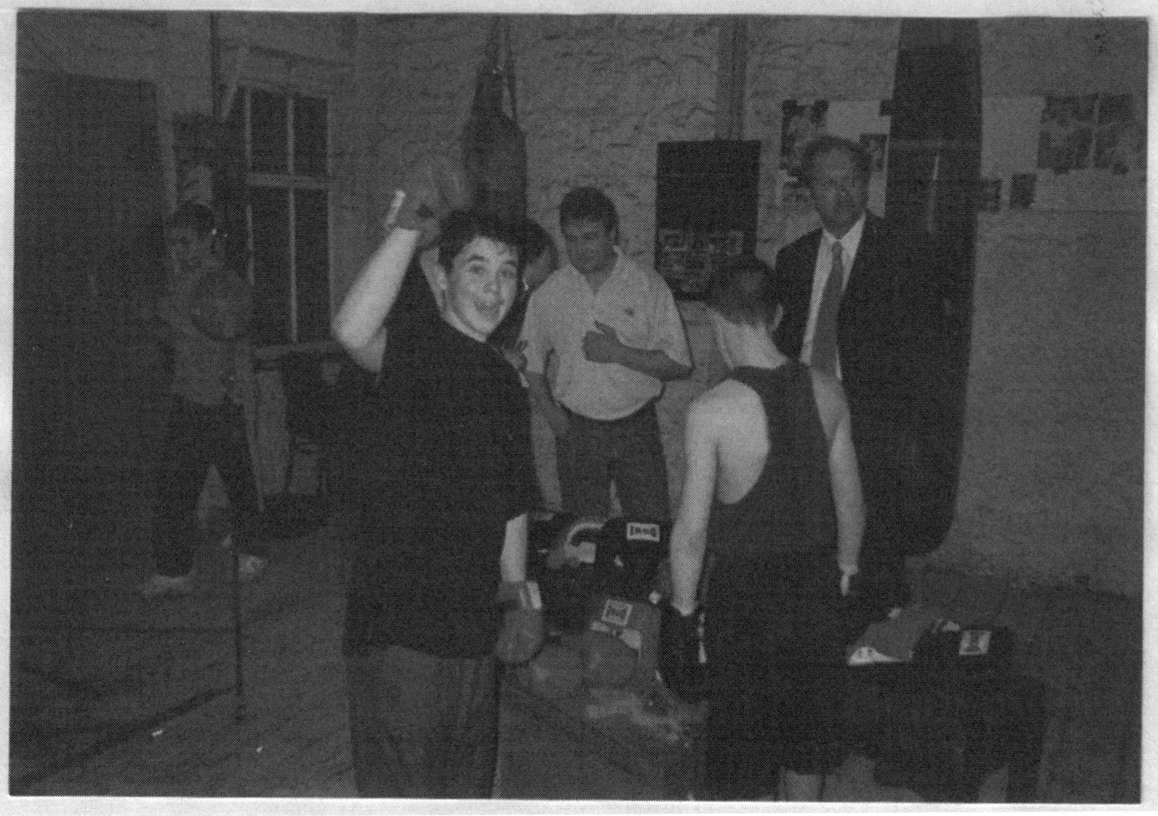

northdevongazette
• February 27, 2008

Seeing stars

Frank's visit is a knock-out!

■ KNOCK-out! Boxing legend Frank Bruno meets one of Bideford's top senior boxers, Richard Grigg and club head coach Dick Kersey

NEVER A DULL MOMENT!

BOXING enthusiasts were given the chance to get "ringside" with one of the true great legends of the sport at a packed sportsmen's gala dinner in Bideford on Thursday night.

The evening with Frank Bruno at the Durrant House Hotel gave fans the chance to quiz the charismatic former WBC world heavyweight champion about his life in the ring, and out.

Bruno spent the evening at the top table with Bideford Amateur Boxing Club head coach Dick Kersey, club treasurer Jeff Facey and up-and-coming senior boxer, 18-year-old Richard Grigg.

After dinner, he spent a good 30 minutes fielding questions from fans on all aspects of his career, from his showdowns with Mike Tyson, to a post-boxing turn as a star of pantomime.

Mr Kersey said that the event was the first celebrity sportsman's dinner the club had put on.

"It was a fantastic success and we would hope to arrange a similar event this time next year," he said.

COME BACK ANYTIME

KNOW WHAT I MEAN GENTS?
WICKED!

Former PROFESSIONAL BOXER, TOMMY LEROY presents Trophies.

FRANK GREENFIELD,
a regular supporter of local boxing presents Trophies.
DB looks on.

CHARLIE WOOTTON, a former LANDLORD of the APPLEDORE INN. BIDEFORD, always a supporter of local boxing.

...in the PUB, CHARLIE and DB.

BIDEFORD PANNIER MARKET SHOW with OLD FRIENDS.

BEST BOUT: Gordon White, secretary of the Square Ring Ex-Boxers' Association (South Devon), presents trophies to Matt Van Emmenis, *(right)*, and his opponent, Lloyd Roberts, at Bideford ABC's Pannier Market show. Van Emmenis, cousin of Bideford-based pro John Van Emmenis, won after claiming a unanimous decision and was also voted boxer of the night

PENNY HAYNES of APPLEDORE takes time out from her busy CHARITY WORK to present trophies at a BIDEFORD COLLEGE SHOW.

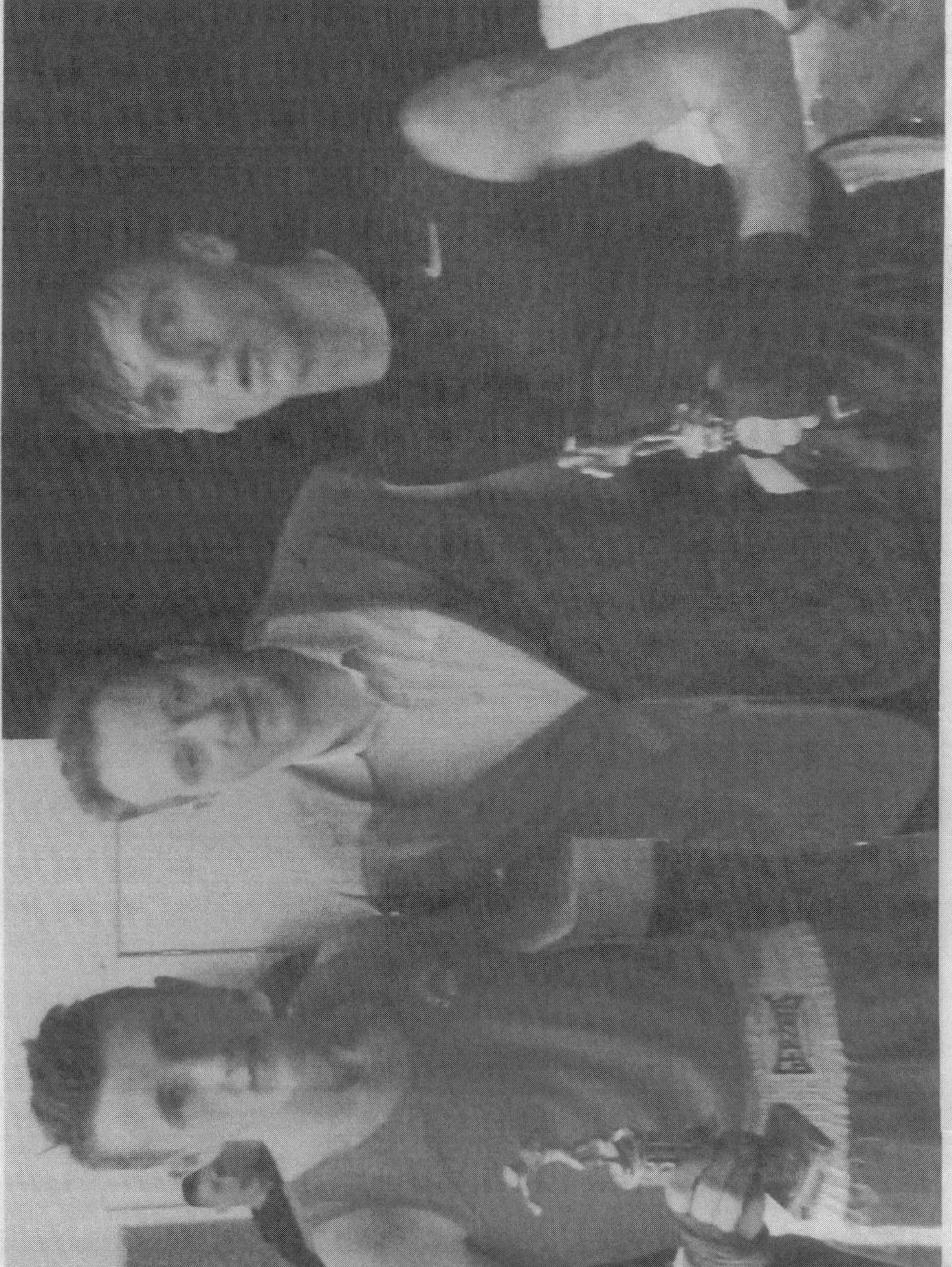

MARK NORTH of APPLEDORE presents Trophies.

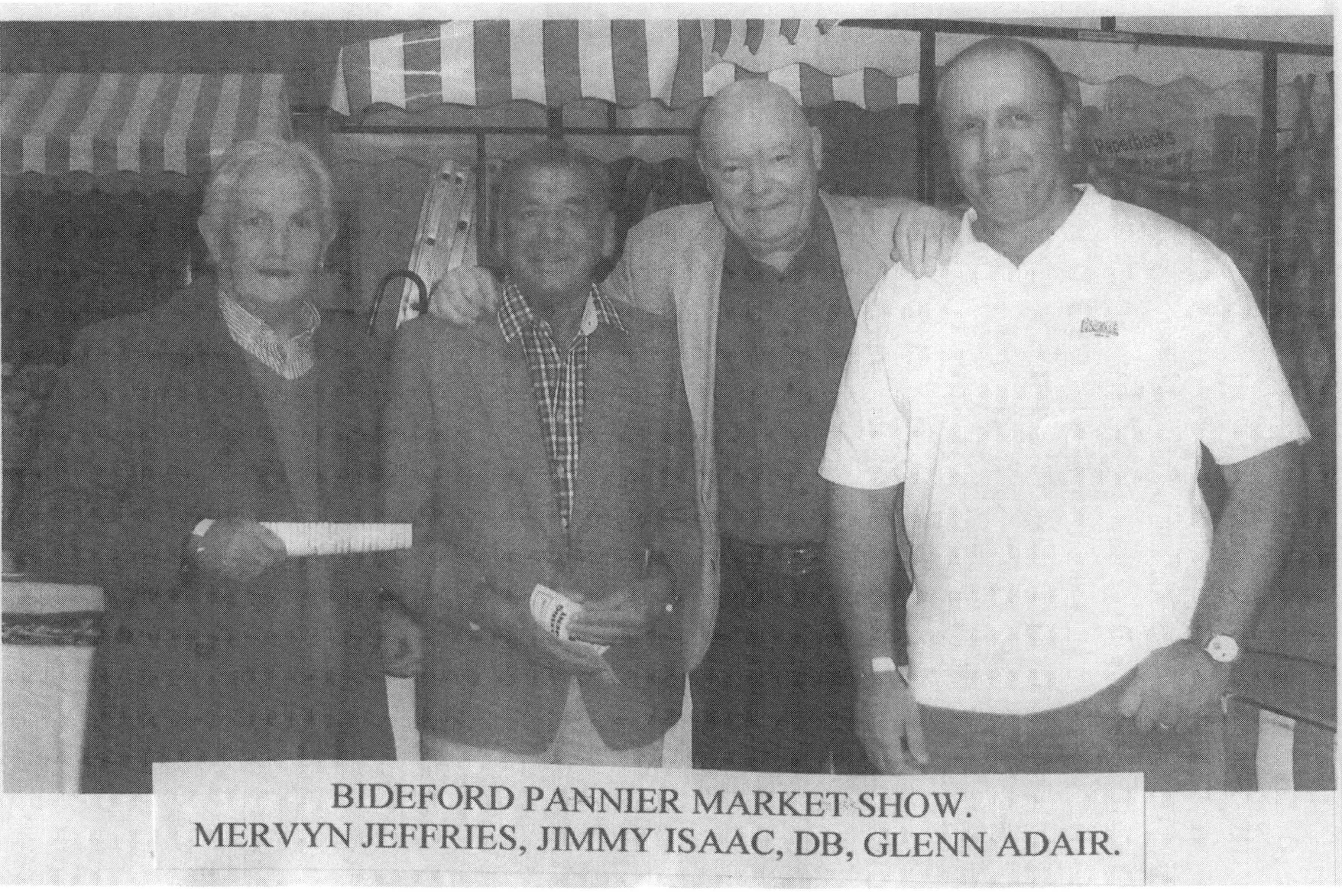

BIDEFORD PANNIER MARKET SHOW.
MERVYN JEFFRIES, JIMMY ISAAC, DB, GLENN ADAIR.

DB and DICK KERSEY with former WORLD PROFESSIONAL CHAMPION, CORNELIUS CARR.

PAUL CASSINNELLI, a great CLUB SUPPORTER over many years, with son FRANK helping to present Trophies.

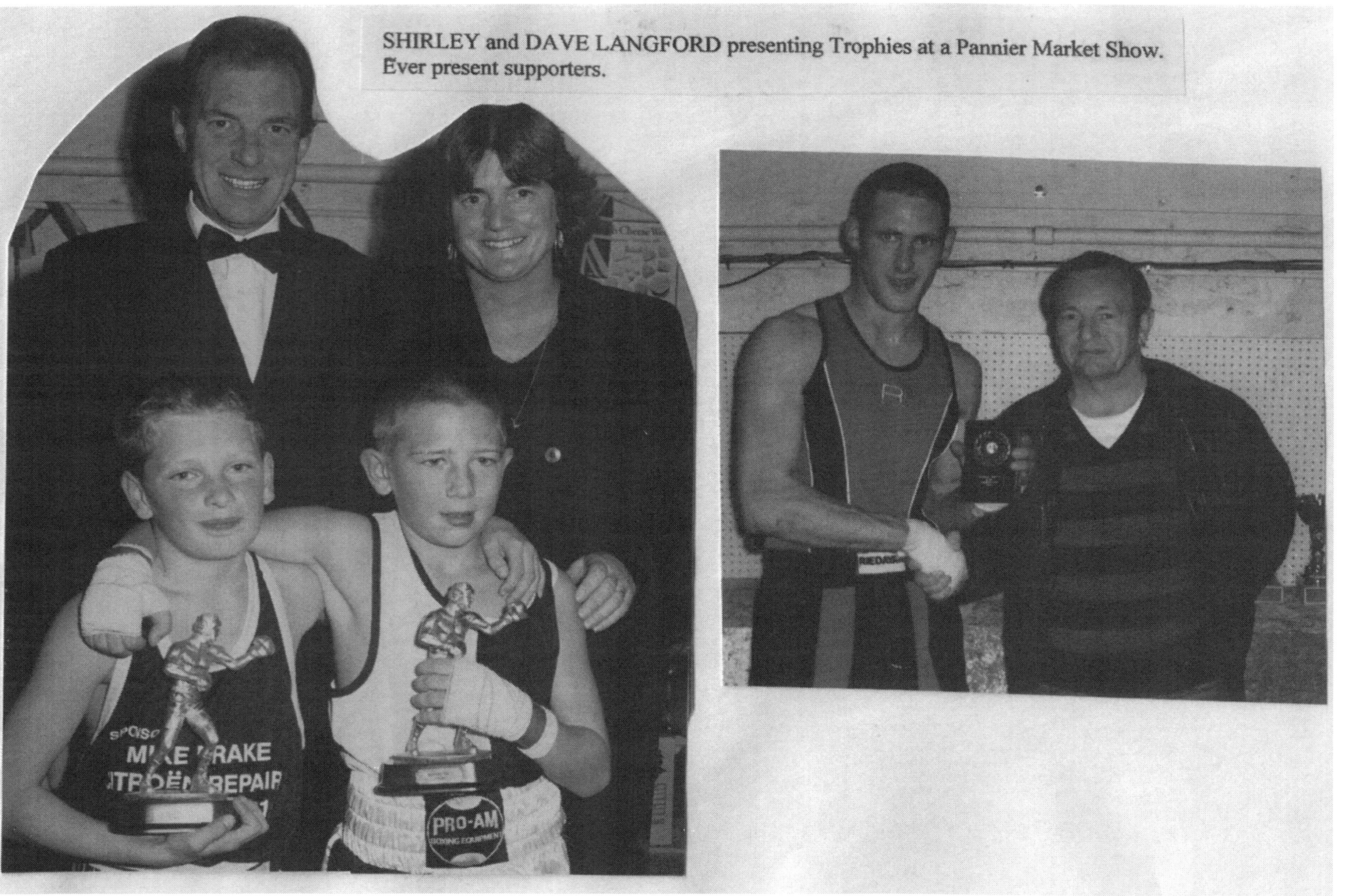

SHIRLEY and DAVE LANGFORD presenting Trophies at a Pannier Market Show.
Ever present supporters.

...and at a BIDEFORD BOXING CLUB PRESENTATION NIGHT.

KEN COURT, H and F FINANCE, LONDON.
KEN has SPONSORED MANY of the BIDEFORD BOXING CLUB SHOWS.

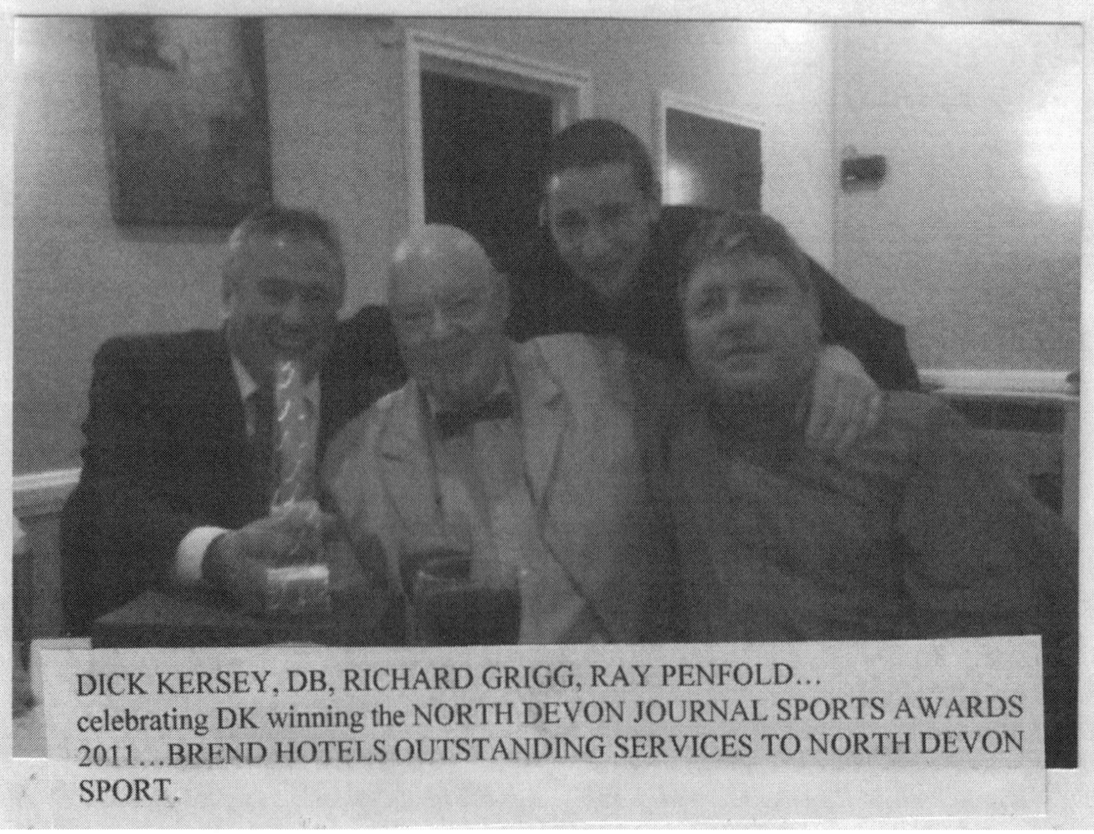

DICK KERSEY, DB, RICHARD GRIGG, RAY PENFOLD…
celebrating DK winning the NORTH DEVON JOURNAL SPORTS AWARDS 2011…BREND HOTELS OUTSTANDING SERVICES TO NORTH DEVON SPORT.

‘FLOWER GIRLS’
BIDEFORD BOXING CLUB PRESENTATION NIGHT.
A ‘Thank You’ to them from the CLUB COMMITTEE.

SALLY JOBSON-SCOTT.

NIKKI BROWNSON.

TERESA FRIENDSHIP

JANET OWEN

ELAINE LESTER.

…ALL EXPERTLY HANDLED, AS USUAL,
by
JEFF FACEY.

Presenting Trophies.

Councillor SIMON INCH.

ALAN MINTER, formerly WORLD MIDDLEWEIGHT BOXING CHAMPION.

JIMMY ISAAC, DAVID GRIGG, BARRY HAWKINS, DB, JOHNNY MOCK,
RONNIE ISAAC.
at the GRAND OPENING of our NEW GYM, POLLYFIELD, EAST-the-WATER,
BIDEFORD, 18th JANUARY, 2014.

Councillor CHRIS LEATHER

CHRIS PRESTON-SMITH, a CLUB stalwart, he never let us down.

EDWARD GASKELL of LAZARUS PRESS
presents the Trophies.
DURRANT HOUSE HOTEL.

DB with 'REGULARS' at a DURRANT HOUSE HOTEL SHOW.

Councillor SIMON INCH.

Councillor TONY INCH.

JOHNNY KINGDOM and DB at a PANNIER MARKET SHOW.

JOHNNY has been a REGULAR GUEST for years and CONTINUES to be as POPULAR as EVER

DERRY BROWNSON presents Trophies.
BIDEFORD'S BEN OWEN is nearing 100 AMATEUR BOUTS.

Councillor DERMOT McGEOUGH,

Councillor PHILIP PESTER,

MICHELLE INCH presents a MEDAL to BOXER LOUIS CLARK at a BIDEFORD BOXING CLUB PRESENTATION NIGHT.

Councillor BARRY PARSONS.

Councillor PETER CHRISTIE presents a WINNERS Trophy to his grandson, JAKE CHRISTIE.

DB with former professional boxer, TOMMY LEROY.

Councillor ROBIN JULIAN.

Councillor DERMOT McGEOUGH.

ALAN McKENZIE presenting Trophies.
A regular supporter of the CLUB.

Here CHEYE SAUNDERS gets his WINNER'S Trophy.

JEFF FACEY and ALAN McKENZIE present Trophies.
BIDEFORD PANNIER MARKET.

BARRY HAWKINS, RONNIE ISAAC, JIMMY ISAAC, DB, at the GRAND OPENING of our NEW GYM, POLLYFIELD, EAST-the-WATER, BIDEFORD, 18th JANUARY, 2014.

'MITCH' WARBURTON, DB, GARTH GOSS.

Councillor DOUG BUSHBY presents Trophies.

Councillor DOUG BUSHBY.

These BOXING GLOVES, AUTOGRAPHED by TOMMY LANGFORD and FRANKIE GAVIN were won in auction by DOUG and donated to the BOXING CLUB. They are now on permanent display in the GYM.

Councillor DERMOT McGEOUGH presents
JACK LANGFORD with the BELT as the...
'MOST OUTSTANDING BOXER.'
DURRANT HOUSE HOTEL SHOW.

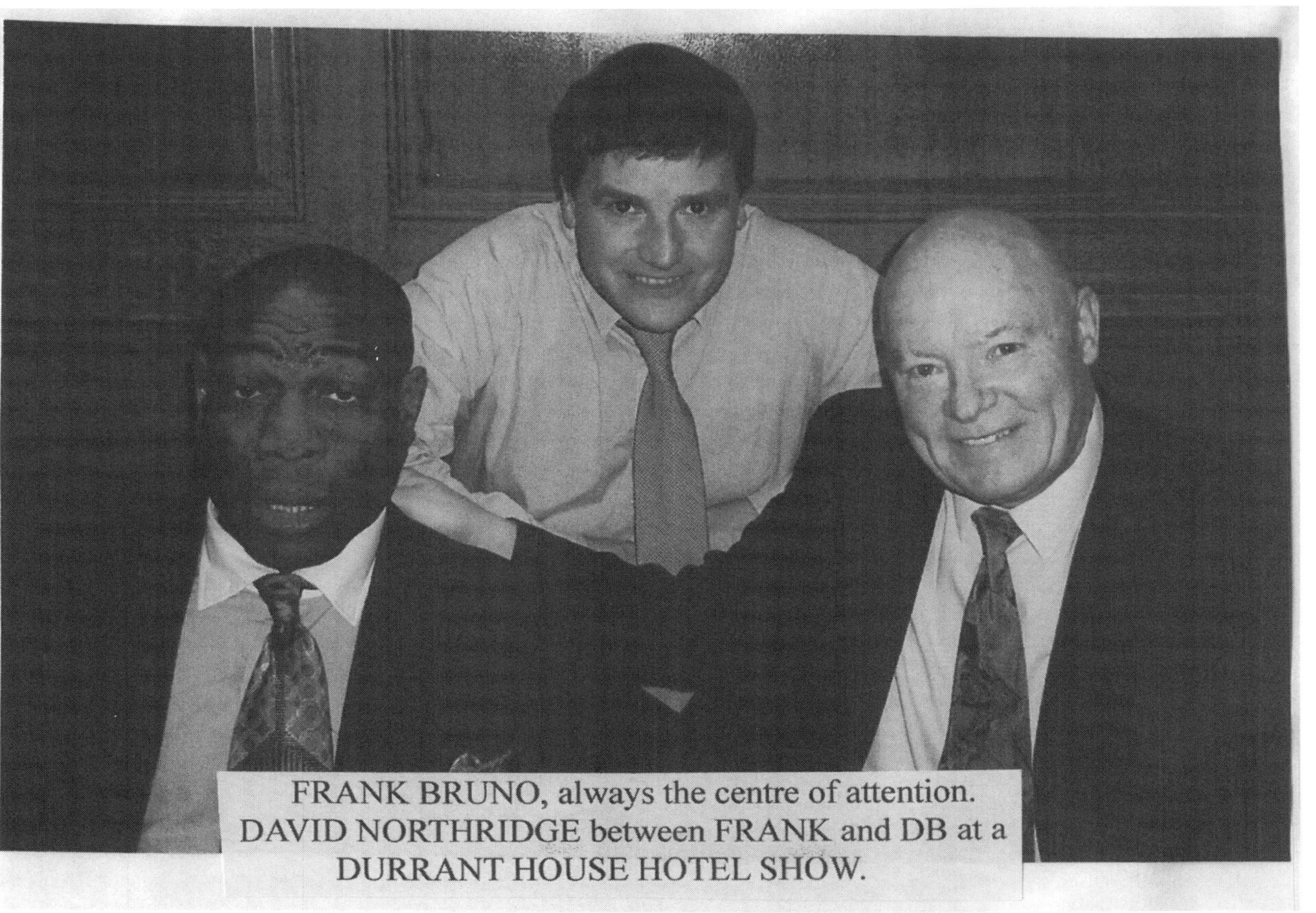

FRANK BRUNO, always the centre of attention.
DAVID NORTHRIDGE between FRANK and DB at a
DURRANT HOUSE HOTEL SHOW.

Councillor MERVYN LANGMEAD.

Councillor SIMON INCH.

DB, DENZIL LEWIS, PROFESSIONAL BOXING REFEREE, BARBARA LEWIS, NIKKI BROWNSON, HEROL GRAHAM.
AT A BIDEFORD PANNIER MARKET SHOW.

DENZIL, GLYN RHODES, BARBARA, DB.

JOHNNY KINGDOM and the GANG !

GLENN ADAIR with KYLE De BANKS formerly of BIDEFORD ABC, now with the ROYAL NAVY.

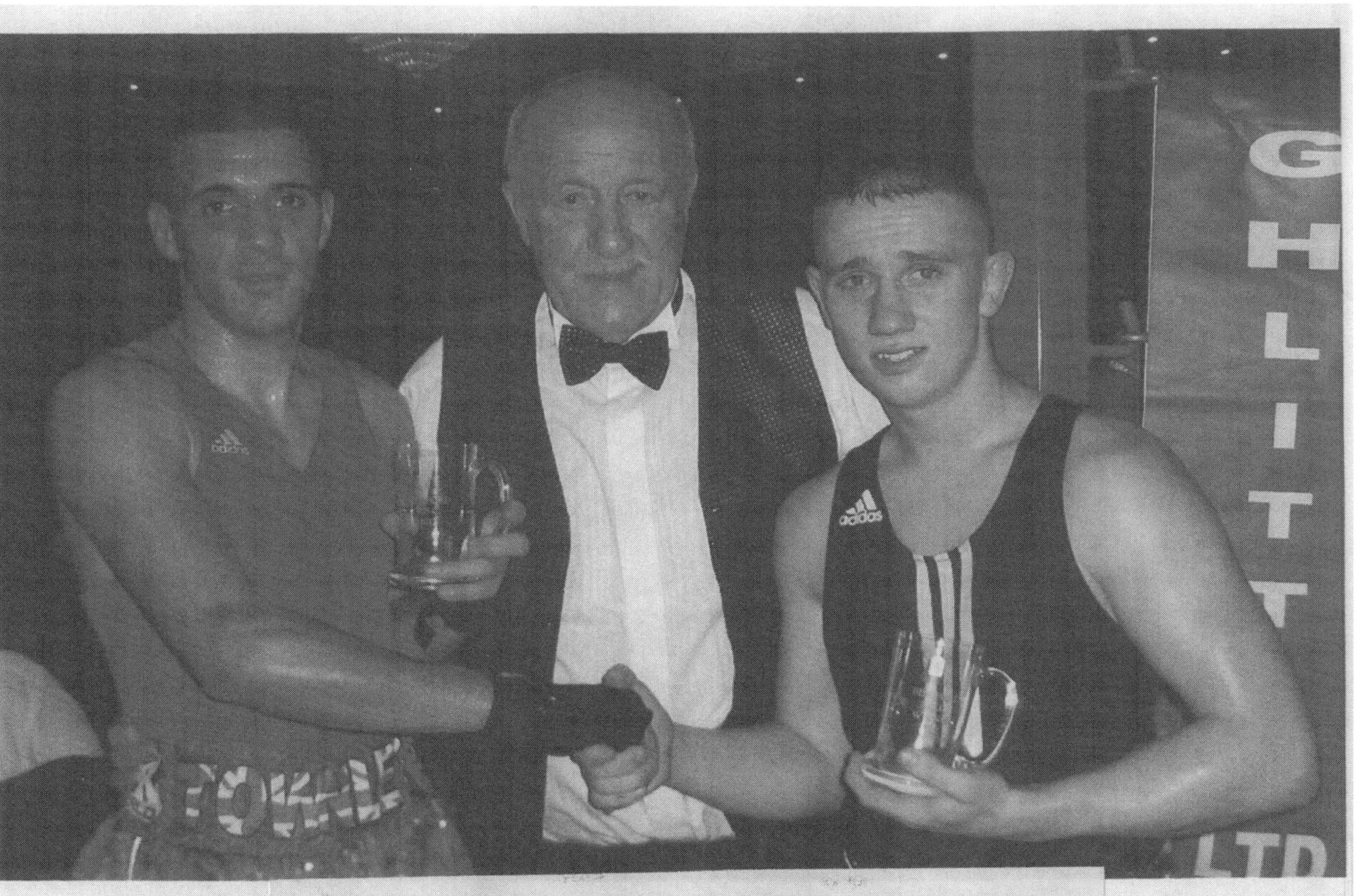

PHIL COX presents Trophies. BIDEFORD'S BEN OWEN is nearing 100 AMATEUR BOUTS.

DB with FAMILY MEMBERS at a DURRANT HOUSE HOTEL SHOW.

The DURRANT HOUSE HOTEL SHOW...
DB with JOHNNY KINGDOM, always a GREAT SUPPORTER of BIDEFORD ABC.

DB with son LEE.

...and DERRY.
STEVE CLARKE and friend nearby.

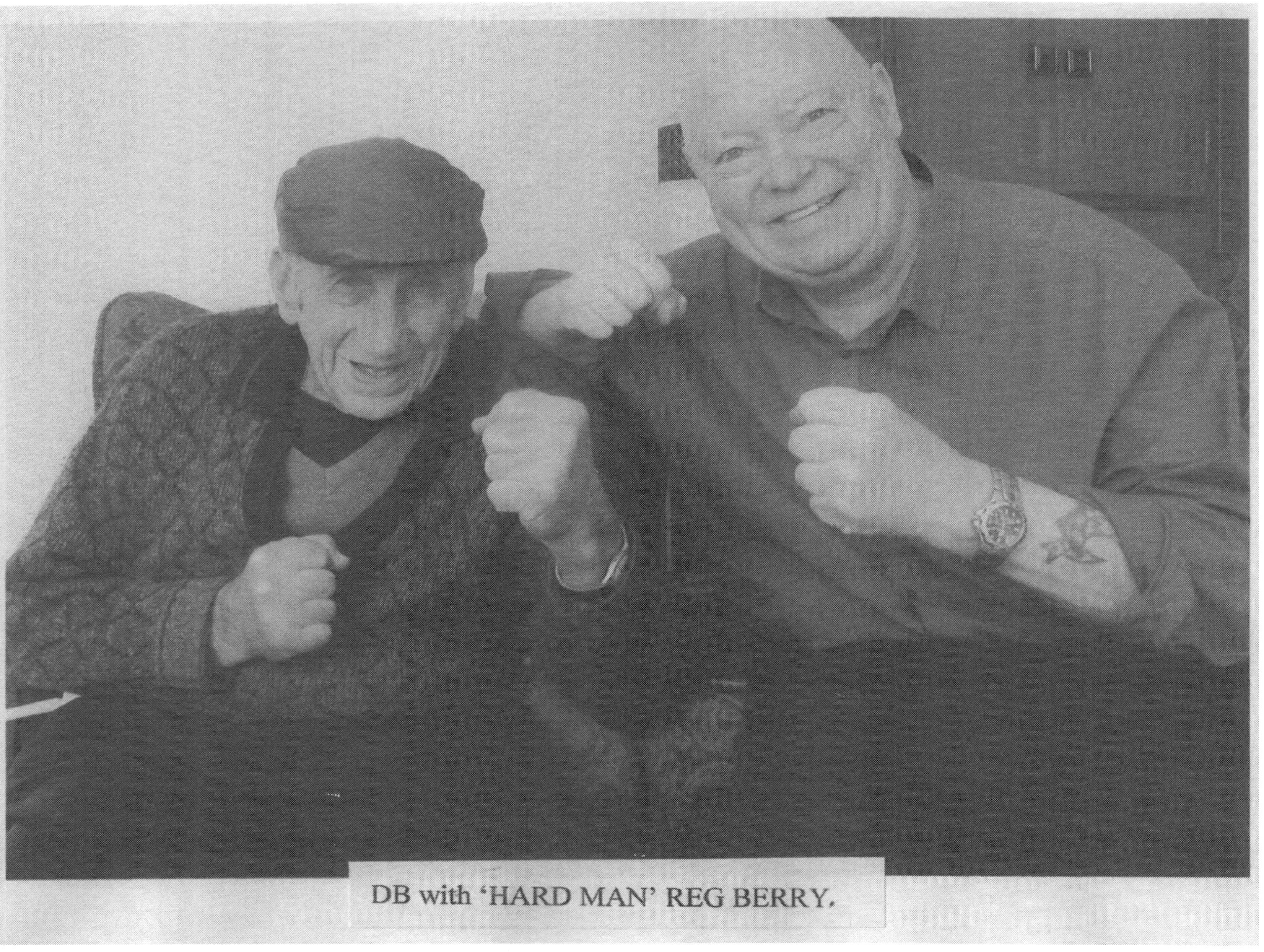

DB with 'HARD MAN' REG BERRY.

ANNUAL CLUB PRESENTATION NIGHT.

Councillor PHILIP PESTER.

BARRY JONES with RAY PENFOLD on his right.

DB and DAVE STACY.

A re-union with PROFESSIONAL MANAGER and TRAINER NIGEL CHRISTIAN after almost 30 years.

JOHN SABIN, JOHNNY KINGDOM, ELAINE LESTER.

KEN WHEATLEY with
AARON HINTON winner of his debut bout in the ring.

A fading REX 'STRANGLER' CASEY...but game to the very end. DB.

Seated…LES BOOTH, MARJORIE BOOTH, JILL GREEN, MERVYN 'MEL' GREEN. Bideford Pannier Market Show.

…with JIMMY ISAAC.

DB in illustrious company…
GLENN ADAIR, former AMATEUR HEAVY WEIGHT CHAMPION of GREAT BRITAIN.
JIMMY ISAAC, lost twice in a FINAL, once to KEN BUCHANAN who went on to win a WORLD PROFESSIONAL TITLE.
I could live with THAT DEFEAT on my record !!!...DB.

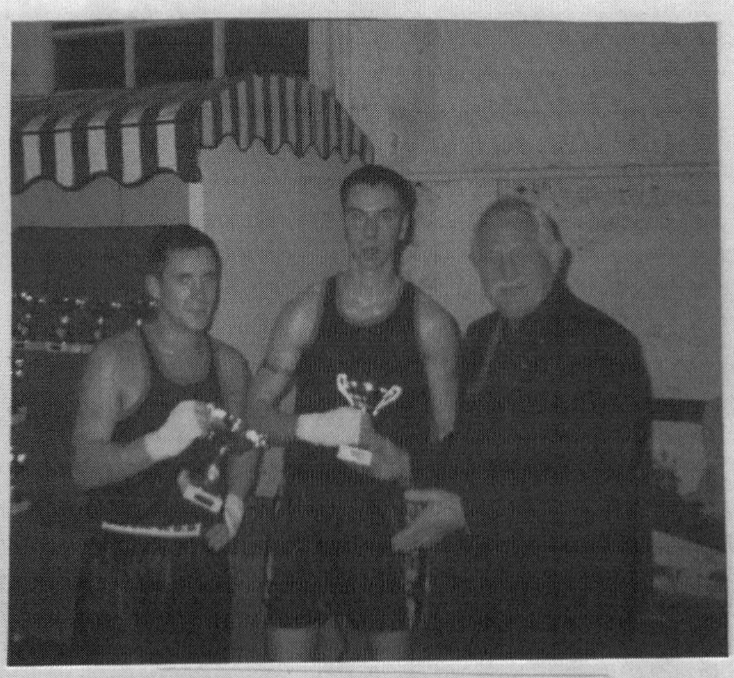

CHRIS PRESTON-SMITH.

RAY PENFOLD, PRESIDENT, BIDEFORD BOXING CLUB.

GARTH GOSS presenting Trophies.

KEVIN FISHLEIGH with the STAN FISHLEIGH MEMORIAL SHIELD.
This SHIELD, in memory of his father, is presented to a BIDEFORD CLUB BOXER to hold for one year at the club's annual presentation night.

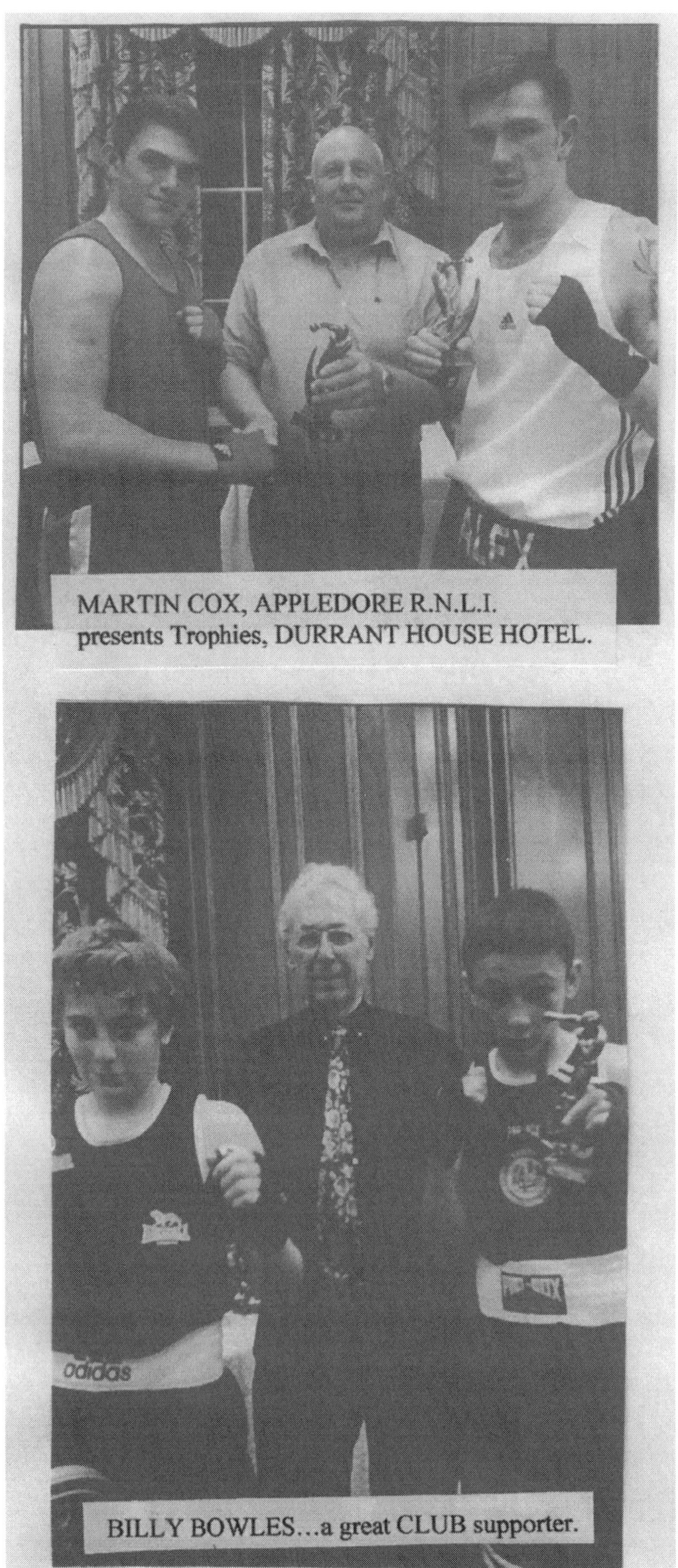

MARTIN COX, APPLEDORE R.N.L.I.
presents Trophies, DURRANT HOUSE HOTEL.

BILLY BOWLES…a great CLUB supporter.

Councillors PHILIP PESTER, MERVYN LANGMEAD, SIMON INCH. Further along the TOP TABLE, Councillor DOUG BUSHBY chats to NDJ reporter, MARK JENKIN.

JONATHAN BARKER of CENTURY GALLERIES, BIDEFORD, DB, DERRY BROWNSON.

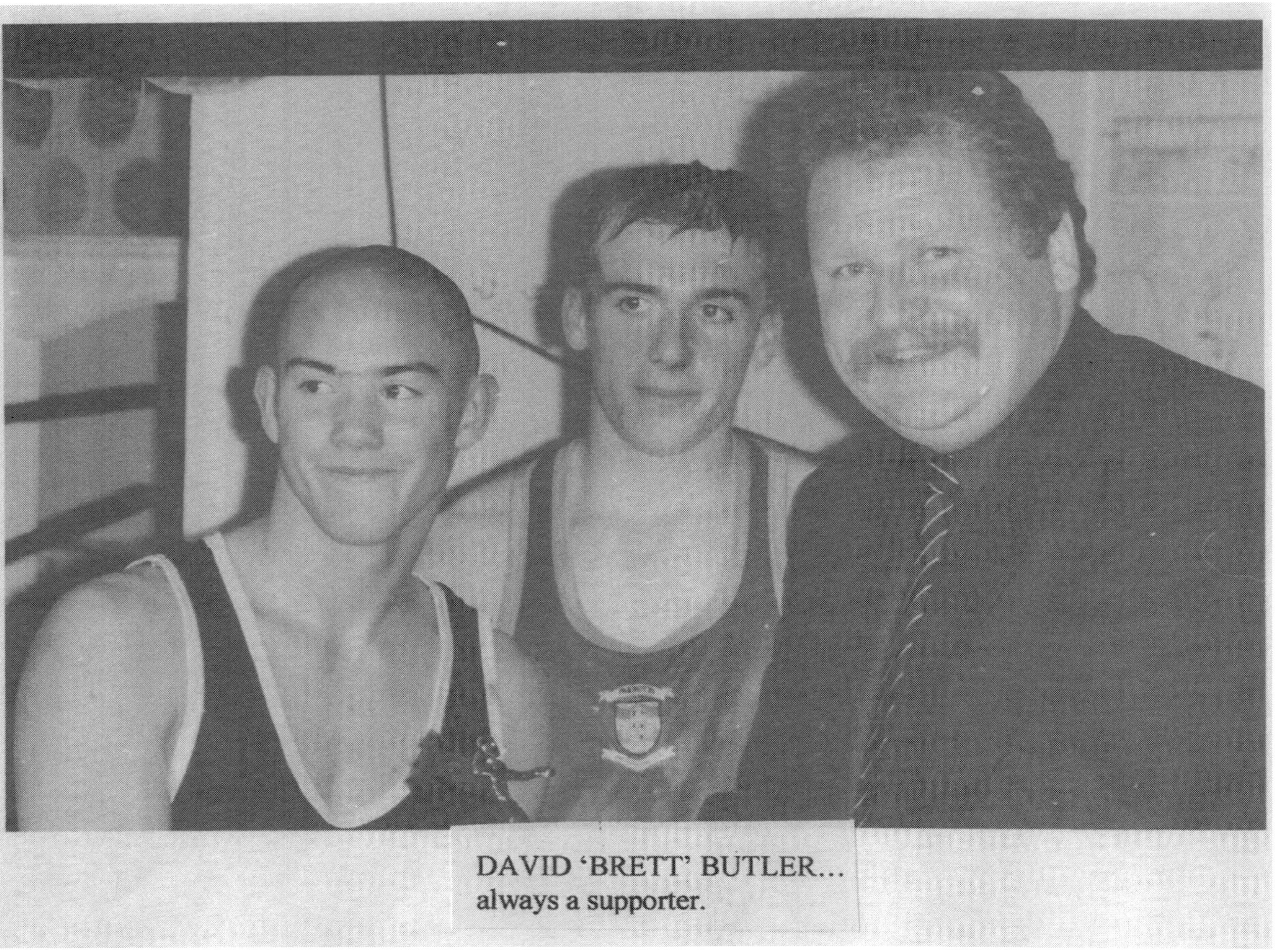

DAVID 'BRETT' BUTLER…
always a supporter.

ARTHUR SCRINE, Landlord of the PATCH and PARROT PUB in BIDEFORD. A dedicated supporter of BIDEFORD BOXING CLUB.

DICK KERSEY, DB, ARTHUR.

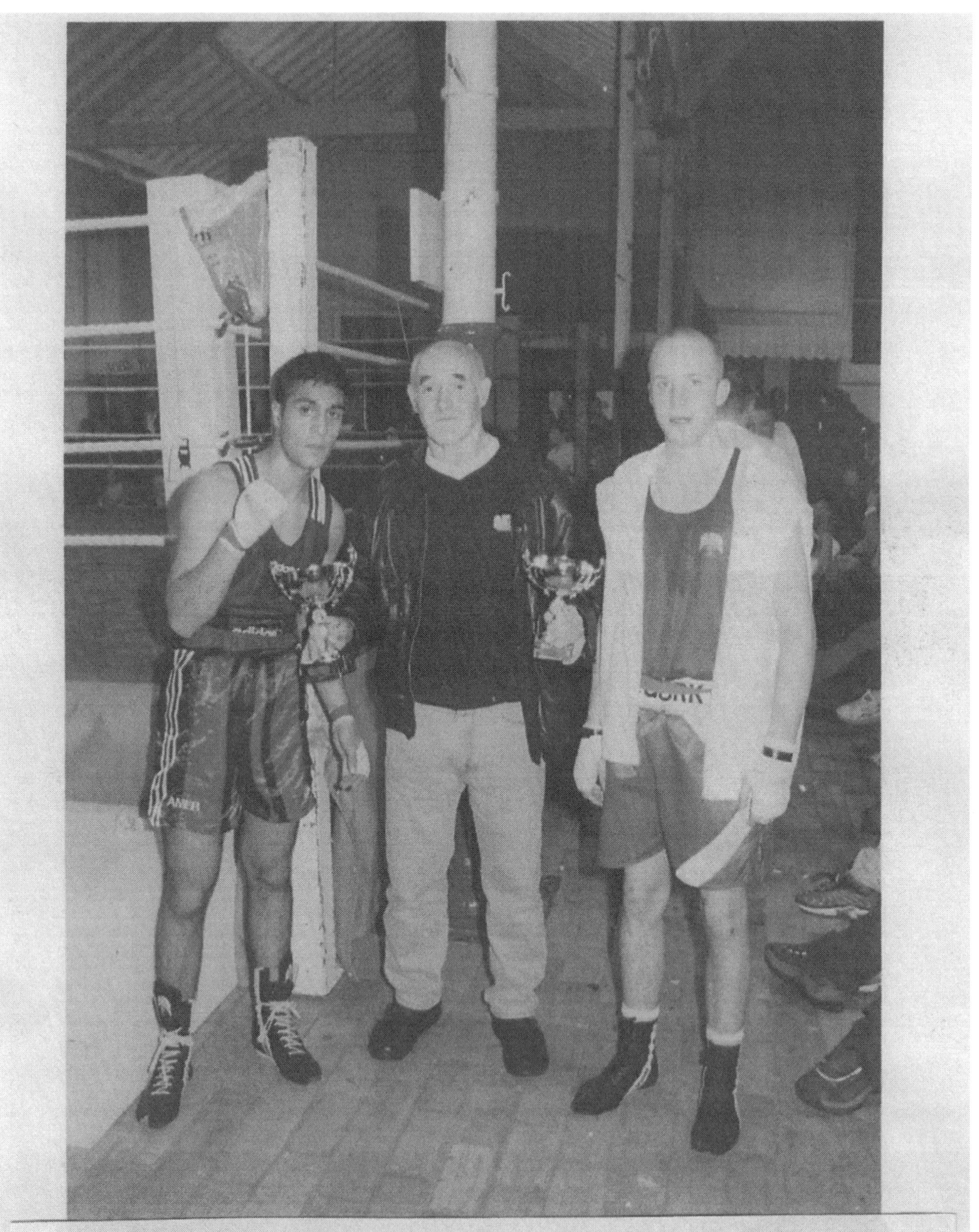

Presenting Trophies at a BIDEFORD PANNIER MARKET SHOW.

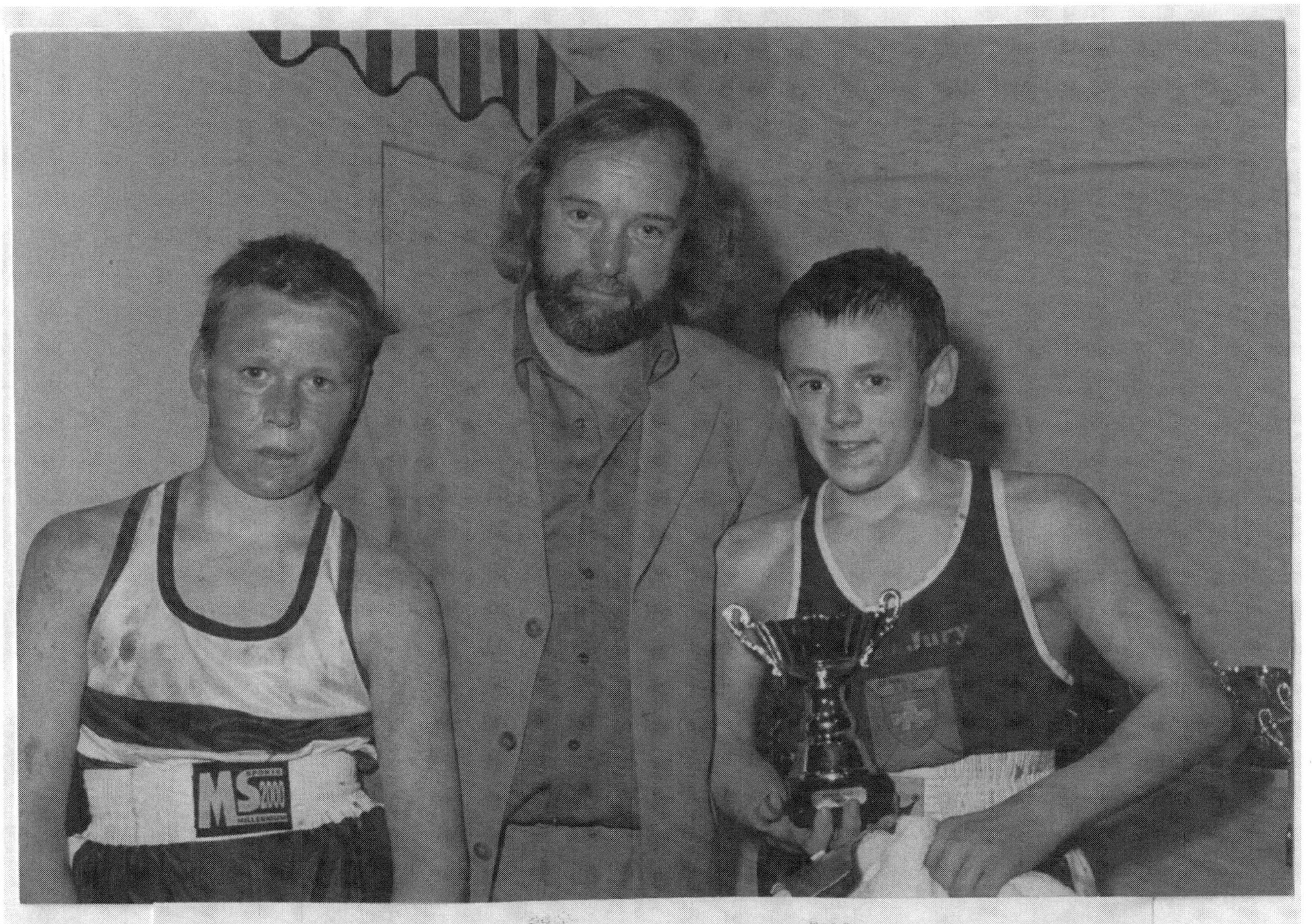

JIM HOPKINS, former LANDLORD of the APPLEDORE INN, BIDEFORD
presents Trophies at a BIDEFORD PANNIER MARKET SHOW.

JOHNNY KINGDOM holds fort at the
DURRANT HOUSE HOTEL SHOW.
DERRY BROWNSON, GLENN ADAIR, JK, DB, JIMMY ISAAC, PHIL COX.

JOHNNY points out CLUB PRESIDENT, RAY PENFOLD for the cameraman.

TED TITHECOTT of TITHECOTT CONTRACTORS,
WESTWARD HO!
A GENEROUS SUPPORTER of the BOXING CLUB over a GREAT MANY YEARS.

LES BOOTH, a former boxer and holder of a PROFESSIONAL TRAINER'S LICENCE.

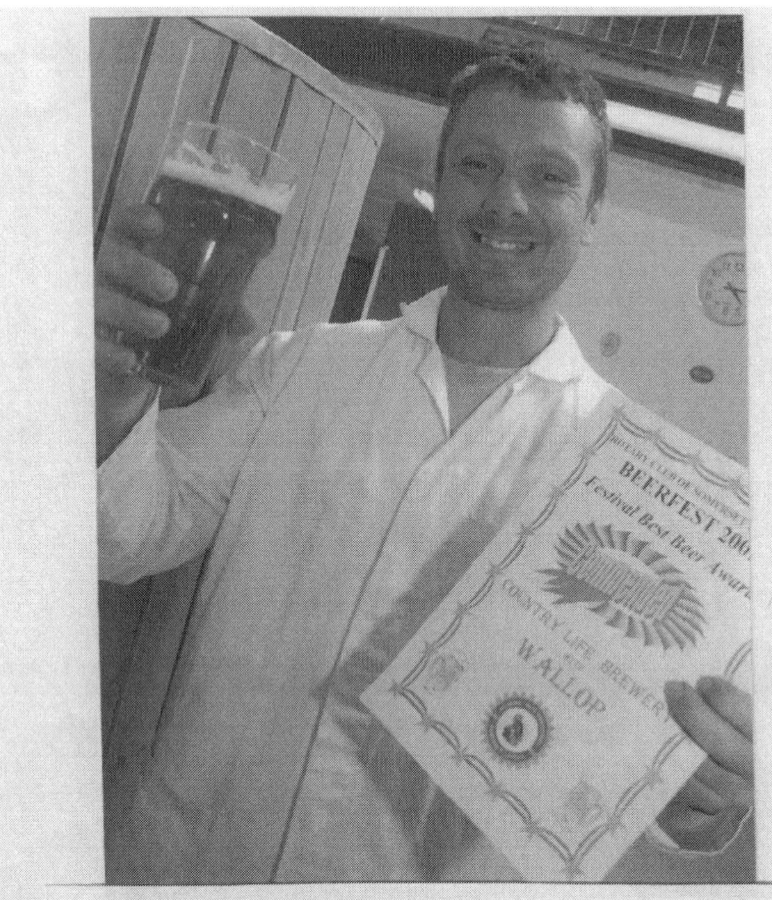

SIMON LACEY, a former boxer with BIDEFORD ABC.

SIMON and ANNA
now run a VERY SUCCESSFUL BREWERY BUSINESS.

COUNTRY LIFE BREWERY

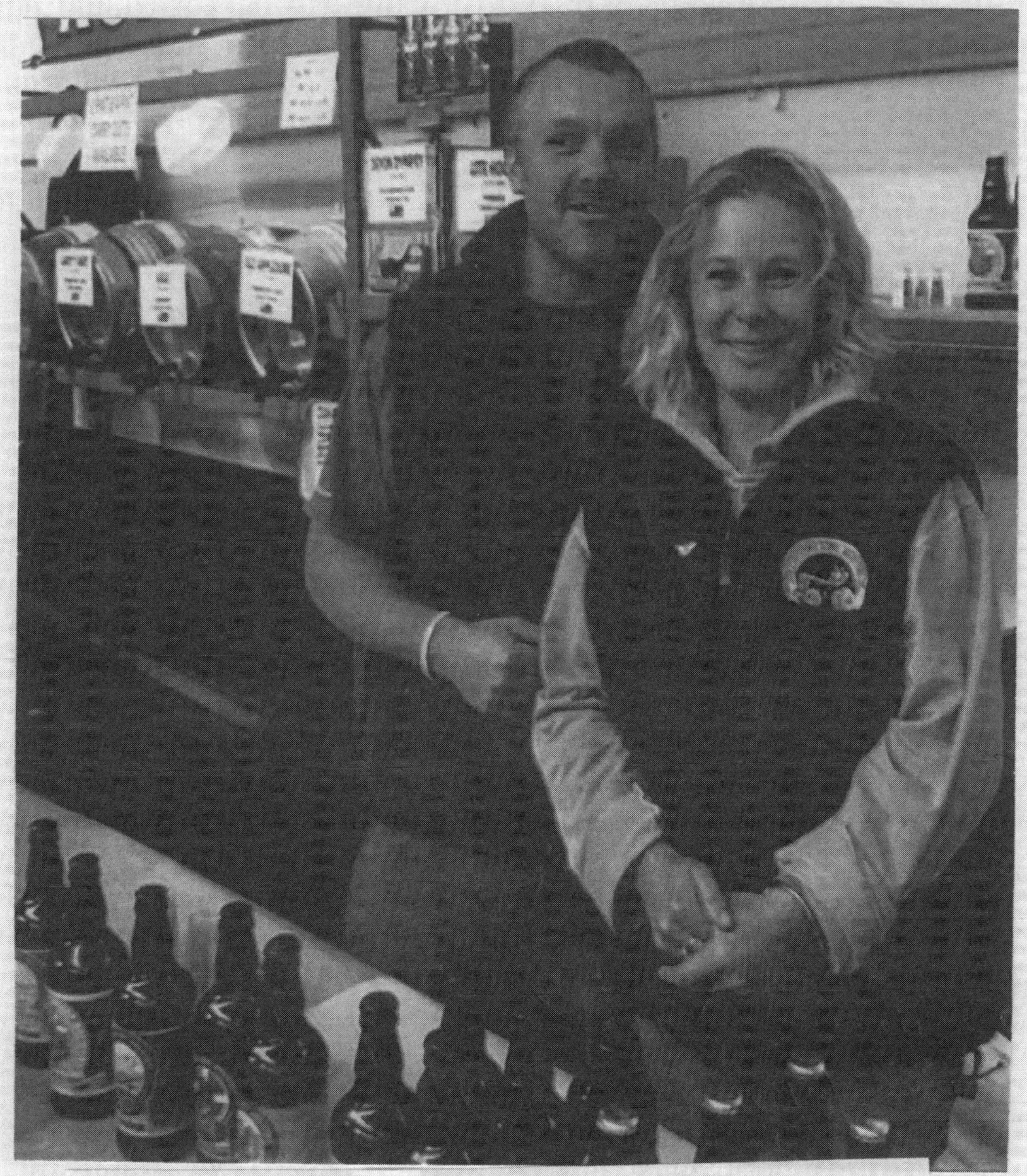

SIMON and ANNA surrounded by their BREWERY PRODUCTS.
What a GREAT BUSINESS to be in !!

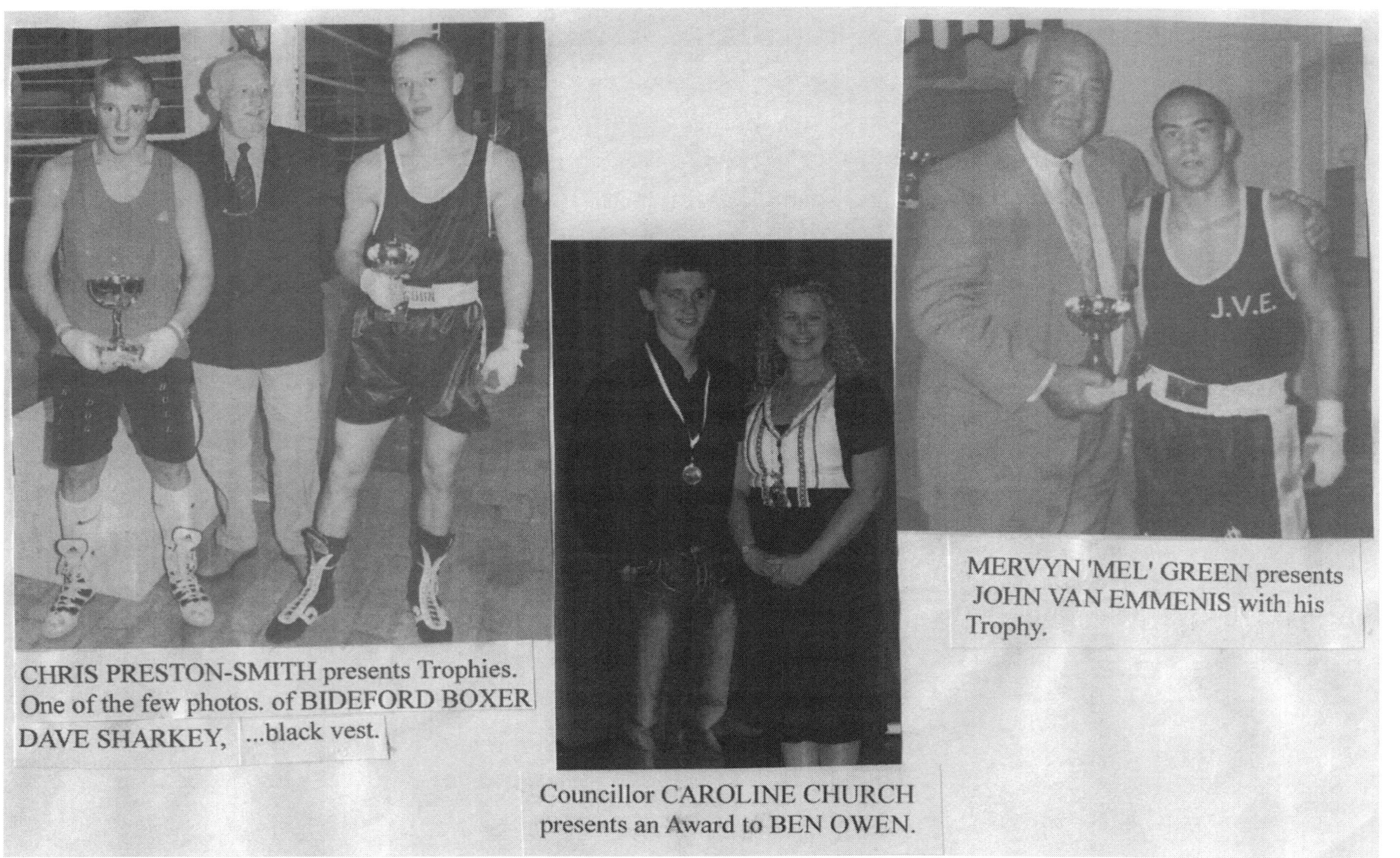

CHRIS PRESTON-SMITH presents Trophies. One of the few photos. of BIDEFORD BOXER DAVE SHARKEY, ...black vest.

Councillor CAROLINE CHURCH presents an Award to BEN OWEN.

MERVYN 'MEL' GREEN presents JOHN VAN EMMENIS with his Trophy.

DURRANT HOUSE HOTEL SHOW.

Always ready to help BIDEFORD BOXING CLUB...
JONATHAN BARKER of CENTURY GALLERIES with DB

Councillor CHRIS LEATHER presents Trophies.

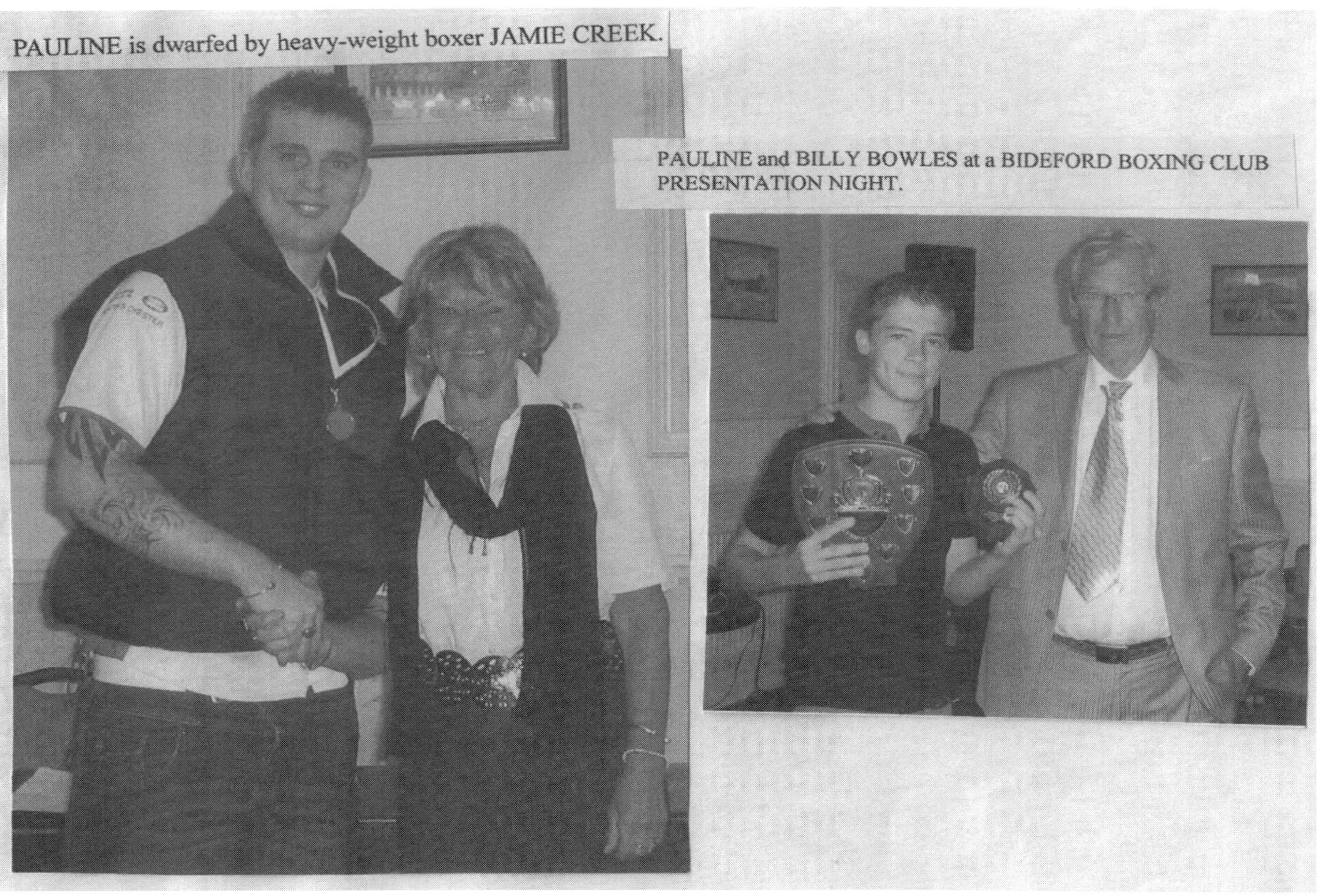

PAULINE is dwarfed by heavy-weight boxer JAMIE CREEK.

PAULINE and BILLY BOWLES at a BIDEFORD BOXING CLUB PRESENTATION NIGHT.

...with boxer VALENTIN BUMBUL.

BILLY PARSONS receives his BELT and SHIELD.

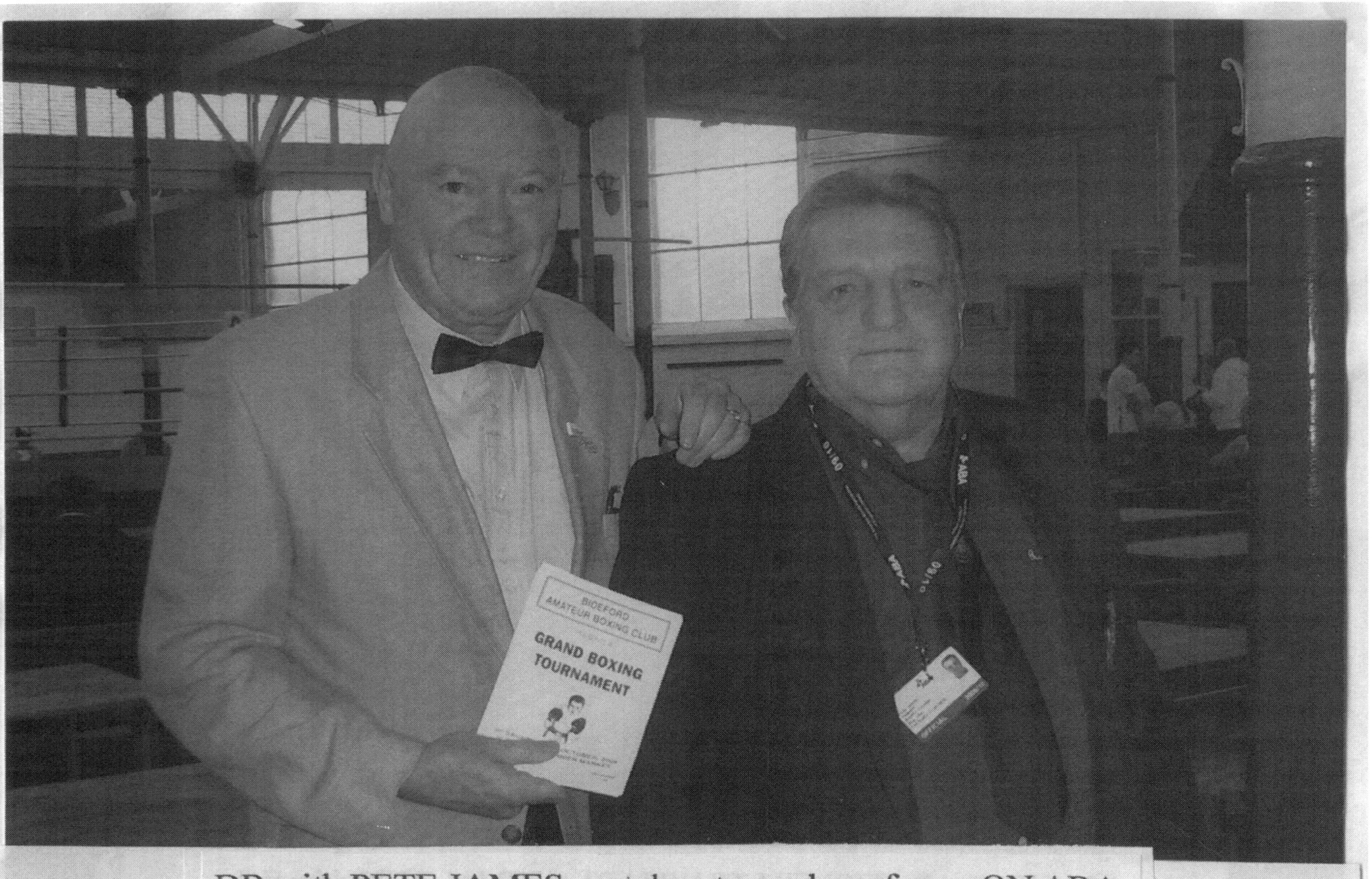

DB with PETE JAMES, a stalwart member of ON ABA.
DEVON ABA.

The 'GANG'...at the CONSERVATIVE CLUB, BIDEFORD, for the BOOK SIGNING, Volume..1 of 'THE STORY OF NORTH DEVON BOXING' I hope they ALL make it for this BOOK LAUNCH !

BOOK SIGNING for 'BATTLE FOR THE BELT'
at
WALTER HENRY'S BOOKSHOP, BIDEFORD.
JULIE GILL of WHB, Councillor MERVYN LANGMEAD, RICHIE WENTON,
former BRITISH CHAMPION who arrived with his LORD LONSDALE BELT, DB.

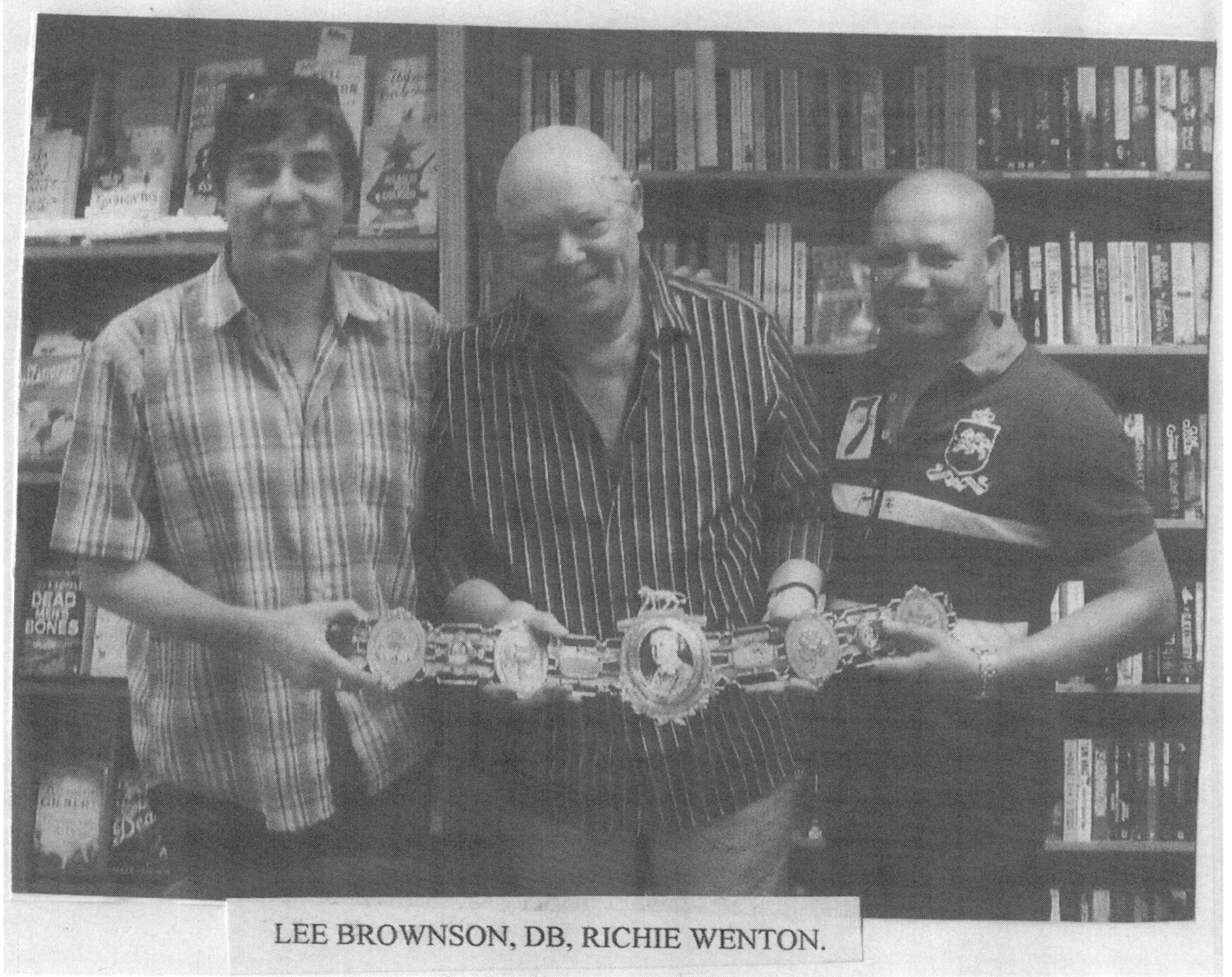

LEE BROWNSON, DB, RICHIE WENTON.

BOOK SIGNING at WALTER HENRY'S BOOKSHOP, BIDEFORD. DICK KERSEY is joined by his mother, VIOLET, DB centre with plaster cover around eye. The result of efforts to put right old injuries.

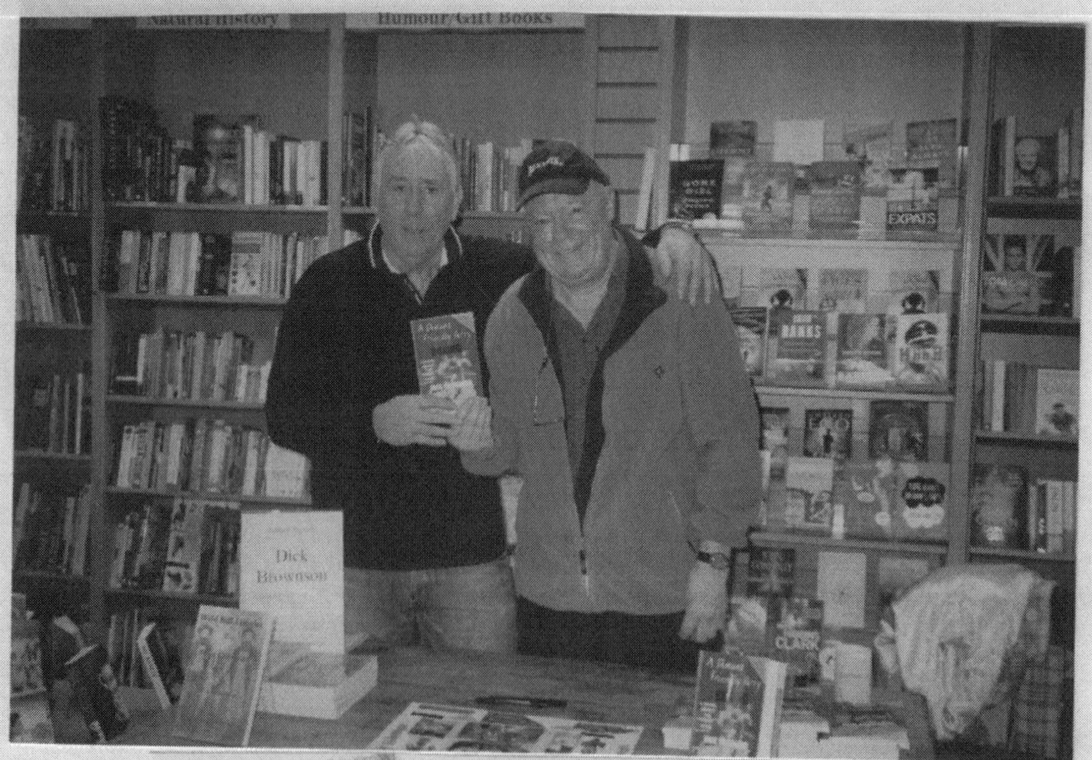

Former boxer SAM ADAIR buys a book.

BOOK SIGNING at WALTER HENRY'S BOOKSHOP, BIDEFORD.
Always great support from PAM and Councillor PHILIP PESTER.
RICHIE WENTON turned up with his LONSDALE BELT.

DB with DICK KERSEY.

LUNDY JOHN ALFORD and DB at the BOOK SIGNING,
BIDEFORD CONSERVATIVE CLUB,
for Volume..1 of
'THE STORY OF NORTH DEVON BOXING'
I would like to write HIS LIFE STORY...
PG RATING would then take on a new significance !

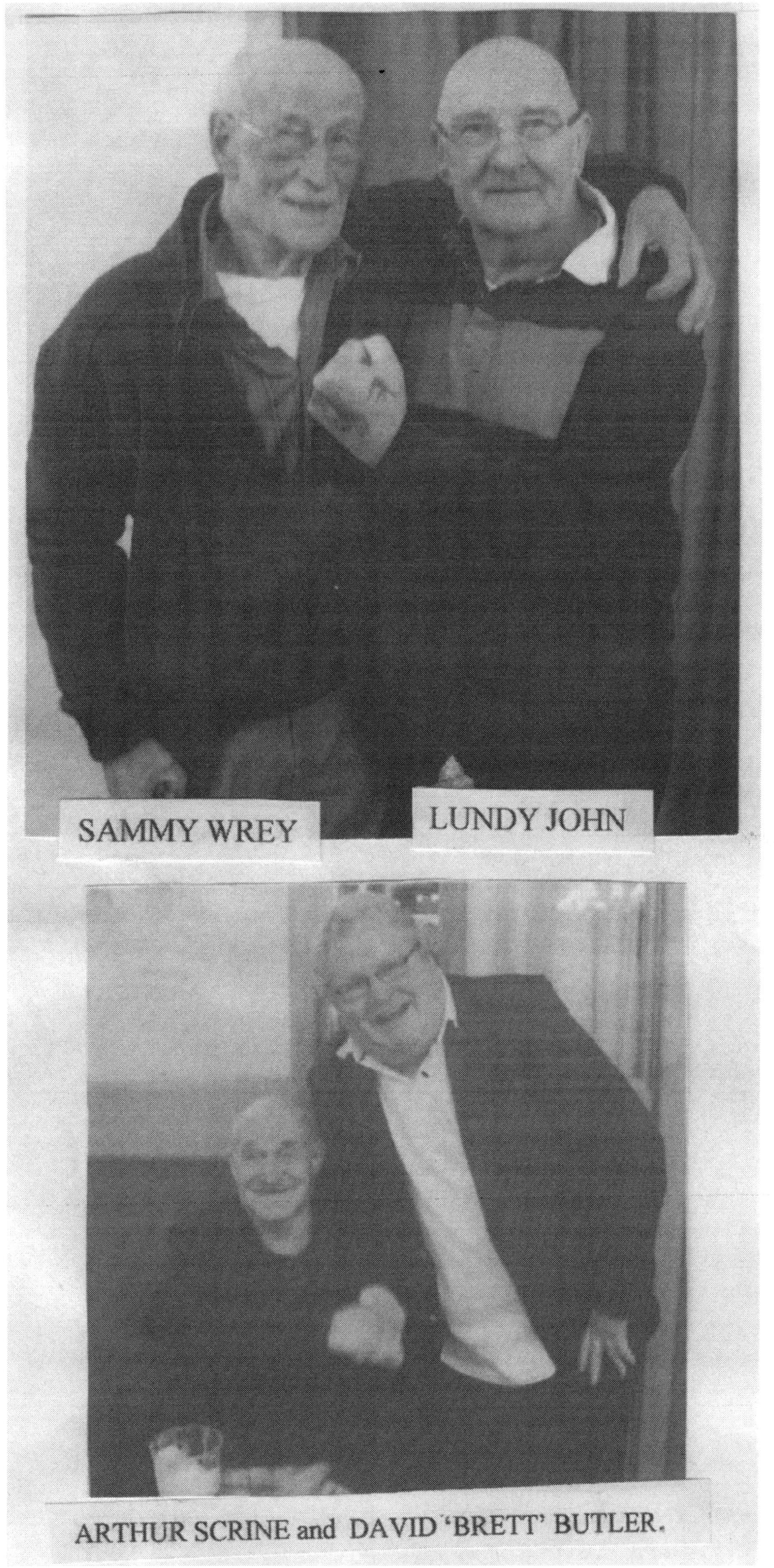

SAMMY WREY LUNDY JOHN

ARTHUR SCRINE and DAVID 'BRETT' BUTLER.

THE ROYAL EXCHANGE PUB. JOY STREET.BARNSTAPLE..
THE STORY OF NORTH DEVON BOXING. by Dick Brownson. 27th Dec.2014.

COMBE MARTIN & DISTRICT A.B.C.

BOXING TOURNAMENT

(UNDER A.B.A. RULES)

AT

COMBE MARTIN TOWN HALL

SATURDAY 17th OCTOBER 1981

COMMENCING 7.30 p.m.

OFFICIALS

OFFICIAL IN CHARGE:	A. French
REFEREES:	B. Pollard & D. Freeborn
JUDGES:	G. Beecham, R. Jenkins, J. Heal, B. Edwards, L. Wetherall, N. Parsons
C.O.S. & M.O.A. :	V. Christian
TIMEKEEPER:	A. Willis
DOCTOR:	Dr. A. Mathison
M.C. :	D. Stephenson

COMBE MARTIN ABC

A great many talented boxers have started their career with this club. As so often happens after a few successful bouts, they move on to a bigger boxing club which they hope will improve their all round performance and lead to greater achievements in the ring. This is not always the case.

	RED CORNER		BLUE CORNER
1.	~~M. Roode~~ [handwritten: J. Birch, Exeter, WON, RSF] ~~Barnstaple~~	3 x 1½ mins v	~~D. Chappell~~ [handwritten: Bennet, Saltash] ~~Saltash~~
2.	M. Burrell [handwritten: WON y] Combe Martin	3 x 1½ mins v	D. Stanbury Saltash
3.	M. Hemming [handwritten: WON y] Combe Martin	3 x 1½ mins v	N. Cox Bideford
4.	Justin Beveridge [handwritten: WON, R.S.F.] Combe Martin	3 x 1½ mins v	M. Worthington Mayflower
5.	M. Theobald Combe Martin	3 x 1½ mins v	M. Barr [handwritten: WON m] Newton Abbot
6.	K. Burgess [handwritten: WON u] Combe Martin	3 x 1½ mins v	N. Gibbons Mayflower
7.	I. Gates [handwritten: WON m.] Combe Martin	2 x 1½ mins – 1 x 2 mins v	C. Cox Exeter
8.	Jason Beveridge Combe Martin	2 x 1½ mins – 1 x 2 mins v	G. McGahey [handwritten: WON y] Exeter

	RED CORNER		BLUE CORNER
9.	J. Thadwald Combe Martin	3 x 2 mins v	
10.	M. Potter Combe Martin	3 x 2 mins v	S. Ward Mayflower
11.	M. Coats Combe Martin	3 x 2 mins v	A. Jones Saltash
12.	A. Draper [handwritten: WON u] Combe Martin	3 x 2 mins v	C. Cook Ford
13.	D. Savage [handwritten: WON RSF] Barnstaple	3 x 2 mins v	~~V. Clare~~ [handwritten: M. Coats C/M] ~~Mayflower~~
14.	M. Boyer [handwritten: WON K.O.] Combe Martin	3 x 2 mins v	D. Lauder Newton Abbot
15	S. Farley [handwritten: WON u] Combe Martin	3 x 2 mins v	R. Jones Bideford

OUR NEXT SHOW 15TH MAY 1982

COMBE MARTIN & DISTRICT A.B.C.

BOXING TOURNAMENT

(UNDER A.B.A. RULES)

AT

COMBE MARTIN TOWN HALL

SATURDAY 15th MAY 1982

COMMENCING 7.30 p.m.

OFFICIALS

OFFICIAL IN CHARGE:	R. Phillips
REFEREES:	B. Pollard & D. Freeborn
JUDGES:	M. Trigwell, J. Heal, J. Upton B. Greenaway, R. Beeston, L. Wetherall
C.O.S.	L. Wetherall
M.O.A. RECORDER:	N. Parsons
TIMEKEEPER:	A. Willis
DOCTOR:	Dr. R.J. Ferrar
M.C.:	R. Wright

	RED CORNER		BLUE CORNER
1.	S. Hammon Station	3 x 1½ mins v	D. Topham Lynton
2.	D. Mayling Combe Martin	3 x 1½ mins v	J. Butler Station
3.	S. Doyle Combe Martin	3 x 1½ mins v	S. Simpson Station
4.	S. Lynch Combe Martin	3 x 1½ mins v	H. Wilson Station
5.	M. Burrell Combe Martin	3 x 1½ mins v	
6.	M. Theobald Combe Martin	3 x 1½ mins v	R. Hancock Station
7.	M. Hemmings Combe Martin	3 x 2 mins v	P. Reed Paignton
8.	S. Swift Paignton	3 x 1½ mins v	P. Coleman Lynton
9.	D. Smith Barnstaple	3 x 1½ mins v	D. Eddolls Station
10.	G. Moore Chepstow	3 x 2 mins v	N. Dickenson Paignton
11.	I. Gates Combe Martin	3 x 2 mins v	J. Wakeham Newton Abbott
12.	D. Dolby Combe Martin	3 x 2 mins v	D. Todd Barnstaple
13.	R. Huxtable Barnstaple	3 x 2 mins v	D. Webber Paignton
14.	A. Draper Combe Martin	3 x 2 mins v	S. Hewitt Newton Abbott
15.	M. Boyer Combe Martin	3 x 2 mins v	D. Lauder Newton Abbott
16	M. Potter Combe Martin	3 x 2 mins v	C. Davey Paignton
17.	A. Coats Combe Martin	3 x 2 mins v	A. Padden Barnstaple
18.	S. Farley Combe Martin	3 x 2 mins v	

Combe Martin ABC
Open Show
Stowford Farm Meadows
16th October 2010

Show Programme

Junior

1. **Jed Pearce** 3x1.0 (skills) **Thomas Burbridge**
   Combe Martin ABC v Barnstaple ABC

2. **Jake Hatch** 3x1.0 (skills) **Jack Brierley**
   Bideford ABC v Paignton ABC

3. **Jordan Keen** 3x1.0 (skills) **Aaron Edwards**
   Combe Martin ABC v Tiverton ABC

4. **David Slade** 3x2.0 **Thomas Capola**
   Combe Martin ABC v Camborne & Redruth ABC

5. **Timmy Pike** 3x2.0 **Anthony Brierley**
   Combe Martin ABC v Paignton ABC
   Bout Sponsor - Northdevonpa

6. **Harrry Sugars** 3x2.0 **Tylar Barwood**
   Barnstaple ABC v Paignton ABC

7. **Callum Dovell** 3x2.0 **Joe Preece**
   Combe Martin ABC v Torbay ABC

8. **Corey Westbrook** 3x2.0 **L Lloyd**
   Tiverton ABC v Always ABC

9. **Billy Stanbury** 3x2.0 **Dylan Cortney**
   Combe Martin ABC v Comborne & Redruth ABC

10. **Lewis Clark** 3x2.0 **Sam Parkins**
    Bideford ABC v Tiverton ABC

11. **Jake Thorne** 3x2.0 **N Asmans**
    Combe Martin ABC v Victoria Park ABC

12. **Jack Taylor** 3x2.0 **Mason Shaw**
    Combe Martin ABC v King Alfreds ABC

Senior

Lightweight Contest

13. **Tony Tucker** 3x2.0 **A Harry**
    Exeter ABC v Nantymoel ABC

Welterweight Contest

14. **Andrius Juknye** 3x2.0 **Tim Cutler**
    Combe Martin ABC v Empire ABC

Featherweight Contest

15. **Danny Waters** 3x2.0 **Matt Vaneminnis**
    Ilfracombe ABC v Bideford ABC
    Bout Sponsor – Justin Francais - Carpenter

Middleweight Contest

16. **Craig Lavercombe** 3x2.0 **Gavin Wyatt**
    Combe Martin ABC v Hamilton Green ABC

Light Middleweight Contest

17. **Faheem Khan** 3x2.0 **Luke Stevens**
    Exeter ABC v Hamilton Green ABC

Cruiserweight Contest

18. **Gary Seldon** 3x2.0 **Neil Rowe**
    Combe Martin ABC v St Austell ABC

Middleweight Contest

19. **Tommy Herd** 3x2.0 **Luke Howells**
    Combe Martin ABC v Hoosh ABC
    Bout Sponsor – Jason Lovelock Construction

Heavyweight Contest

20. **Vaneltin Bumbul** 3x2.0 **Craig Kennady**
    Combe Martin ABC v Llamrumney Pheonix ABC

COMBE MARTIN AMATEUR BOXING CLUB

WELCOMES YOU TO A

BOXING OPEN SHOW

AT COMBE MARTIN VILLAGE HALL

SATURDAY 5TH SEPTEMBER

PRESENTATION TO INTERNATIONAL ULTRA ATHLETE: **VICKY SKELTON**

RED CORNER:		BLUE CORNER:
1. **BILLY STANBURY**	**Vs** (3x1 1/2 min)	**REECE BURNETT** (TIVERTON)
2. **CALLUM DOVELL**	**Vs** (3x1 1/2 min)	**JOE PREECE** (TORBAY)
3. **SAM WATTS** (TORBAY)	**Vs** (3x1 1/2 min)	**JACK KNAPTON** (TIVERTON)
4. **TYLER BARWOOD** (PAIGNTON)	**Vs** (3x1 1/2 min)	**SAM PARKINS** (TIVERTON)
5. **REECE HALE**	**Vs** (3x2 min)	**CORUM HOLDEN** (MAYFLOWER)
INTERVAL		**(RAFFLE)**
6. **JACK TAYLOR**	**Vs** (3x2 min)	**RYAN FISHER** (BODMIN)
7. **BRADLEY RICHARDS**	**Vs** (3x2 min)	**BRAD BUGDALE** (DEVONPORT)
8. **DAMIEN KNILL**	**Vs** (3x2 min)	**YANIS TYLER** (DEVONPORT)
9. **MARK PEACH**	**Vs** (3x2 min)	**JESSE HARVEY** (TIVERTON)

February 4, 2009

● TOM Herd is pictured with Combe Martin's ABA senior team coach Tim Pike

Tom's big Valentine date

TOM Herd ,18, from the Combe Martin ABC is preparing for the Western Counties Clubs for Young People Championships at Bristol's Broadplain ABC on February 14.

After receiving a walk-over in the early round, Tom is how training hard for his Valentine's night contest.

Ricky Hatton, Amir Khan, Joe Calzaghe, Enzo Maccarinelli and Naseem Hamed are all former CYP boxing champions and they continue to support what is considered the leading voluntary youth organisation in the UK.

More information about Combe Martin Boxing Club from Lloyd Chappell 07891896728.

● Valentin Bumbul

Combe Martin heavyweight Valentin Bumbul brought home his club's first Western Counties title with victory over Nathan Madge, also from Forest Oaks.

Although his opponent did not allow Bumbul to settle and avoided his explosive punch power, the Combe Martin boxer remained determined and gained a points victory.

November 19, 2008

The North Devon Gazette

Mallander is instant hit in first bout

The Journal Thursday January 28, 2010

BOXING

By MARK JENKIN
mjenkin@c-dm.co.uk

IT TAKES courage and character to step into a boxing ring.

And both attributes were clear to see during Saturday's Village Hall Show hosted by Combe Martin ABC.

On a night when most lads did themselves proud with their desire and sportsmanship, a new name emerged in the claret and blue of the host club.

Joe Mallander, in his first bout, served up an instant classic against fellow rookie Shaun Southwell of Paignton ABC.

The pair went to war from the opening bell, maintaining that intensity for three breathtaking and brutal rounds.

Bloodied an exhausted, at times their clash was like a scene from *Rocky*.

Fans love nothing more than two boxers giving absolutely everything, and they were at fever pitch in the atmospheric venue.

With any thoughts of defence long gone, the speed of the fight seemed to increase in round two when both lads required standing counts.

How they were still standing at the end of the third is anyone's guess.

The final bell provoked a standing ovation and Mallander celebrated a majority victory on a debut he will never forget.

Very much in the Valentin Bumbul mould, hard-hitting and shaven-headed, Damien Knill has the potential to become another crowd pleaser.

His second-round knockout of Corey Langdon was a case in point.

Forced to wait while the Penzance visitor had a new gumshield moulded, Knill was eager to make up for lost time when the opening bell sounded.

Unleashing heavy hits off both hands, Damo had the visitor covering up on the ropes and needing a standing count.

In the second round, Knill's jarring left sent Langdon crashing to the floor and the writing was on the wall.

On the next attack, a speedy right cut through the Cornishman's defences, toppling him for a second time and, on this occasion, unable to beat the count.

Callum Dovell's destruction of Jack Briely was equally emphatic.

Fast-improving Dovell got the job done inside two rounds with his sweeping rights a constant danger to the Paignton boy.

Starting round two with a volley of stinging shots, he then feigned to go with the right before unleashing a sturdy left downstairs.

Briely pressed on but was caught by another combination and by the time his corner flung the towel into the ring, Dovell's arms were aloft.

It was that sort of evening. In fact the first punch thrown by a Combe Martin boxer set the tone.

David Slade let go a stealthy left-hander to plant Paignton's George Bedford on his backside in the first few seconds of the opening bout.

Bedford recovered and the two technically skilled youngsters produced a cracking contest.

A couple forceful rights from Slade helped him through to a unanimous triumph. He later picked up the award for best Combe Martin junior of the night.

Callum's older brother Alex, fighting Ilfracombe ABC's Noel Grommett, ensured there was a double celebration for the Dovell family.

Dovell got the decision from all three judges and showed just how much it meant to him, leaping into the air with excitement.

The host club won the other all-North Devon clash too, as Reece Hale had the measure of Bideford ABC's Kyle England in some frantic exchanges.

Holding a height and reach advantage, Hale moved quickly in and out with swiping body shots while England stood his ground with some forceful single shots of his own.

Caught by a combination of right to the ribs and left to the head, England needed a 10-second breather at the end of round two before Hale's energy and enthusiasm finally gave him a unanimous win.

Maintaining a tight guard and counter-punching with tidy left leads, Jake Thorne boxed maturely against skilful Poole opponent Kieren Gilmour. The visitor's quick combinations gave him the edge in a close contest 12-7, 10-8, 8-5.

Billy 'The Kid' Stanbury was always looking to fight on the front foot against Poole's Dean Hecford and the home youngster was rewarded with a unanimous win in another tight bout.

And Bradley Richards missed out in a tactical all-southpaw clash with Downend's Kyle Cockram.

Promising displays from North Devon newcomers weren't just reserved for the Combe Martin crew.

Barnstaple ABC's Henry Swain won his debut bout with a composed performance against Paignton's James Smith.

While Smith charged forward at the start of each round and punched himself out, Swain took his time, scoring with a succession of swift lefts to the head and body.

There was disappointment for Tommy Herd when he lost to Paignton's Conner Jones after having points deducted.

Keen to impress, Herd was the busier over three two-minute rounds but paid the price after being warned by the referee for holding.

Jack Taylor was also the architect of his own defeat, disqualified in the second round against Bodmin's Ryan Fisher for directing a punch long after the referee had asked the pair to stop.

See a slideshow of photos from the show at www.thisisnorthdevon.co.uk

■ BODY BLOW: David Slade strikes George Bedford.

1001-103_03

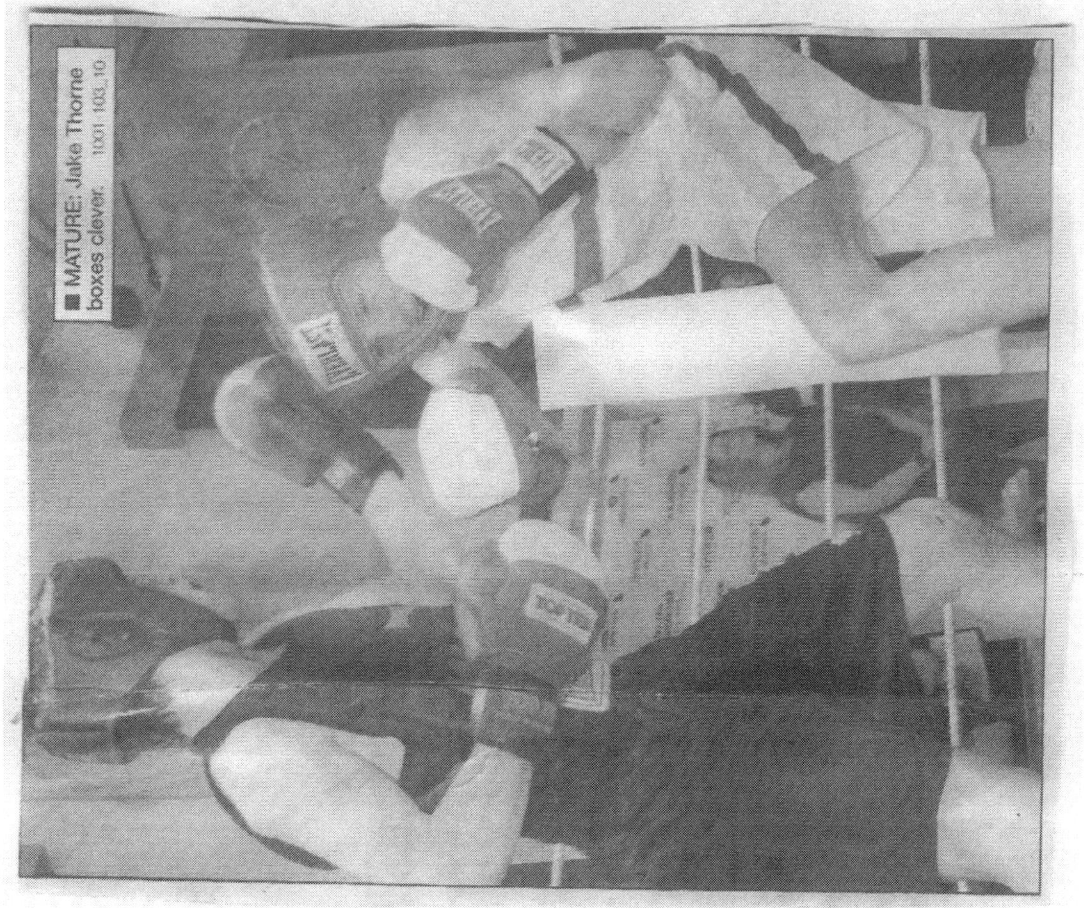

■ MATURE: Jake Thorne boxes clever. 1001 103_10

The orphan who grew into a ruthless fighter

Thursday January 28, 2010 **The Journal**

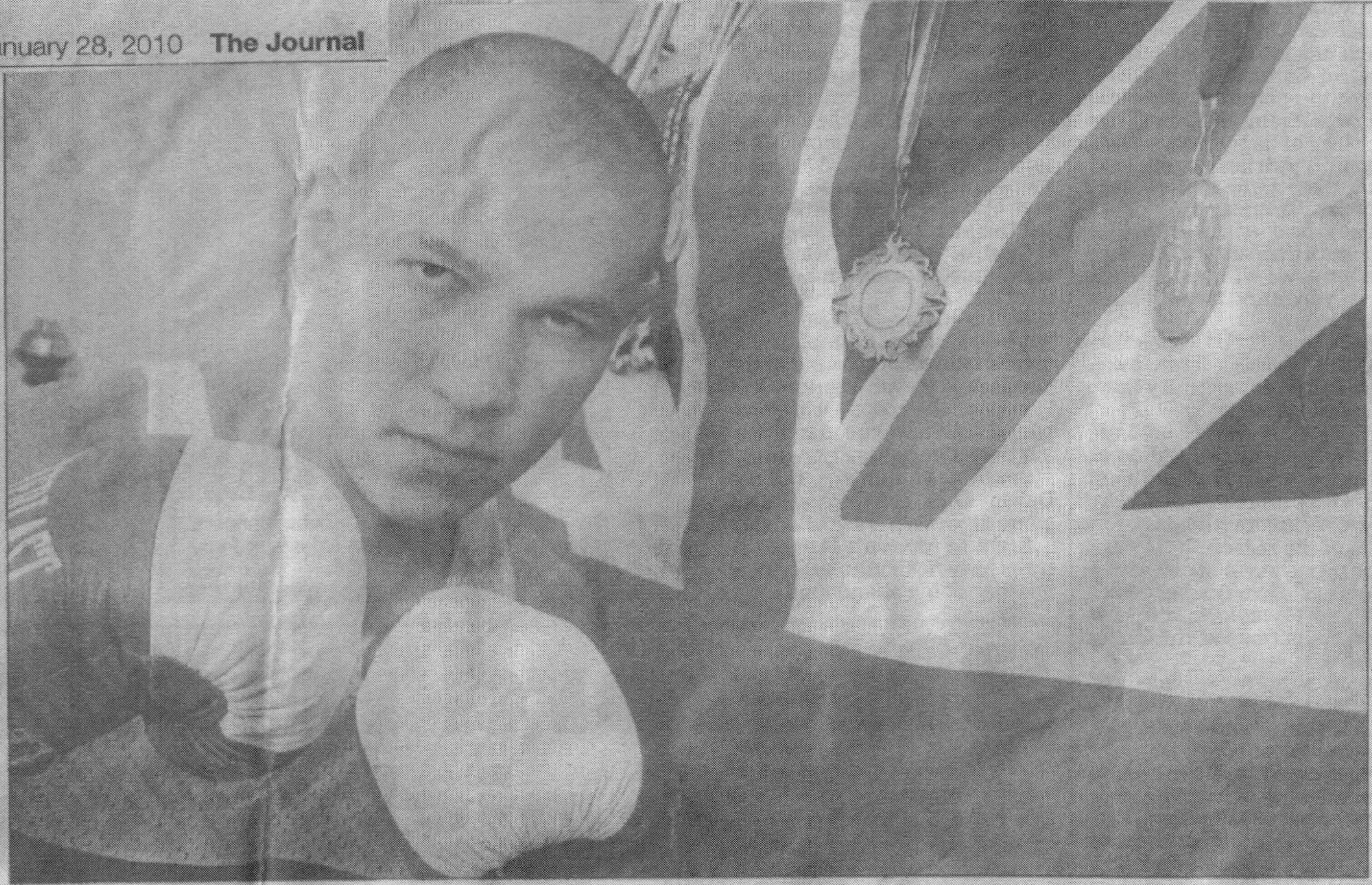

■ ADOPTED COUNTRY: Valentin Bumbul is considering switching nationality in 'the best country in the world'. Picture: Mike Southon 1001-03_04

VALENTIN BUMBUL remembers fondly his eight years in a Lithuanian orphanage, his refuge from the beatings.

Abandoned by his father and then his mother, the North Devon boxer is a graduate from the school of hard knocks.

Yet it doesn't take long in Bumbul's company to see the warmth of his personality.

"A lovely fella, a gentleman," is how his trainer, Tim Pike, describes him.

Educated too. Val, as his friends call him, speaks five languages.

Inside a boxing ring, though, Bumbul carries a ruthless streak. He has won 15 of his 18 contests, six by knockout.

The West's top heavyweight/cruiserweight over the last two years, his ambition is to win an ABA title and turn professional.

He may be known for his big hitting, but victory over Ross Chard, close to midnight in Combe Martin on Saturday, was more about a big heart.

It was a classic contest with both men climbing off the canvas twice after being sent down by their opponent's shuddering power.

Bumbul got through with a booming straight shot which left his Launceston rival requiring a count.

Back came Chard with a left of his own, leaving Bumbul on one knee and the home fans concerned.

Floored again, this time by Chard's right cross in the second round, Bumbul looked groggy. But he cleared his head and was back on the attack in the third, stopping his rival with a typically potent attack.

At the time the referee stepped in, Bumbul was actually trailing on at least one scorecard. A rematch already looks an intriguing prospect.

Many a lesser man would have used his skill and strength as a boxer to exact retribution on the stepdad who was violent towards him as a boy. And many would not have forgiven his mother for walking out on him.

That Bumbul has resisted revenge on his stepdad and keeps in touch with his mother in Russia underlines his value as a role model at Combe Martin Amateur Boxing Club.

The man from the Baltics, now six years a resident in North Devon, sets an example in behaviour as well as dedication to his sport.

Never knowing his father, young Bumbul was no better off with the new man in his mother's life.

"He didn't really like me, so he kept punching me and I always went to school with black eyes," he said.

Now that the physical advantage is reversed, hasn't Bumbul been tempted to hit back? "No, no, no," he insisted.

Unless the day comes when he needs to protect his mother, Valentina.

"I was visiting Mum in Belarus three years ago and I woke up and heard this argument in the next room," said Bumbul.

"I went to the room and said: 'What is the problem?' My Mum was crying and I just took my stepdad like that (he motions a tight grip of the collar) and said: 'If I see my Mum crying one more time you've got a problem'."

And his mother? When Bumbul was 10 she put him and his brother into an orphanage in Zarasai, some 60 miles from the Lithuanian capital Vilnius, where the boys were born, and moved to Belarus.

"It was a difficult situation for her and I understand," said Bumbul. "It was better for me when I moved to this children's house because I was happy there — no more stepdad."

After eight years in the orphanage — "nice people, nice food three times a day" — Bumbul returned to Vilnius at 18 and fed himself by training as a chef. "I got food for free at college," he said.

"I found a job in security but it was little money, about £300 a month." This in a country where the cost of living is similar to England.

Then what was intended to be a one-week holiday visiting friends in Barnstaple changed Bumbul's life. One suggested he stay and he agreed to give it a go, taking a job processing scallops at Coombe Fisheries.

"I hated this job because of the stink, wet and cold," said Bumbul. "I decided I would go home the next week but, after working one week, the money was not bad — £250 a week.

"In Lithuania I got £250 for one month, so I stayed for one more week. I saved a lot of money and thought: 'I like this.' So I stayed."

Now 25, Bumbul has been joined by his sister, Irina, in Barnstaple and he found love among the scallops, meeting Polish girlfriend Magdalena.

Back in Zarasai, Bumbul started bodybuilding at 12 and was fascinated by Mike Tyson.

Asked by the orphanage director one Christmas what he would like for a gift, he said a punch bag and gloves.

"Every morning, every evening, I started punching this bag — I was really happy," said Bumbul.

But there was no boxing club and it was not until he came to Barnstaple that he had his first contest.

Within four months of joining Barnstaple Boxing Club in 2006, Bumbul had won his first tournament trophy.

In 2008 he moved with Pike to the newly-formed Combe Martin club.

Brian Mulholland was thrilled. "I could see the potential Val has to go right to the top in British boxing," said the club official.

Bumbul's greatest achievement so far is his 2008 ABA Senior Novices Nationals runner-up success at heavyweight. His main goal this year is the ABA Open cruiserweight title.

Now a machine operator at Norbord, South Molton, Bumbul would love the sponsorship that would give him more time to train.

With backing, Pike believes that he could break into the Great Britain squad for the 2012 London Olympics.

So he's considering switching nationality from Lithuania to Britain?

"I'm thinking about this," said Bumbul. The Union Flag hanging up in his living room is testimony to his inclination.

"I like this flag," said Bumbul, turning towards it. "It's like it is my country, the best country in the world. It's given me a good job, a good life."

Not to mention a new home and adopted boxing family. Complete with two men — Pike and Mulholland — whose caring qualities the young Bumbul was denied in a father.

One of the stars from this club and an exciting fighter. I'm certain he could have found success in the professional ranks.

The North Devon Gazette
March 31, 2010

Champion guest at C Martin show

THE fighters of Combe Martin Amateur Boxing Club put on an exciting show for their home fans at the Village Hall on Saturday.

They were joined by guests of honour Scott Dann, Plymouth's former British and Commonwealth champion boxer and North Devon's ultra marathon runner and international competitor Vicky Skelton.

With the majority of Combe Martin boxers winning, the fans did not leave disappointed.

In just his third bout, 11-year-old David Slade continued to impress, claiming a unanimous decision against Ben Saterley from Poole ABC in a spirited match which saw the local fighter dominate from start to finish. Young David was also named junior boxer of the evening, by Scott Dann, who said he was impressed with his natural talent and movement.

Reece Hale's majority victory against experience visitor Ross Dann from Pilgrims ABC was, in the words of Combe Martin coach and chairman Lloyd Chappell "an extraordinary performance."

There were two senior bouts on the evening, with Combe Martin's Mark Peach matched against the tall and awkward Yanis Tyler from Devonport. It was a hard evening for the home fighter, with both landing heavy shots, but Mark's power and determination carried him through to a majority victory.

Tommy Heard could not overcome the visiting Adrian Campbell from Devonport, whose greater speed and accuracy gave him a majority verdict in a close bout.

See more pictures at www.northdevongazette.co.uk.

Juniors: Timmy Pike, CMABC v Ellis White, Wells ABC (skills contest); David Slade CMABC beat Ben Saterley Poole ABC unanimous pts; Sidney Longworth bt Lewis Clarke Bideford ABC unan pts; Callum Dovell CMABC bt Joe Simpson Pilgrims ABC (disq.); Billy Stanbury CMABC bt Dene Heckford Poole ABC maj pts; James Hobson Launceston ABC bt Jack Taylor CMABC maj pts; Reece Hale CMABC bt Ross Dann Pilgrims ABC maj pts; Ryan Cook Launceston ABC bt Jake Thorne CMABC unan pts.

Seniors: Mark Peach CMABC bt Yanis Tyler Devonport ABC maj pts; Adrian Campbell Devonport ABC bt Tommy Heard CMABC maj pts.

■ YOUNG David Slade was named Junior Boxer of the Night

■ COMBE Martin club president Matt Bacon, former British champion Scott Dann and Combe Martin boxer Mark Peach.

Southern division success for Combe

TWO Combe Martin boxers reached the Western Counties Southern Division finals at the weekend — and a third has gone marching on.

Popular Combe Martin ABC member Valentin Bumbul, 24, was crowned the Southern Division champion by walkover and will contest the Western Counties Championship tomorrow (Thursday) in Torbay.

Clubmates Joe Davis and Tommy Herd both won through to their respective finals, but it was not to be for them this year.

Joe, 22, gritted his teeth in the closing moments of his semi-final against Ben Smith from Oakmead after suffering a shoulder injury, but had done enough in the earlier rounds to ensure a good victory. He was denied a crack at the title after the ringside doctor decided to pull him out of the competition.

Tommy Herd recently moved into the four by two minute round division and raised his game for a gritty semi-final against Robert Smith of Lympstone.

His opponent in the final was the experienced Adam Tanner from Truro, who has an impressive record of 16 wins and only one defeat. Tom, an 18-year-old trainee Ilfracombe carpenter, began well, but was caught by a right hand to the head and the referee stepped in.

Now it is up to Norbord machine operator Valentin to carry the torch onwards.

● TOM Herd, Valentin Bumbul and Joe Davis put up a great effort for Combe Martin ABC at the Western Counties Southern Division event in Weymouth.

20·10·2010

County award for David at Combe tourney

COMBE Martin Boxing club celebrated a successful show at their new venue at Stowford Farm Meadows, with a total of 17 bouts, a dozen of them involving Combe Martin boxers.

The evening opened with skills bouts for Jed Pearce and Jordan Keen, who gave good accounts of themselves on their first time in the ring.

During the evening, David Slade, 12, was presented with the Devon ABA Kurt Ernest Shield for the most skilful young up and coming boxer in the county. He showed just why with a unanimous points victory in his bout, his fourth win in four contests.

A unanimous victory for Billy Stanbury earned him the title of best junior boxer of the night while Tommy heard took the senior award, with a unanimous verdict in his top-of-the-bill middleweight contest against a good Welsh opponent.

In the junior section there was also a unanimous win for Jack Taylor, while Timmy Pike and Jake Thorne both gained majority verdicts in their first competitive bouts. Callum Dovell lost a tight contest on points.

Craig Lavercombe won his senior middleweight bout on points. There were points defeats for welterweight Andrius Juknye and cruiserweight Gary Seldon.

There was a strong contingent of opponents from Wales and others from across Devon and Cornwall.

Combe Martin BC's next show is a Christmas special back at the town hall on December 11.

The North Devon Gazette

Thursday March 8, 2012 The Journal

Stanbury shades big bout

BOXING

By MARK JENKIN
mjenkin@c-dm.co.uk

BILLY STANBURY was not concerned about reputations with his latest victory for Combe Martin Amateur Boxing Club.

The teenager traded shots with Mateusz Ziolkowski, the Clubs for Young People national champion, in a thrilling tear-up on Saturday night.

And the visitor from the Heart of Portsmouth club returned to the south coast knowing all about Stanbury's stamina.

The volume in the village hall always goes up a notch when Billy The Kid walks into the ring.

If the atmosphere had been a little subdued earlier in the evening, it soon lifted when the pair went at each other from the opening bell.

Prepared to take a punch in order to land one, they wowed the crowd with their attacking instincts.

Stanbury shaded a majority win and both boys took the plaudits for bout of the night.

It was another successful show for Combe Martin with four victories from the five contests involving their boxers.

Jack Taylor was named best boxer after finishing his job in super-quick time.

Fighting on the front foot, he made his presence felt with powerful right hooks against Steve Parry, of Sturminster Newton.

The visitor damaged a hand in the opening exchanges and was unable to continue beyond the first round.

Timmy Pike showed how the momentum of a fight can shift in an instant.

Patiently probing with the left jab, he was up against it when Toby Davis banged shots to the body in a frantic first round.

But by the end of the second the visitor from Sturminster Newton was the one in the firing line.

He was left wincing with pain and the referee stepped in to halt the contest, handing the hosts their first triumph.

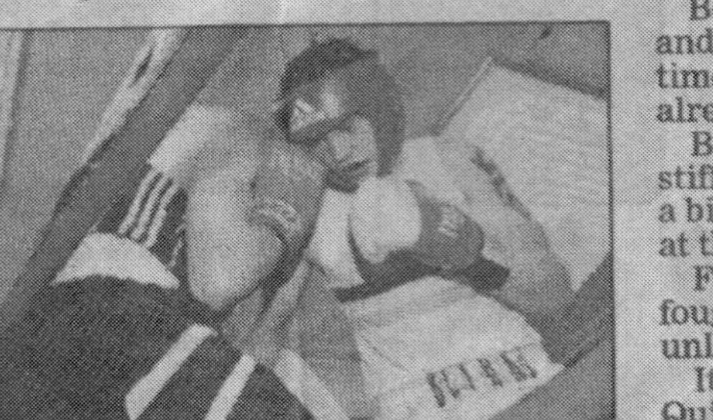

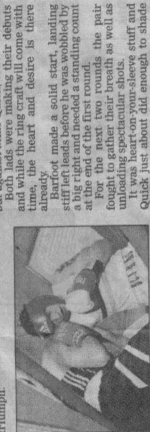

■ MAJORITY WIN: Billy 'The Kid' Stanbury.

Jordan Keen carried on the good work in a slug-fest against Jake Varley, of Apollo ABC.

Keen proved he has plenty of clobber with his recent KO victory at the Pollyfield Centre show.

And with Varley also prepared to bang, the pair traded forceful shots for three rounds.

Forced back against the ropes early on, Varley had to compose himself after losing his footing.

As Keen continued to press forward, the visitor was warned in the second round for holding on.

It was not always pretty but the Combe Martin lad stuck at it and was good value for his majority win.

Richie Barfoot was beaten but not disheartened after a barnstorming debut against Mike Quick, of St Ives.

Both lads were making their debuts and while the ring craft will come with time, the heart and desire is there already.

Barfoot made a solid start, landing stiff left leads before he was wobbled by a big right and needed a standing count at the end of the first round.

For the next two rounds the pair fought to gather their breath as well as unloading spectacular shots.

It was heart-on-your-sleeve stuff and Quick just about did enough to shade the majority decision.

Wesley Smith, of Launceston ABC, was the other Cornishman celebrating following his tight victory over Anthony Coles.

Smith won the Senior ABA southern division title in a skilful contest with his Camborne opponent.

Coles on his return after a year out of the ring, missed out 13-11, 15-11, 15-12.

It was tight, too, when Ben Owen, of Bideford ABC, faced Chris Adams, of Sturminster Newton.

The North Devon boxer showed patience and poise to take the unanimous verdict 16-13, 15-10, 14-13.

Adams, with height and reach advantage, looked threatening in the opening round but Owen stayed out of trouble by maintaining a tight guard.

Twice in the second round Owen had to stop for a wipe-down after being splattered by blood oozing from his opponent's nose.

Stronger down the finishing stretch, the Bideford boxer added another win to go with his recent success at Pollyfield.

There was disappointment for his club-mate Jake Hatch, however, with a narrow defeat to Ashley Holder, of Weston-super-Mare.

● Bideford ABC will host the next boxing show in North Devon at Bideford Pannier Market on March 24.

Tickets cost £5 and can be ordered from Dick Kersey on 07841 846552.

● Results: page 94.

COMBE MARTIN A.B.C PRESENTS

BOXING

OPEN SHOW

★ COMBE MARTIN VILLAGE HALL ★ SAT 23RD MARCH 2013 ★

EVENING PROGRAMME

Thank you to all the local people
and businesses that support our club

Junior boxers

	Skills	
Bayley Ratcliffe Combe Martin ABC		Charlie Barber Portland ABC
Hosna Adenas H.O.P ABC	3 x 1.5 (Girls)	Elizebeth Bools Trowbridge ABC
Connor O'Toole Combe Martin ABC	3 x 1.5	Haydon Riskilly Torpoint & Rame
Jesse Douglas H.O.P ABC	3 x 2	Ainsley Adams Margate ABC
James Ward Trowbridge ABC	3 x 2	Paul Commins Margate ABC
Matthew Porter Combe Martin ABC	3 x 1½	Joshua Carter Paignton ABC
Ricky Diamond Bideford ABC	4 x 2	Ben Bendal H.O.P ABC
Kline Ruterford AIDLY St Ives ABC	3 x 2	Alex Stockley Margate ABC
Timmy Pike Combe Martin ABC	3 x 2	Jamie Hood Margate ABC

OPEN CLASS
NATIONAL
CHAMP.

Senior boxers

9/	Chris Tuson Torpoint & Rame	3 x 2	Khaleel Graham Portland ABC
10/	Jordan Keen Combe Martin ABC	3 x 2	Bradley Parsons Trowbridge ABC
11/	Alex Dovell Combe Martin ABC	3 x 2	Callum Trudgon St.Ives ABC
12/	Ben Owen Bideford ABC	3 x 2	Claude De Lang Portland ABC
13/	Steve Martin Combe Martin ABC	3 x 2	Jamie Drummond Exmouth ABC
	Reece Hale Combe Martin ABC	3 x 2	Liam Laird Barnstaple ABC
14/	Jack Taylor Combe Martin ABC	3 x 2	Paul Brown Margate ABC
15/	Billy The Kid Stanbury Combe Martin ABC	4 x 2	Ross Aylett Margate ABC

OPEN CLASS
NATIONAL CHAMPION

The Journal

Boxing talent emerges

FIRE DRILLS: Young boxers are put through their paces at the makeshift gym in Ilfracombe Fire Station.

BEHIND the fire engines lining the forecourt is a fire station filled with burning ambition.

As a bell sounds loudly in the corner of the room, it is not an alarm prompting firefighters into action but rather youngsters into the boxing ring.

For two nights every week, Ilfracombe Fire Station is transformed into the home of the town's emerging boxing club.

With fewer than 20 members and no established committee, it is still early days for the group that came together four years ago.

But Ilfracombe ABC are already starting to punch above their weight.

Darren Franks, one of the three ABA-qualified coaches, said: "We are a very small club compared to some around here but we are just as enthusiastic. We are all totally mad on boxing.

"We have quite a high turnover of kids of all ages. They find it difficult, go off to university or college, get a job or just lose interest. But we have got a small nucleus of boxers to keep us ticking over."

From the current group, only Danny Waters and Heidi Such are registered to box competitively.

The rest, aged ten and over, are happy to train regularly and hone their basic skills.

And that enthusiasm is clear to see as they get stuck into a session of circuits, pad work and punch bags.

"Everyone who turns up works solidly," said Franks. "They never slack.

"We put the music on and we like them to have a good time at the same time as working hard.

"You get a nice rapport. It's almost like a family atmosphere."

Thanks to Franks's dad, Chris, the club's immediate future is in safe hands.

Chris The Real Ale Man has provided new kit and is paying the rent at the station for the next year.

Ilfracombe ABC moved to the station in 2009 after outgrowing their previous home, the Vision Community Centre at Slade.

Trevor French, a fireman and boxing coach, helped set up the move and Combe are grateful that Lee Howell, the chief fire officer for Devon and Somerset, is happy to accommodate them.

French said: "I've been in the fire brigade for 20 years and if you had said there would be boxing in the fire station I would have laughed at you."

Having represented England while he served in the Marines, French never imagined he would end up as a coach either.

"It beats sitting at home watching EastEnders," he said.

"We try to keep it, not lighthearted, but as relaxed as possible."

The kids looked focused as French took them through a series of exercises to improve their core strength.

Despite the physical demands they keep coming back for more.

Bayley Ratcliff, 11, said: "I saw there was a boxing club and I just thought maybe I should try it. I came down, had a go and really enjoyed it. Everybody is really friendly here."

Kenny Jones, 11, said: "My dad has wanted me to come since I was 8.

"I was doing aikido and because I quit he wanted me to do boxing.

"When you're sparring it keeps you fit. You just get healthy."

Nicola Rennie, 14, is the only girl who trains regularly.

"There used to be more girls but they don't do it now," she said.

"I don't mind it, I just get on with it. They are all really nice here."

Initially started by Tony Jordan, the club was kept going by Dax Mayling when the founder member moved away.

Mayling, the third qualified coach, said: "There were a few times when I thought, 'I've had enough', but then you come in and see the faces.

"A lot of kids these days need a bit of discipline. We get a bit of cheek but we tell them, 'You are here to work, you are here to listen'.

"It's not all about just throwing a left or a right.

"You can't go in half-hearted. You have got to be totally committed to the sport."

Sessions take place on Mondays and Wednesdays at 6.30pm and cost £1.50 for juniors and £2 for seniors.

To find out more call Darren Franks on 01271 883389.

ALEX MASON tried hard to get BOXING going in ILFRACOMBE as have others over the years. Many boxers represented ILFRACOMBE and CAPSTONE BOXING CLUB, and are mentioned in NEWSPAPER CUTTINGS and seen in photos., mostly groups.

DB.

ANY JIMMY ISAAC HERE? Well, there could be, if enthusiasm and potential mean anything. This big-smile and big-glove group consists of the 18 junior boxers of Ilfracombe Sports Club, with chairman, Mr. Reg Boyen (left) and secretary, Mr Alex Mason (right).

LYNTON AND LYNMOUTH ABC

To Phil
All Good Wishes
Joe Erskine

LYNTON AND LYNMOUTH
A.B.C.

LYNTON AND LYNMOUTH A.B.C.

PRESENT THEIR FIRST

B O X I N G T O U R N A M E N T

AT

THE TOWN HALL, LYNTON

ON

SATURDAY 8TH NOVEMBER, 1980.

Bout No.1 — Schoolboy Contest

M. Hoad (Lynton and Lynmouth A.B.C.) V D. Keift (Ford A.B.C.)

Bout No.2 — Schoolboy Contest

B. Russell (Minehead A.B.C.) V B. Penfold (Wellington A.B.C.)

Bout No.3 — Schoolboy Contest

S. Cotterell (Lynton and Lynmouth A.B.C.) V L. Woodward (BidefordA.B.C.)

Bout No.4 — Schoolboy Contest

S. Dower (Virginia House A.B.C.) V S. Fuller (Lydney A.B.C.)

Bout No.5 — Schoolboy Contest

J. Hallums (Lynton and Lynmouth A.B.C.) V D. Saunders (BarnstapleA.B.C.)

Bout No.6 — Schoolboy Contest

S. Woods (Chepstow A.B.C.) V P. Squires (Bideford A.B.C.)

Bout No.7 — Schoolboy Contest

P. Coleman (Lynton and Lynmouth A.B.C.) V S. Butson (Ford A.B.C.)

Bout No.8 — Schoolboy Contest

D. Gallini (Virginia House A.B.C.) V P. Kane (Watchet A.B.C.)

Bout No.9 — Schoolboy Contest

D. Jones (Lynton and Lynmouth A.B.C.)	V	M. Gibbs (Combe Martin A.B.C.)

Bout No.10 — Schoolboy Contest

A. MacDonald-Brown (Lynton and Lynmouth A.B.C.)	V	M. Russell (Ford A.B.C.)

Bout No.11 — Junior Contest

K. Saunders (Barnstaple A.B.C.)	V	G. Tremayne (Lydney A.B.C.)

Bout No.12 — Schoolboy Contest

J. MacDonald-Brown (Lynton and Lynmouth A.B.C.)	V	A. Courtis (Ford A.B.C.)

Bout No.13 — Junior Contest

A. Paddon (Barnstaple A.B.C.)	V	K. Bale (Wellington A.B.C.)

Bout No.14 — Junior Contest

J. Hallums (Lynton and Lynmouth A.B.C.)	V	S. Barnett (Lydney A.B.C.)

Bout No.15 — Junior Contest

D. Brady (Chepstow A.B.C.)	V	S. Dingle (Virginia House A.B.C.)

Bout No.16 — Senior Contest

S. Copp (Ford A.B.C.)	V	M. Coates (Combe Martin A.B.C.)

Master of Ceremonies - Mr. I.C.L. Dawkins

DESPITE FREQUENT LOCAL NEWSPAPER APPEALS for BOXING EPHEMERA over the last six years and visits by me to LYNTON and LYNMOUTH, very little came in about the BOXING CLUB.

DB.

LYNTON schoolboy Gavin Dawkins receives his trophy from former World featherweight champion Howard Winstone after outpointing Robert Shaddick of Barnstaple — they are in action on the right — in the Lynton Boxing Club show on Saturday.

Barnstaple's Michael Roode won the 'Boxer of the Night' award for his display in outpointing M. Jones of Bristol.

A large crowd packed the Town Hall for the 12-bout programme and the results of the other North Devon boxers in action were:

Dave Short (Barnstaple) beat S. McCabe (Jersey) points; Darren Todd (Barnstaple) lost to M. Brady (Chepstow) points; Scot Bartlett (Lynton) beat J. le Cheminant (Jersey) points; Darren Berry (Lynton) beat J. Grandson (Tottenham) points; Rob Irlam (Lynton) beat C. Powell (Bristol) points; Phil Wyness (Lynton) lost to M. Ward (Guernsey) stopped.

Pictured are (left) Paul Coleman and Andrew MacDonald Brown (right) after presentation of shields by Howard Winstone

Entertaining Boxing at Lynton

A large crowd packed the Town Hall, Lynton where former World Featherweight Champion Howard Winstone, M.B.E., was the Guest of Honour at the local Boxing Club's Tournament.

North Devon boxers were in action in eight of the twelve bouts. Scot Bartlett had to work hard for his majority points win over Jason Le Cheminant of Guernsey, as did a much improved Darren Berry, who won a majority verdict over Jason Grandson, of New Enterprise ABC, Tottenham.

In a return match, Gavin Dawkins also had a majority points win over Robert Shaddick of Barnstaple, with Gavin picking up points with his left jab and some useful body punches at close quarters, although he was shaken at times by the solid right crosses of his opponent.

The left jab was Rob Irian's main weapon in a battle of young giants as he outpointed Clive Powell of National Smelting Co. ABC, Bristol. Powell barely 16 years old but 6'2" and 12½ stone, was dwarfed by the 15 year old Lynton boxer who stands 6'5" and weighs 12 stone 4lbs, but it was by no means one-way-traffic and Irian had to survive several flurries of hard punches by Powell before being declared a unanimous points victor.

Phil Wyness, however was not so fortunate, as he was stopped in his debut bout with Michael Ward of Guernsey.

David Short of Barnstaple beat Steve McCabe of Jersey Leonis ABC on points, and Michael Roode outpointed Michael Jones of National Smelting Co. ABC, Bristol to earn the "Boxer of the Night" award. Darren Todd however, lost on points to Nick Brady of Chepstow ABC.

At the end of the evening's boxing Howard Winstone presented commemorative shields to Paul Coleman and Andrew MacDonald-Brown to mark their achievements in winning Schools ABA Western Counties titles this season.

Afterwards he complimented the host club on a very entertaining night's boxing.

He is to pay a return visit to Lynton later this year, with his family, as guests of club coach Glyn Dawkins.

Pictured are (left) Paul Coleman and Andrew MacDonald Brown (right) after presentation of shields by Howard Winstone

Entertaining Boxing at Lynton

A large crowd packed the Town Hall, Lynton where former World Featherweight Champion Howard Winstone, M.B.E., was the Guest of Honour at the local Boxing Club's Tournament.

North Devon boxers were in action in eight of the twelve bouts. Scot Bartlett had to work hard for his majority points win over Jason Le Cheminant of Guernsey, as did a much improved Darren Berry, who won a majority verdict over Jason Grandson, of New Enterprise ABC, Tottenham.

In a return match, Gavin Dawkins also had a majority points win over Robert Shaddick of Barnstaple, with Gavin picking up points with his left jab and some useful body punches at close quarters, although he was shaken at times by the solid right crosses of his opponent.

The left jab was Rob Irian's main weapon in a battle of young giants as he outpointed Clive Powell of National Smelting Co. ABC, Bristol. Powell barely 16 years old but 6'2" and 12½ stone, was dwarfed by the 15 year old Lynton boxer who stands 6'5" and weighs 12 stone 4lbs, but it was by no means one-way-traffic and Irian had to survive several flurries of hard punches by Powell before being declared a unanimous points victor.

Phil Wyness, however was not so fortunate, as he was stopped in his debut bout with Michael Ward of Guernsey.

David Short of Barnstaple beat Steve McCabe of Jersey Leonis ABC on points, and Michael Roode outpointed Michael Jones of National Smelting Co. ABC, Bristol to earn the "Boxer of the Night" award. Darren Todd however, lost on points to Nick Brady of Chepstow ABC.

At the end of the evening's boxing Howard Winstone presented commemorative shields to Paul Coleman and Andrew MacDonald-Brown to mark their achievements in winning Schools ABA Western Counties titles this season.

Afterwards he complimented the host club on a very entertaining night's boxing.

He is to pay a return visit to Lynton later this year, with his family, as guests of club coach Glyn Dawkins.

SOUTH MOLTON ABC

BOXING TOURNAMENT

(under A.B.A. Rules)

NEW ASSEMBLY ROOMS
SOUTH MOLTON

Thursday, December 11th

AT 7.45 P.M.

OFFICIALS :

A.B.A Official in Charge—JACK GARDNER

Referees & Judges—B. Treeby, S. E. S. Thompson, G. Parsons, R. Punchard, W. D. Cornish.

Hon. Medical Officer—Dr. R. A. Dubery.

M.C.—W. Wheeler. Timekeeper—K. Mock.

Whip—G. Kingdon.

South Molton & District Amateur Boxing Club.

Chairman—E. J. Kingdon.

Hon. Treasurer—H. E. Chudley

Hon. Secretary—H. J. Cross

PRICE 6D.

S. W. LYDDON, "TOWER" PRINTING WORKS, SOUTH MOLTON

Thanks . . . .

- To all Sportsmen who donated towards Prizes.
- To R.A.F. Chivenor, for loan of Ring.
- To Messrs. E. J. Kingdon Ltd., for Transport.
- To Mr. Jack Gardner, who arranged this Programme and to all the Officials who so readily offered their services.

Apart from the SOUTH MOLTON BOXERS FEATURED IN Volume...1 of 'THE STORY OF NORTH DEVON BOXING' only this one undated programme came in for Volume...2. Urgent appeals in LOCAL NEWSPAPERS and many visits to the Town from me failed to produce anything.
DB.

1. Junior Class A. 2-1½ min. and 1-2 min. rounds

C. FROST v. E. FURSDON
Apollo S.C., Torquay — Teignmouth A.B.C.

2. Junior Class A.

D. THOMPSON v. J. BAKER
Apollo S.C. — Sidmouth K.F.C.

3. Bantamweight.

R. SIMS v. J. BERGIN
Apollo S.C. — Barnstaple A.B.C.

4. Light Welterweight.

J. TURNER v. G. APLIN
South Molton A.B.C. — Teignmouth

5. Lightweight.

K. JACKSON v. K. BECK
Apollo — Teignmouth

6. Middleweight.

A. COURT v. A. CHARLES
Exeter A.B.C. — Barnstaple

7. Light Middleweight.

J. CARTER v. J. ALLEN
South Molton — Barnstaple

INTERVAL.

8. Junior Class B.

E. DREW v. B. STOCKER
Exeter — Apollo

9. Featherweight.

M. O'CONNOR v. G. VOUGHT
Sidmouth — Teignmouth

10. Welterweight.

C. TURNER v. S. SMITH
Exeter — Barnstaple

11. Middleweight.

R. SMITH v. S. BRIGHT
Teignmouth — Barnstaple

12. Lightweight.

D. JOHNS v. J. CRIMMONS
Exeter — Teignmouth

13. Bantamweight.

R. BALDWIN v. T. HOGAN
Sidmouth — Barnstaple

14. Heavyweight.

J. BECKLAKE v. D. STOCKER
South Molton — Apollo

NOTE. All Senior bouts are three rounds of two minutes unless otherwise announced.

TIVERTON AMATEUR BOXING CLUB.

In Volume...1 of 'THE STORY OF NORTH DEVON BOXING' a great many fighters from the TIVERTON AREA took part in Shows in NORTH DEVON. ALL of these promotions were under PROFESSIONAL RULES and it was not until after the 1939-45 WAR that the word AMATEUR began to appear on BOXING POSTERS. This fact is WELL DOCUMENTED in the individual BOXING CLUB histories.

In view of TIVERTON'S contribution to NORTH DEVON BOXING I am pleased to include them in this book.

The AMATEUR CLUB came into existence in the late 1940's although I am certain there was a BOXING CLUB operating locally in the 1930's but my research has failed to establish when and where. The early 1940 to 1950 rather faded photos. indicate the AMATEUR CLUB had re-formed but seemed to have disappeared by 1960.

Then in 2007 PAUL HARVEY stepped in.

In over 65 years of being around BOXING GYMS it has usually been one man with vision who starts things off. Other TRAINERS come forward but fall by the wayside for numerous reasons. PAUL'S dedication to TIVERTON BOXING cannot be over-estimated and today he operates a vibrant and successful CLUB, no doubt with unstinting help and advice from father, PAUL Snr., May they go forward to greater achievements.

Book these Dates . . . .

Special Attraction—TWO GREAT

BOXING SHOWS

JUNE 8th, *at* 8 p.m.
at Factory Yard

★

An All Professional Show
on JULY 25th

BOTH OPEN AIR SHOWS

TIVERTON HOSPITAL BOXING ASSOCIATION
and
TIVERTON BOXING ASSOCIATION

In Tiverton Boxing Tournament

February 6th 1952 – Devon and Somerset News

Seven local boys took part in the TIVERTON AMATEUR BOXING CLUB TOURNAMENT at the NEW HALL, TIVERTON on THURSDAY. They are seen with Mr. R. MILLMAN (left) Joint Secretary and Mr J. SNOW, Trainer.

CAPTION READS-
GOOD FIGHTERS...A group of TIVERTON AMATEUR BOXERS who featured in the programme at the NEW HALL on SATURDAY.

GOOD FIGHTERS.—A group of the Tiverton amateur boxers who featured in the programme at the New Hall on Saturday.

FEBRUARY 9th 1949

Some of the MEMBERS of the TIVERTON AMATEUR BOXING and PHYSICAL TRAINING CLUB at their new headquarters in the SCOUT HUT next to the SWIMMING BATH. The SECRETARY, Mr L. MILLMAN is seen on the left.

TIVERTON AMATEUR BOXING CLUB.

1949

ON GUARD.—L. King, of Tiverton (right) counters S. Schofield, of Dunster, whom he k.o'd. later in the bout. The M.C. was Mr. A. S. Leggatt.

■ SOME of Tiverton's sporting youngsters watch a boxing demonstration. The picture was taken in 1954 at Tiverton Boxing Club's headquarters above the stables of the Swan Inn in Westexe South. Les King, pictured squaring up to the punchball, is watched by a group of 10 and 11-year-olds including Alan Hunt, on the left, who submitted the picture. The group of youngsters used to take part in boxing competitions in the Heathcoat Hall, and the club trained for many years at the Swan Inn, where the landlord was Dick Grant. Watching Les train are (back row, from left) club committee members Les Hookway, ?? Newberry and Reg Millman and boxing coaches Jack Snow and ?? Broomfield. Kitted up are youngsters Alan Hunt, David 'Walt' Hole, John Cottrell, Terrence 'Toby' Gillard, David Simpson and David 'Bungy' Main. Can you help with the missing names or tell any tales about the boxing club? If you can, or have any other memories you would like to share, contact the *Gazette* at 29 Bampton Street, Tiverton or call 01884 252725.

"Tiverton Gazette"
03 June 2003

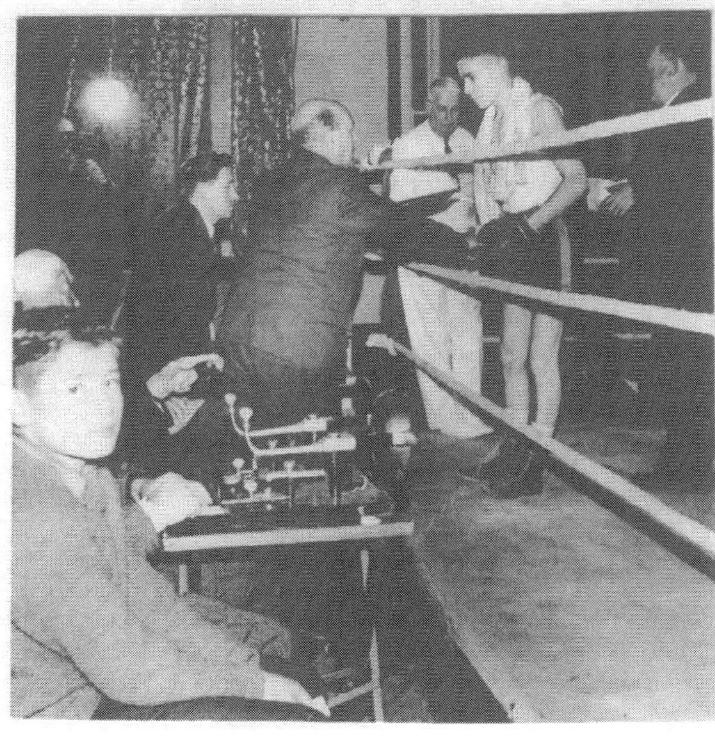

5th October 1949.

Boxing

TIVERTON CLUB'S NEW H.Q.

More help wanted

TIVERTON Amateur Boxing and Physical Training Club has just moved to new headquarters in the scout hut next to the Tiverton Swimming Baths.

The hut has been re-equipped with new lighting arrangements, and a portable boxing ring has been installed, the cost for this being partly covered by a generous donation by the club president, Sir John Amory.

Earlier in the season the club had some difficulty in starting up, owing to the lack of support, and acting committee members, but now it is on its feet with a membership of fifty, under the trainers, Messrs. J. Snow and J. Pow, and the masseur, Mr. Hockin. There is, however, an insufficient number of acting committee members, and as Mr. L. Millman said, "There is at present so much work for so few that we would welcome new enthusiasts."

Boys from the age of ten years can join the club on the payment of a small subscription, and the membership is still going up, especially since the club has moved to the scout hut.

The club is to hold a boxing tournament on March 18th at the New Hall, Tiverton, where the members of Exeter, Taunton, Bradninch, Exmouth and several other clubs will take part. The proceeds of this event and other social activities arranged by Mr. L. Hookway, one of the club's committee members, are for the club funds.

Boxing

TIVERTON CLUB CARRYING ON

Offer of H.Q. hut accepted

DESPITE a poor attendance at the resumed annual meeting of the Tiverton Amateur Boxing and Physical Training Club on Thursday, it was decided to carry on and that attempts should be made to procure a hut as headquarters.

Sir John Amory remains president, with Mrs. D. Butlin and Mrs. Moncrieff as vice-presidents. Mr. F. Smith retains his post as chairman with Mr. O. Murphy as vice-chairman. Mr. W. R. Millman and his brother, Mr. L. Millman, were re-elected joint secretaries, and the treasurer is to be elected later. The trainer is Mr. L. King. New committee members were Messrs. W. J. Stone, J. W. Greenaway, O. Bennett, and A. Baker.

It was the Chairman's suggestion that the club should make an effort to buy a hut, and thus have a permanent room in which the club's activities could take place. The club, he thought, would benefit in several ways, especially financially.

Mrs. Moncrieff generously offered to loan the club the money for the project, free of interest. Her offer was gratefully accepted. The club will open for training on Mondays and Thursdays.

The RINGSIDE BELL,
NOW definitely an ANTIQUE!
Still on display in the
TIVERTON ABC GYM.

meet the COACH

Today's self-penned profile is by Tiverton Amateur Boxing Club coach...

PAUL HARVEY

How many years have you been involved in boxing?
I used to watch the big fights on Sportsnight with my Dad when I was growing up. Later I went into the Army and represented the Parachute regiment in Army Boxing Championships in the lightweight division.

Which boxer inspired you most?
Marvin Hagler, I liked him because he was so single-minded in his pursuit of success. He came up the hard way, no-one ever did him any favours but he had to be one of the greatest middleweight champions of all-time.

Have you seen any funny or strange incidents in the ring?
It was not one of our boys, but I went to a bout once and there was a little lad there from Bideford I think and every time he got punched in the ring, he would swear at his opponent. The referee warned him to stop using bad language or he would be disqualified. I make it clear from the outset to our fighters that they have to show respect to the referee and their opponent.

What do you like most about being a boxing coach?
It is satisfying to see a youngster who started out very raw develop and become a good boxer. They don't necessarily have to win, just to see them boxing well is pleasing.

Are there any rule changes you would like to see in amateur or junior boxing?
I would like judges to be more consistent. I know it is a hard job to do and I guess it is a gripe common to many coaches.

How has the sport changed since you competed?
When I boxed, there were no headguards. That was pre-1990 before guards came in, which has made the sport safer. I think the boys are more skilful now if anything.

How do you relax outside of the ring?
I go running a lot which I have always found to be a good way of beating any stress. I also like to spend time with my wife, whose support I am grateful for, as I have been away at the weekends so much recently going to lots of different bouts.

MEET ANOTHER OF THE AREA'S COACHES NEXT WEEK

TIVERTON AMATEUR BOXING CLUB

members' TALK

We asked members at Tiverton Amateur Boxing Club...

What's boxing about?

Zac Jones 11
I'm still waiting for my first fight but never scared when getting into the ring for training. Everything in there is down to you. I just want to box. Luckily we have a good coach and he works you hard. He's always here to help you.

Aaron Edwards 15
I've only been boxing for about a year now but already won six out of seven fights. I got through to the Western county finals. Apart from the mates you make and the fitness side of boxing you get a real adrenaline rush.

Jack Knapton 15
I've won about eight of 16 fights but I did beat the Welsh Champion in Cardiff last December. I beat him on points and it felt good. At first I just joined the boxing club because I thought it would be a bit of a doss but then you get into it.

Alex Jones 15
I like both sides of boxing, there's the training and then the fighting. Out of ten fights I've won four but I'm very competitive and this just makes me want to box more. One of my best moments was taking on the British champion.

Corey Westbrook 15
At the moment I'm 56 kilos and have had 28 fights, 17 I've won. One of the best moments of my boxing so far is taking on the British Champion at my weight in London, I lost on points but proved I was good enough to be there.

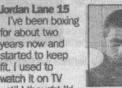

Jordan Lane 15
I've been boxing for about two years now and started to keep fit. I used to watch it on TV until I thought I'd give it ago myself. When I started there weren't many of us here but now the club's really grown. It's much better.

INTERVIEWS BY MARCUS THOMPSON

Alex Jones, Phil Pearce, sponsor John Burnell, Zack Jones and Bradley Davey of Tiverton ABC

TIVERTON ABC has a smart new kit thanks to sponsor John Burnell of JP Burnell Roofing.

The new kit, which will be worn for the show at the Heathcoat Social Club, on Saturday, May 30, is in the club's traditional claret and blue colours – with the cross of St George on the shorts, Tiverton ABC on the back of the vest, and JP Burnell Roofing on the front.

"John's helped us no end over the last few years," said Tiverton ABC coach Paul Harvey. "He always sponsors bouts and is keen to help in any way he can."

Tickets for the show can be obtained from the Heathcoat Club or by calling 01884 256282 / 07535 544197.

RISING STARS: From left, Tiverton ABC's Zack O'Loughlin, Barnaby Butt and John Penfold, with Zack's belt at the Port Talbot show Photo: Submitted

Western Counties

Amateur Boxing Association

(Affiliated to England Boxing)

England Boxing Youth Championships

This is to certify that

Harry Davey

of

Tiverton ABC

is

Western Counties Class A Champion

At

LightHeavyweight 75-81kg

Regional Association Secretary

Saturday 25th January 2014 at the St Agnes Show

Jones' showtime finale

Boxing

TIVERTON ABC holds its final tournament of the season on Saturday night at the Heathcoat Social Club with a bill featuring 16 bouts.

Topping the bill will be Alex Jones, boxing in his 42nd and final bout for the club.

The 19-year-old joins the Army in July.

Jones, who joined Tiverton as a 12-year-old, reached the ABA semi-finals as a schoolboy and became the Western Counties champion as a junior.

More recently as a senior boxer he beat London champion Alex Zendra from Finchley.

Coach Paul Harvey said: "It is the end of a truly remarkable journey for both Alex and Tiverton ABC.

"We have had some wonderful moments and memories which I will always cherish.

"Never one to disappoint, Alex has never been in a bad bout. He's got a brilliant style and is renowned for his body punching."

"People like Alex Jones don't walk through your gym doors that often. I can't praise him enough as a person and a boxer and we wish him well in his forthcoming army career."

TIVERTON'S Alex Jones with his trainer and mentor, Paul Harvey.

Jones delights supporters as he bows out with hard-fought win

IN his final fight for Tiverton ABC, a vociferous home crowd roared boxer Alex Jones to an impressive victory.

Jones' bout was one of 15 on a bumper night of boxing at the Heathcoat Club, in Tiverton, on Saturday evening.

Jones, who was representing the Mid Devon club for the 42nd and final time before he joins the army in July, was pitted against Plymouth's Ryan Hibberd.

As soon as Jones walked into the ring, the whole of the Heathcoat Club erupted in a show of support for the popular Tiverton boxer.

Hibberd had beaten Jones in Plymouth only last month, but it was clear from the outset that the Mid Devon man was determined the result would be rather different this time.

It quickly became apparent neither boxer was going to give an inch. And while Hibberd is nobody's fool and was happy to wait patiently for his opponent to make an error, the home fighter was clearly in the ascendancy.

When the judges' decision was announced, the whole of Heathcoat Club erupted for a second time to bring the curtain down not just on another great Tiverton ABC show but also on Jones' career for the club.

"You couldn't really have written the script any better," reflected coach Paul Harvey afterwards.

"Winning in front of your home fans, with them singing your name throught the whole three rounds, is just about as good as it gets."

"When Alex looks back on this in years to come, he's sure to have a great big smile on his face."

Stevenson makes up for market defeat

JACOB Stevenson won his rematch with Liam McCluskey at the Tiverton ABC Show.

The Bideford ABC boxer was on the wrong end of a split decision at the Barnstaple Pannier Market Show.

Less than a week later, however, he left the result in no doubt by dominating every round against the same Torbay opponent.

Stevenson started aggressively, landing combinations, and kept the tempo up in the second round when he bloodied McCluskey's nose by using his right uppercut when in tight.

Carrying his momentum into the third, Stevenson put in a big effort and trapped his opponent on the ropes with fast combinations to seal the win, capping a great season in which he has won six of his eight bouts.

Josh Short also had a rematch and beat Torbay's Kai Draper for the second time.

Big hooks rocked Draper in the first round and, after taking his foot off the gas in the second, Short went through the gears in the last to record his fifth win in six outings this season.

Lewis Cornish showed potential in his skills bout with Dylan Willis, of Tiverton. Cornish showed good footwork and punch variety, ending up the stronger of the two in a well-matched contest.

A week on from his Pannier Market victory over Chris Banks, Dave Curry was edged out by the Tiverton boxer's better workrate in a competitive bout.

Read more online at northdevonjournal.co.uk

16 - June 2016

Bank avenges recent defeat

TIVERTON ABC

TIVERTON ABC held their final show of the season in a marquee on Elmore Football Club's Horsdon Park ground on Saturday night.

In the first bout of the night, Tiverton's Zack O'Loughlin put up a fantastic performance to avenge his recent loss to Port Talbot's Efan Williams on a unanimous points decision.

However another home fighter, John Penfold, was on the wrong end of a unanimous points decision against Devonport's Noel Revell.

Tiverton's Zack Jones put up a tremendous effort against his nemesis, Cwmgor's James Parker, but after three rip-roaring rounds it was the Welshman that was given the verdict.

Another Tivvy fighter Chris Banks did gain revenge for a recent defeat in his fight against Barnstaple's Dave Curry. Having lost to Curry seven days earlier, Banks left no doubt in the judges' eyes this time around as he dominated from start to finish.

Tivvy's Brad Riggs fought reigning champion Jordan Ruth for the Western Counties Middlewight Challenge Belt. Riggs put in a tremendous effort, showing buckets of heart and courage, but was beaten on a points decision.

Earlier in the evening, two Mid Devon youngsters, Dylan Burston and Edward Fry had performed with distinction in their respective skills bouts, impressing coach Paul Harvey in the process.

O'Loughlin was ajudged best junior boxer of the night with Banks picking up the seniors' award.

Afterwards, Harvey expressed his gratitude to all the sponsors and everyone who went along to support it, as well as Elmore Football Club for their help in staging the event.

Tuesday June 14, 2016 The Gazette

the latest breaking news middevongazette

North Devon Gazette | Wednesday, June 15, 2016

Follow us on Twitter @ndgazettesport

BOXING

Boxers fight in Tiverton

Members of Bideford and Barnstaple's amateur boxing clubs were in action on Saturday at Tiverton Amateur Boxing Club's home show.

There were plenty of rematches on the card, with two of the bouts being rematches from last week's show in Barnstaple.

Bideford's Jacob Stevenson was looking for revenge as he took on Liam McCluskey for the second time in a week.

McLuskey edged the contest in Barnstaple, but Stevenson didn't allow such a close contest this time around.

Using his right hand well, Stevenson landed combinations early and didn't let up, maintaining a quick tempo and doing more and more as the bout went on.

Another rematch from Barnstaple's show was David Currey against Tiverton's Chris Banks.

The Barnstaple fighter edged an entertaining fight last week, but was on the wrong side of the decision this time around.

Banks edged the fight with a better work rate in the close and very competitive bout.

Bideford's Josh Short got a second win over Kai Draper of Torbay thanks to a blistering first round.

Short put in some big hooks early on but allowed Draper to come back in the second round before assuring a points victory in the last.

Lewis Cornish showed potential in his skills bout with Dillyn Wallis of Tiverton.

Cornish showed good footwork and punch variety in a well-matched contest.

BIDEFORD BOXERS Lewis Cornish, Jacob Stevenson and Josh Short.

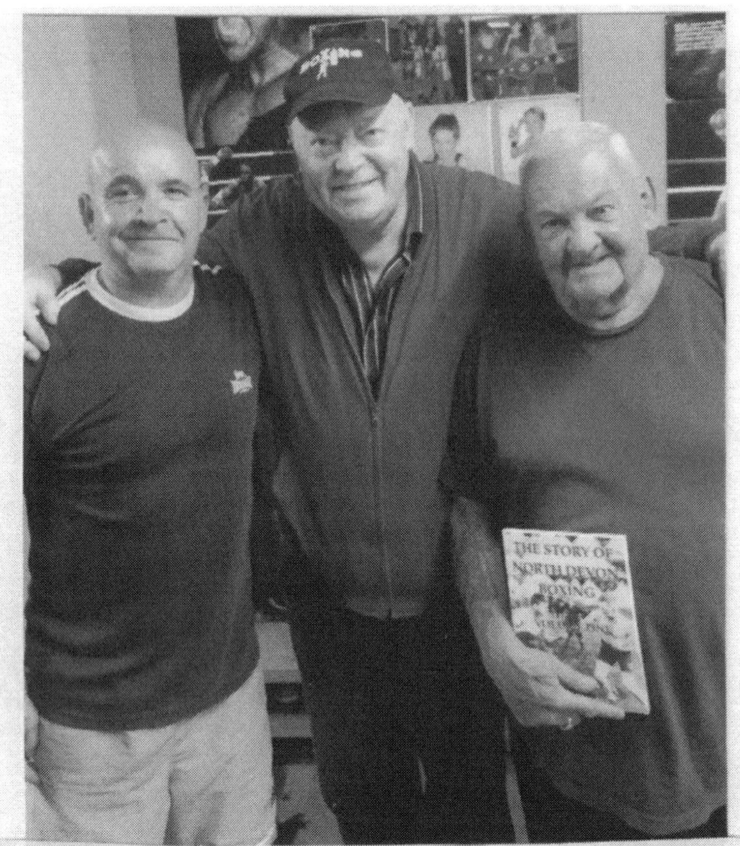

TRAINER and HEAD MAN, PAUL HARVEY, DB, PAUL Snr.

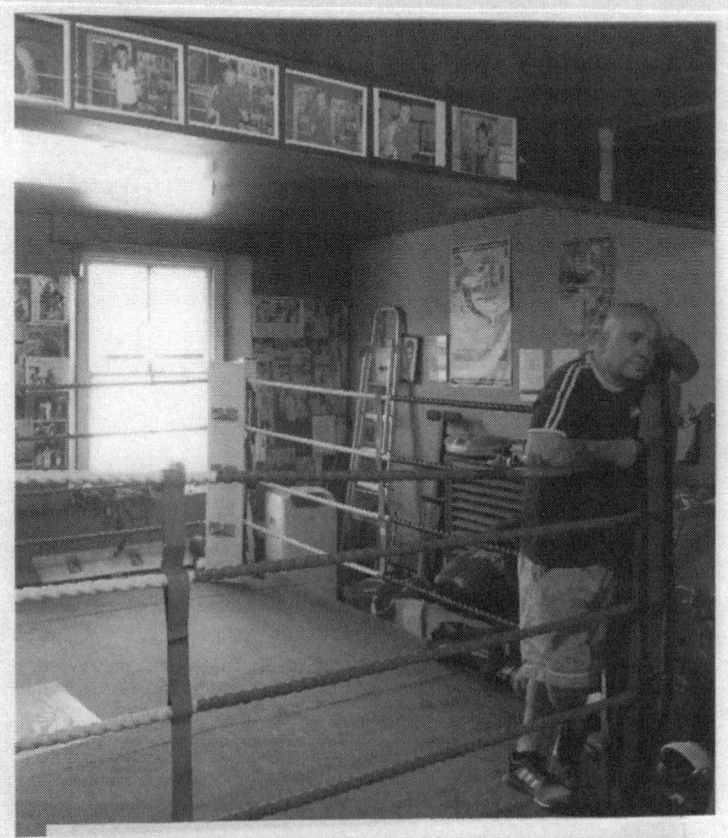

PAUL HARVEY in a thoughtful moment.

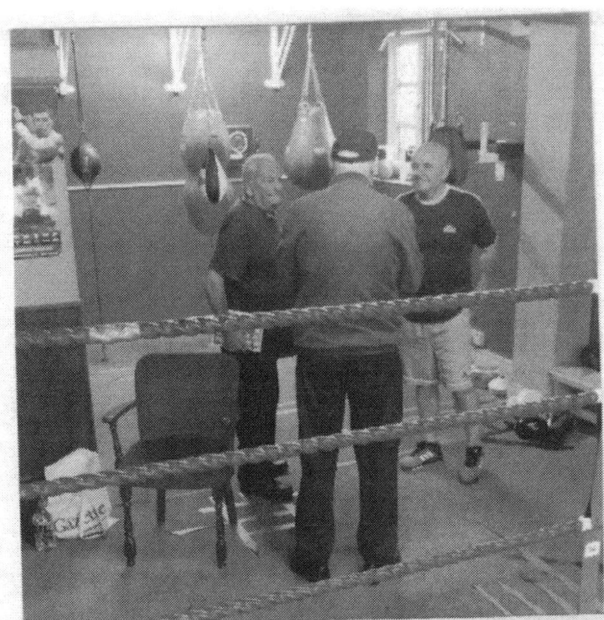

DB visits TIVERTON AMATEUR BOXING CLUB'S GYM.
So much work has gone into creating this gym, it has an atmosphere reminiscent of the 'old days' but with every modern facility.

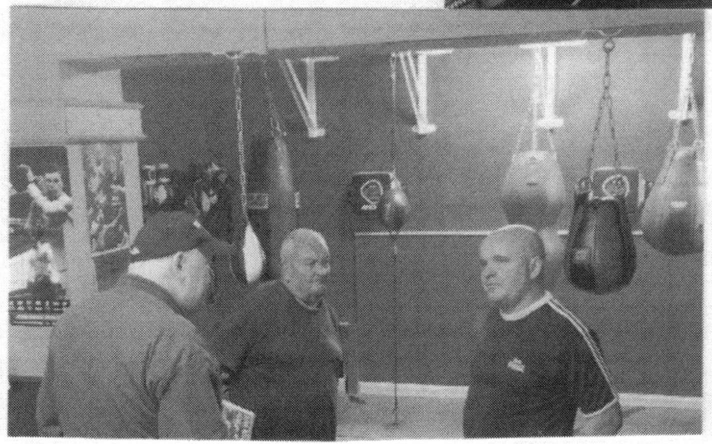

TORRINGTON POLICE ABC

The Journal Thursday April 11, 2013

■ AT RISK: Torrington Boxing Club faces homelessness unless members can find a new home by the end of April.

Boxing club in urgent need of new premises

By NICOLE TRAVERS-WAKEFORD

A FLEDGLING sports group in Torrington faces homelessness for the second time in a year.

Torrington Police Amateur Boxing Club was formed last year and is searching for a permanent home to hold training sessions.

The club was forced to leave its former base at the Globe Hotel in January when the hotel closed its doors.

Coaches and members have been using a room inside Torrington Town Hall since.

However, this was only a temporary arrangement. The club has until Tuesday, April 30 before they have to vacate.

With less than three weeks until the group has to leave their temporary accommodation, coaches are on the hunt for a permanent home.

Since the club was set up, members have trained in four venues including a local garage, a village hall and at Function Fitness.

Club coach Heathcliffe Pettifer said the club has never been able to properly set down its roots.

Mr Pettifer said: "This issue has been a constant worry and distraction.

"Frustratingly and despite the relative numbers of vacant properties in the town, the biggest challenge for the club is finding a new home.

"The committee members, boxers and their supporters including Function Fitness and Torrington Cavaliers have worked tirelessly to make the club a success.

"The club attracts up to 30 members at any one time, training three times a week. They have more than half a dozen of their boxers with medical cards ready to compete in tournaments."

Sharon Smith's son Ade Smith Jones is 15 and trains and competes with the club. Her husband Stephen is a club coach.

She said: "All the coaches are very passionate about the boxing and Torrington. Many have lived here many years so they are familiar with a lot of the community.

"Its great they give their spare time three times a week plus attending competitions. I have watched this club grow in size dramatically over the last eight or so months.

"They are seen out training in the town supporting and encouraging each other. I have seen all these kids self esteem grow which in turn has improved their confidence."

Mr Pettifer said: "It takes huge amounts of courage, commitment and dedication to step into a ring and box for your club and your town."

NEWS SATURDAY APRIL 13 2013 WESTERN MORNING NEWS

Boxing club coaches search for new home as deadline looms to leave hall

BY NICOLE TRAVERS-WAKEFORD

Some of the members of Torrington Police Amateur Boxing Club which must find a permanent home by the end of this month

A fledgling North Devon sports group faces homelessness for the second time in a year.

Torrington Police Amateur Boxing Club was formed last year and is searching for a permanent home to hold training sessions.

The club was forced to leave its former base at the Globe Hotel in January when the hotel closed its doors.

Coaches and members have been using a room inside Torrington Town Hall since.

However, this was only a temporary arrangement. The club has until Tuesday, April 30, before it has to vacate.

With less than three weeks to find temporary accommodation, coaches are on the hunt for a permanent home.

Since the club was set up, members have trained in four venues including a local garage, a village hall and at Function Fitness.

Club coach Heathcliffe Pettifer said the club has never been able to properly set down its roots. Mr Pettifer said: "This issue has been a constant worry and distraction.

"Frustratingly and despite the numbers of vacant properties in the town, the biggest challenge for the club is finding a new home.

"The committee members, boxers and their supporters including Function Fitness and Torrington Cavaliers have worked tirelessly to make the club a success.

"The club attracts up to 30 members at any one time, training three times a week. They have more than half a dozen of their boxers with medical cards ready to compete in tournaments."

Sharon Smith's son Ade Smith Jones is 15 and trains and competes with the club. Her husband Stephen is a club coach.

She said: "All the coaches are very passionate about the boxing and Torrington. They are familiar with a lot of the community. It's great they give their spare time three times a week plus attending competitions. I have watched this club grow in size dramatically over the last eight or so months.

"They are seen out training in the town supporting and encouraging each other. I have seen all these kids' self-esteem grow which in turn has improved their confidence."

Mr Pettifer said: "It takes huge amounts of courage, commitment and dedication to step into a ring and box for your club and your town."

Early problems with finding suitable premises for a gym have now been solved and the club is beginning to produce some talented boxers.

The Journal Thursday May 16, 2013

Green giants rise to the occasion at market show

By MARK JENKIN
mjenkin@northdevonjournal.co.uk

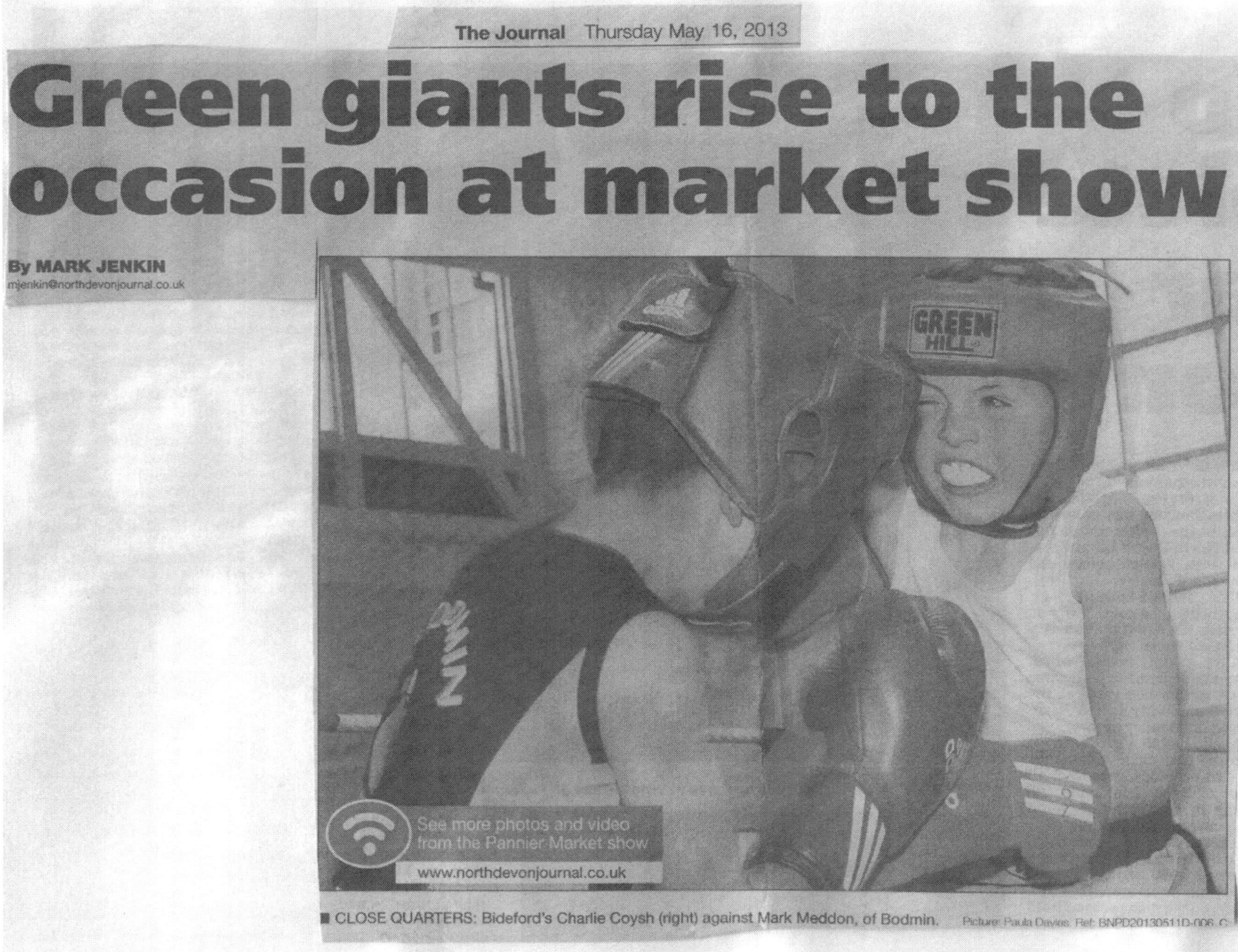
GREEN HILL
See more photos and video from the Pannier Market show
www.northdevonjournal.co.uk

■ CLOSE QUARTERS: Bideford's Charlie Coysh (right) against Mark Meddon, of Bodmin. Picture: Paula Davies Ref: BNPD20130511D-006_C

TWO Torrington teenagers relished the opportunity to perform at an historic boxing venue for the first time.

Joe Tarrant and Ade Smith-Jones made it a memorable occasion for Torrington Police ABC at Bideford Pannier Market on Saturday night.

Proudly wearing the green vest of the emerging club, the 15-year-olds made their moment count with battling victories.

As the amateur scene in North Devon continues to thrive, Bideford ABC were keen to highlight the talents of young boxers from across the area.

With members of the host club, Barnstaple, Combe Martin and Torrington impressing in the 13 bouts, it was mission accomplished.

Wildlife presenter Johnny Kingdom was a guest of honour and will have particularly enjoyed the clash between Tarrant and Barnstaple's Brandon Maddock.

Like two stags on Exmoor, the North Devon rivals went head to head in uncompromising style.

Ever the competitor, Maddock was willing to stand and trade as both boys had spells on the front foot, throwing punches in flurries.

There was nothing to separate them until Tarrant sneaked ahead in the third round, landing two cracking right hooks in a unanimous win.

Only a few points made the difference and a rematch has been agreed for the Barnstaple Pannier Market show on June 2.

Smith-Jones boxed with composure for his majority win against Rob Latham-Willows, of Torpoint and Rame.

Holding a high guard, he stepped in on numerous occasions to score with left-jab, right-hook combinations.

Having only started training this year, Smith-Jones has improved dramatically since making his competitive debut last month.

For the home fans, there were victories to savour for three of their most experienced seniors – Ben Owen, Ray Penfold and Soane Coysh

A measured approach was the key for Penfold and Owen, who both displayed technical skills in their unanimous results.

After a cagey opening spell, Penfold rocked Kyle Gargett with a forceful right hand towards the end of the second round.

The visitor from the Pilgrims club in Plymouth remained cautious but gradually his defences were unpicked.

With a drop of the shoulder, Penfold began the fourth and final round by landing another stealthy right hook to the head.

Gargett was unable to offer much in reply as Penfold moved smartly and maintained a tight guard.

Ever the showman, Owen took on Dan Daws with familiar feigns and low slung hands.

He proved too elusive for a Yeovil opponent who was caught on numerous occasions by fast, straight lefts to the head. Coolness and composure gave Owen the edge.

For Coysh it was a war of attrition over four rounds against Christian Spangle, of the Mayflower club in Plymouth.

The pair refused to let their energy levels drop in a strength-sapping contest notable for the intensity of the shot-making.

And Coysh showed his stamina down the stretch, taking a majority decision thanks to his relentless work ethic.

In the junior ranks, Soane's young cousin Charlie Coysh proudly celebrated his first win for Bideford.

A month after losing narrowly against Bodmin's Mark Meadon in Cornwall, he turned the tables in a rousing rematch.

Kye Cook impressed with his ringcraft after Aaron Robinson started at a thunderous tempo. Cook rode out the early storm, blocking many of the Lympstone boxer's two-handed attacks before replying with the more measured punches. It was enough for a majority win for the Bideford boy.

A split decision went the wrong way for Chey Saunders but the home boxer can take heart from his performance against Tobias Hacker.

Round two was one of the highlights of the night, with Saunders keeping up the pace and Hacker responding with body shots that left his rival needing a standing count.

All the action between Bideford's Billy Parsons and Bradley Axe, of Yeovil, was confined to three explosive minutes.

After a rip-roaring first round, Parsons was caught by three powerful right hooks early in the second. He was given a count and, when Axe attacked again, the referee stopped the contest.

The evening came to a painful and premature end for home heavyweight Jamie Creek who suffered a dislocated shoulder in his heavyweight bout with Matt Leslie, of Downend.

● Youth sport: pages 78-79.

RESULTS

Red corner 1st (Bideford ABC unless stated): Bailey Ratcliffe (Combe Martin) v Connor Merson (Portland) skills bout; Charlie Coysh beat Mark Meadon (Bodmin) U 6-5, 7-3, 7-7; Zack Jones (Tiverton) lost to Owen Pirret (Downend) U 6-10, 6-10, 9-10; Kye Cook beat Aaron Robinson (Lympstone) M 13-8, 11-10, 8-8; Ade Smith-Jones (Torrington Police) beat Rob Latham-Willows (Torpoint Rame Peninsula) M 10-7, 8-7, 7-8; Cheye Saunders lost to Tobias Hacker (Downend) M 9-12, 12-14, 16-13; Joe Tarrant (Torrington Police) beat Brandon Maddock (Barnstaple) U 11-7, 13-12, 11-10; Billy Parsons lost to Bradley Axe (Yeovil) R2 stoppage; Corey Westbrook (Tiverton) lost to Ben Demmery (Downend) U 6-8, 11-15, 10-12; Ben Owen beat Dan Daws (Yeovil) U 15-14, 15-12, 22-10; Ray Penfold beat Kyle Gargett (Pilgrims) U 8-7, 12-7, 12-9; Soane Coysh beat Christian Spangle (Plymouth Mayflower) M 15-14, 18-16, 7-10; Jamie Creek lost to Matt Leslie (Downend) R3 stoppage.

Torrington Police Amateur Boxing Club

PRESENT AN

★ AMATEUR BOXING ★
SHOW

GREAT TORRINGTON SCHOOL
SPORTS HALL

Hatchmoor Road, Devon EX38 7DJ

SAT. 1st FEB 2014 doors 7:00pm

A FULL CARD OF AMATEUR BOXING FEATURING LOCAL TORRINGTON BOXERS

BAR, LIGHT REFRESHMENTS & FOOD AVAILABLE

Entry by ticket only

TICKETS - £10.00 AVAILABLE FROM

Ask here for tickets or telephone - 07901654999: 07958 788 589: 07890902919: 07786075052

● TOM HUTCHINGS impressed for Torrington Police ABC with a composed display at the Paddy Johns Show in Bristol.

In only his third bout, the teenager showed his potential with a rousing win against Shaughnessy Abrahams, of King Alfred ABC.

The Torrie boxer finished strongly with a burst of shots to head and body.

Two boxers from Barnstaple ABC were beaten by split decision at the Blandford Show in Dorset. Tom Allum lost to Harry Cracknell, from the hosts, and Jake Hooper missed out against Portland's William Barber.

Grant Stone proved his fighting spirit in a tough debut for Bideford ABC against John Cooper, from Lawrence ABC.

The Journal Thursday March 20, 2014

Torrington boxers put on show to please fans

SAM Gilbert and Dan Langdon entertained the crowd at the Torrington Police ABC Show.

Both produced impressive victories for the host club at Great Torrington School.

Twelve bouts were scheduled, featuring nine Torrington boxers.

Langdon began the entertainment following the interval by stopping his opponent in the second round, having himself taken a standing count in the first round.

Gilbert headlined the show and did not let his supporters down as he narrowly beat his opponent from Sydenham on points.

Ned Pettifer opened the show with an entertaining and confident three rounds.

Charlie Golder picked up valuable experience in his first skills bout.

Fergus McLean and Matt Gray put in tough debut performances but lost on points to stronger opponents from Plymouth and Reading respectively, while Jack Pledger worked hard in defeat.

Torrington boxers Nathan Board and Trai Sheppard gave everything in their bouts to win against opponents from Sydenham and Bude respectively.

A big performance in the third round secured a points victory for Ben Owen at the Torrington show.

The Bideford ABC boxer was well matched against Alex Jones, of Tiverton.

Jones went into the fight in fine form, having beaten Barnstaple ABC's Liam Laird the week before.

He started well, edging the first round in a tactical affair by countering Owen's jabs with flurries.

In the second round, Owen began scoring with straight punches catching Jones on the way in as he tried to work inside.

It was tight going into the final round but, as the boxers locked horns in the middle of the ring, Owen proved the stronger. He landed big hooks and uppercuts to split Jones's nose and win the fight on points.

Callum Cunningham, one of Bideford's brightest young prospects, continued his education with a mature performance.

In the past he has shown his power to blast three of his four wins out inside the distance, but this time he showed his all-round ability.

Against undefeated Devonport boxer Tyler Dyer, a tall opponent with good feet, Cunningham took his time, moving his head and going in at angles to score with fast flurries and avoid getting countered on the way in.

In the second round, Cunningham switched to body and head, showing a good range of shots and frustrating Dyer, who could not read his opponent's work.

Cunningham continued to move through the gears in the last round, showing great movement to set up clean counter punches and take a unanimous points win.

Owen and Cunningham will be in action in Bideford's dinner show at the Durrant House Hotel on Friday, November 20.

Limited tickets for the show are available from Dick Kersey on 07841 846552.

Torrington Police ABC hailed the show as a success and thanked the community for its support.

● BIDEFORD ABC boxer Jack Langford has passed his level-two coaching course.

The Journal Thursday November 5, 2015

■ BIG HIT: Ben Owen, of Bideford ABC, put in an excellent performance to win on points at the Torrington Police ABC Show.

TORRINGTON POLICE ABC 2016.

Under the expert guidance of BOB ELLIS, his right hand men HEATH PETIFER and STEVE JONES run the boxing side of the gym activities. WAYNE HILL is in charge of recreational training. The present Club facilities are a clear indication of what can be achieved by group planning and hard work. With the gym now situated on 2 floors and every piece of modern training equipment available the Club can accommodate young and old of both sex.

What a great asset for TORRINGTON.

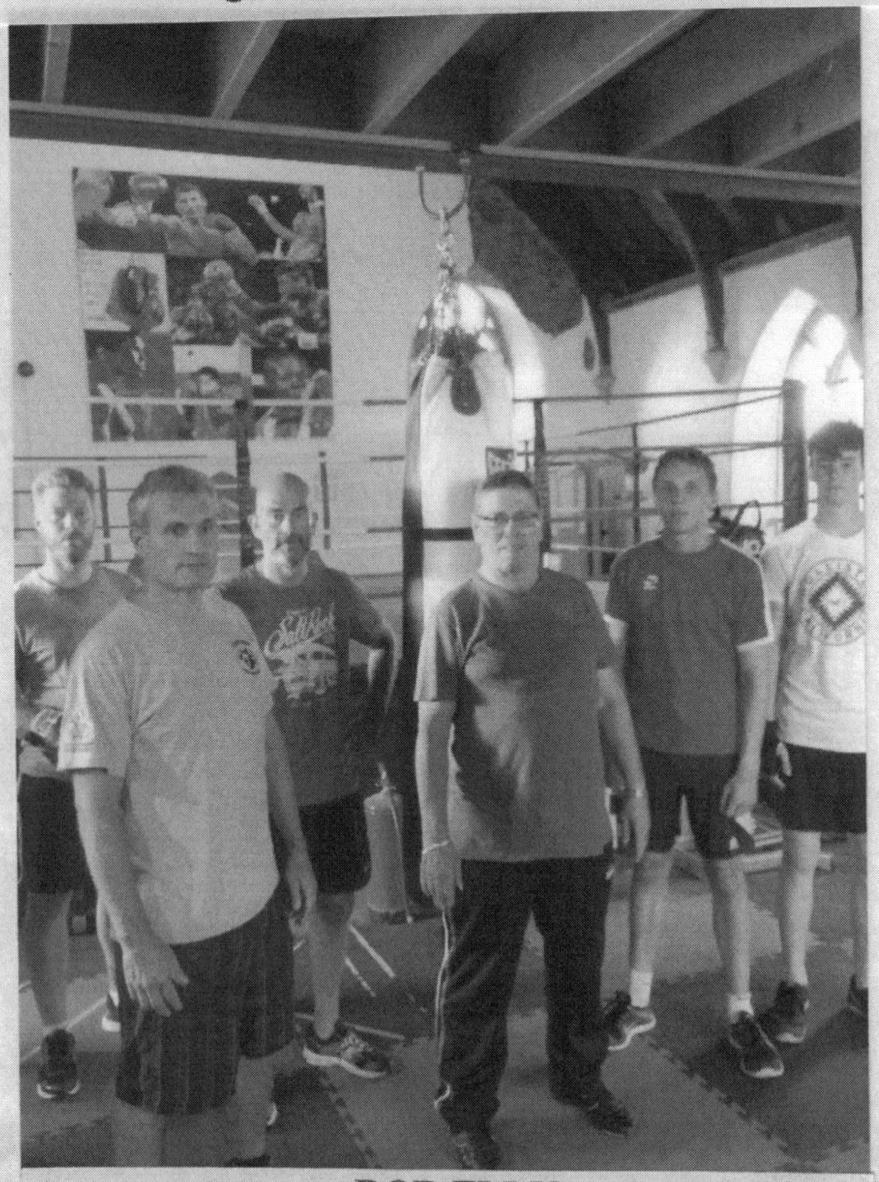

BOB ELLIS,
in blue shirt, with members of his Team.

Participants celebrating their success.

Boxers brave big hill for challenge

By Joe Bulmer
joe.bulmer@northdevonjournal.co.uk

BOXERS from Torrington braved bad weather and managed 123 laps of one the town's steepest hills in a mammoth eight-hour challenge to raise money for terminally ill children.

The Torrington Police Amateur Boxing Club raised more than £1,000 for Children's Hospice South West by running up and down Mill Street for eight straight hours.

Participants started the challenge on Saturday, August 20, at 8am and didn't finish until 4pm.

The charity challengers ran down the hill and back up again 123 times without stopping or walking.

Boxing coach Wayne Hill came up with the idea and would like to thank everyone who helped make the challenge a success.

He said: "I had the idea in my head for some time but it's not something you can spring on people as it needs lots of thought and some decent training.

"When I told boxing club members what I was expecting there was a bit of colourful language but I knew it was the challenge they needed and they didn't let me down, enthusiastically running up and down in the wind and rain.

"I would like to take this opportunity to thank all those involved and all of those people who generously gave donations."

Most people ran around five laps each but Jake Wright completed the most with 11 laps run.

The length of Mill Street is 0.44 miles, so one lap is not far off a mile.

Collectively members ran more than 100 miles.

A variety of members from the club participated including juniors, men, women, mums, dads and also some members of Torrington Running Club donated money and ran some laps.

Support for the challenge was "overwhelming" with drivers stopping their cars in the street to donate and local businesses sending donations in.

Boxing club chairman Shaun Kenneally thanked the community for the support.

"Well done to everyone who took part and particular thanks to Wayne for coming up with the idea for such a good cause," he said.

"The support from the Torrington community was truly outstanding both in terms of encouragement and donations. It helped a gruelling challenge seem ever so slightly easier."

Read more online at northdevonjournal.co.uk

TORRINGTON POLICE ABC.

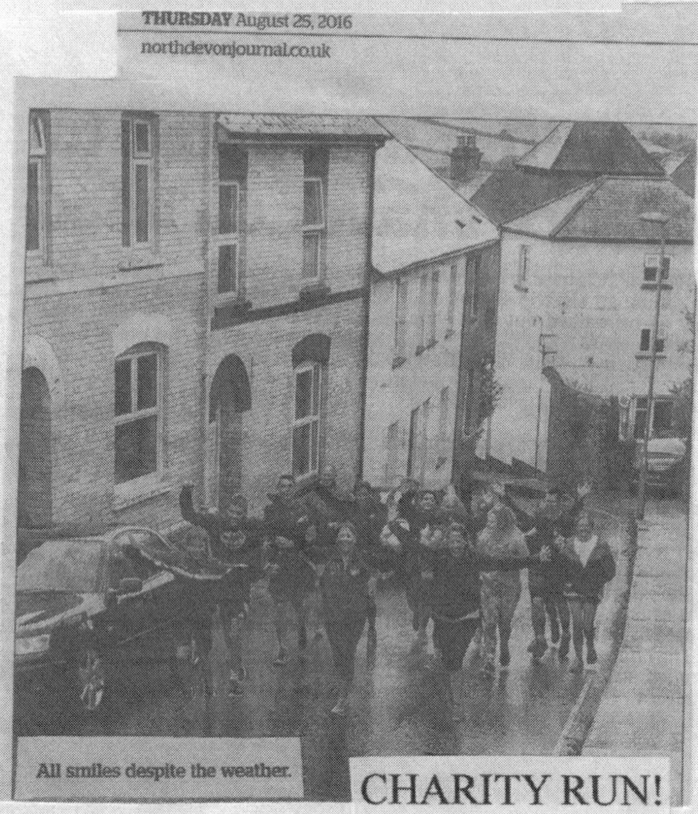
THURSDAY August 25, 2016
northdevonjournal.co.uk

All smiles despite the weather.

CHARITY RUN!

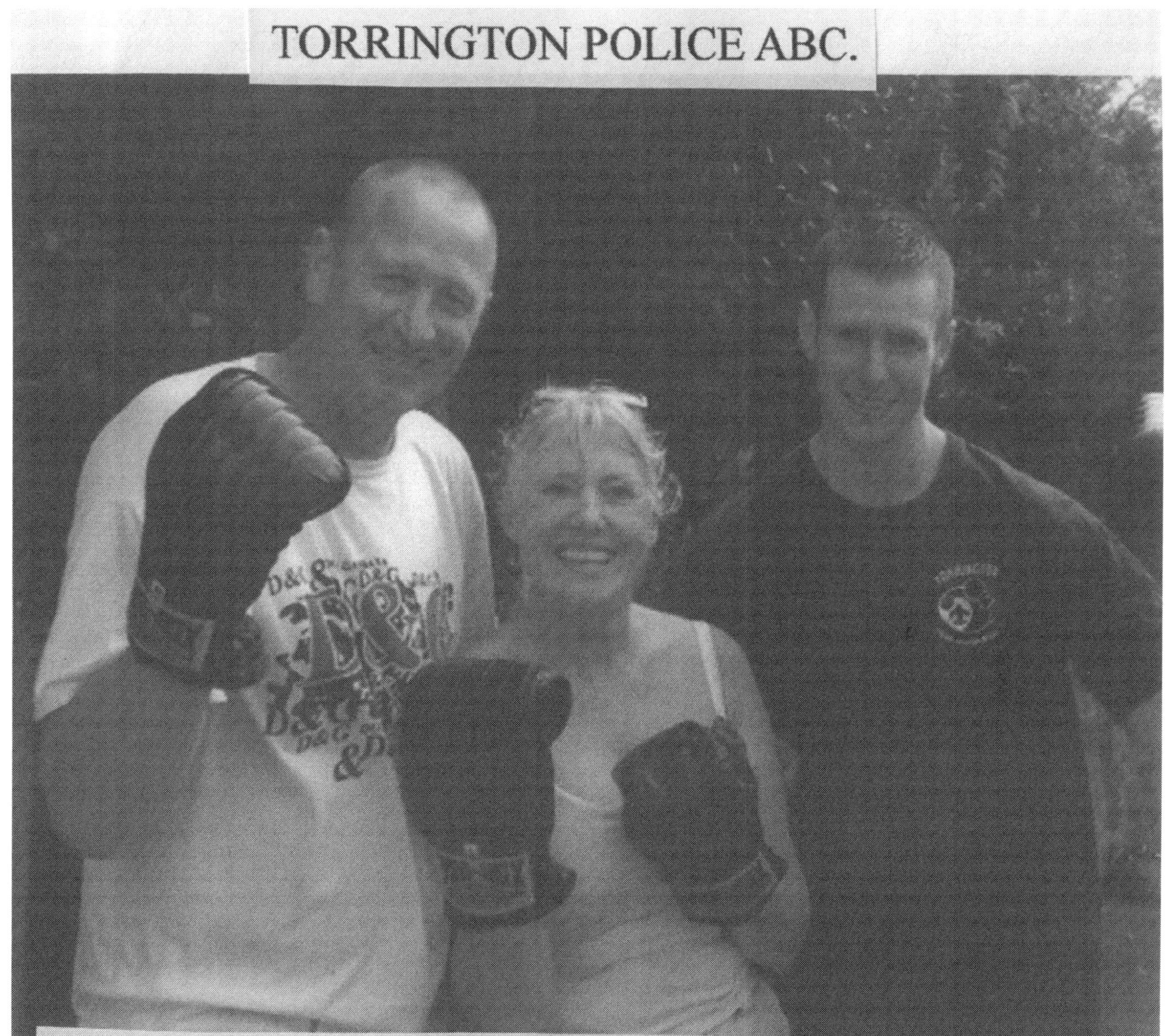

TORRINGTON POLICE ABC.

GLOVED UP! BUT RUNNING FOR CHARITY!!
STEVE JONES, ANNE TATTERSALL, JAKE WRIGHT.

NORTH DEVON BOXING 2016

NORTH DEVON BOXING..2016

BIDEFORD
AMATEUR BOXING CLUB

PRESENTS

An Evening of
Amateur Boxing

Sponsored by
ANDY'S AUTO 01237 237170

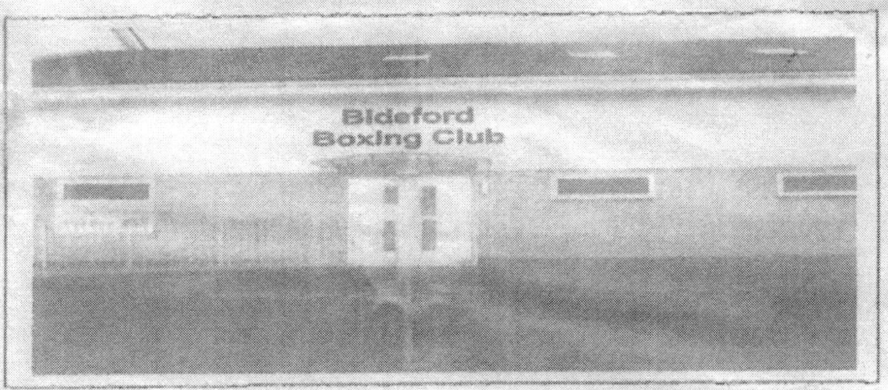

SATURDAY 12 March 2016

BIDEFORD COLLEGE

Thank you for your support

Programme
50P

North Devon Gazette | Wednesday, March 16, 2016

Bideford showcases local boxing talent

■ Gabriel Silva in action for Bideford against Shane Skilton and (inset) Billy Stanbury takes a blow from Max Earle. Pictures: MATT SMART

BOXING

Bideford Amateur Boxing Club had plenty of fighters in action at their home show on Saturday.

The event, which took place at Bideford College, featured 15 fights in total, with 13 fighters from the club on the card.

Billy Stanbury was top of the bill but the heavyweight was unable to end the show with a win.

Stanbury was able to knock down his opponent, Max Earle of Mayflower, but could not capitalise in the later rounds as he lost by split decision.

Gabriel Silva put in an explosive performance in his light heavyweight bout against St Austell's Shane Skilton.

Silva went out fast and didn't relent, knocking his opponent down twice before sealing the win in the first round via technical knockout.

Unfortunately Ben Owen's final home bout wasn't a fairytale ending, losing on a split decision.

Pete McDonald, Matt Wade, Josh and Andy Short and Lewis Mackenzie all picked up wins for the amateur club.

BIDEFORD ABC

Trainer, RICHARD GRIGG.

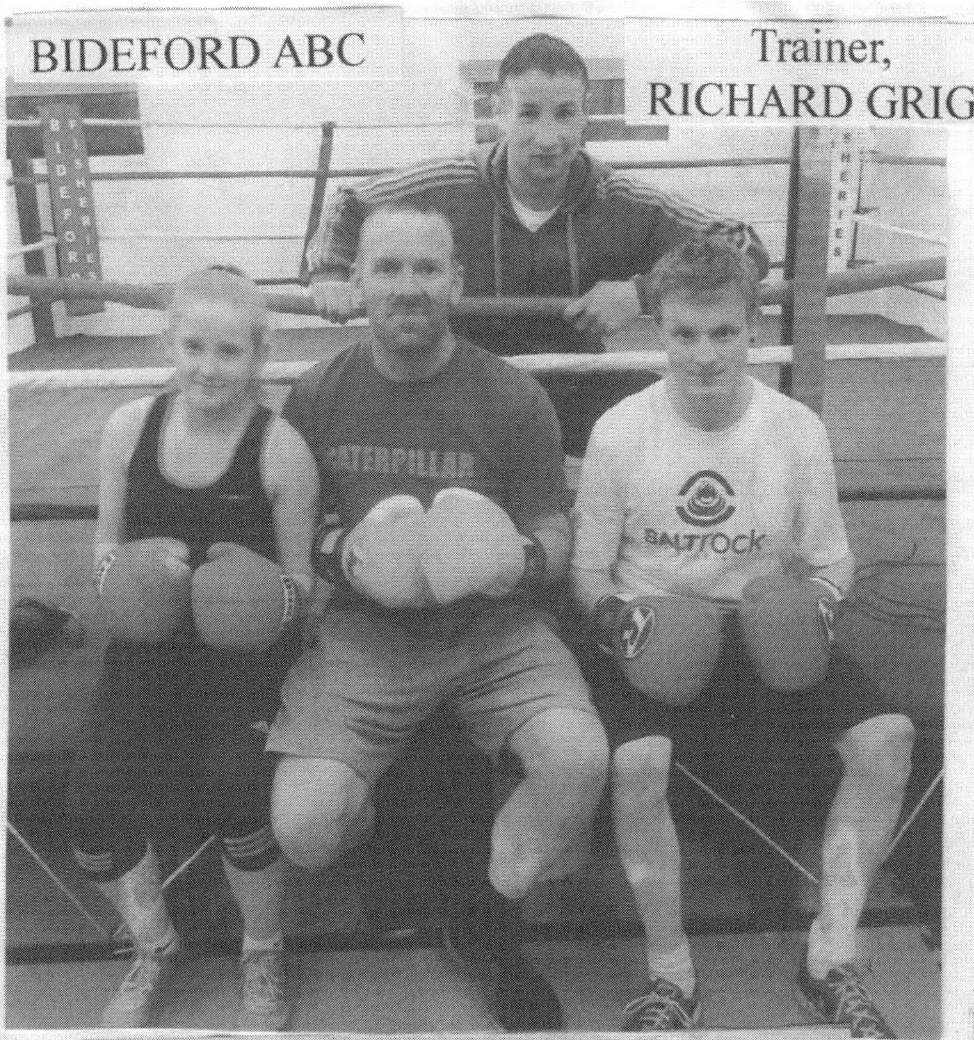

■ Josh, Andy and Grace Short will all be boxing at Bideford College on Saturday.

North Devon Gazette | Wednesday, March 9, 2016

BOXING

Bideford Amateur Boxing Club's show on Saturday promises to be one for all the family.

That's especially true for a family from Appledore.

Andy Short, his son Josh and daughter Grace all feature on Saturday's bill, a feat that has rarely been seen in boxing.

Richard Grigg, who trains the family, said: "We've never had three people from the same family on the bill and I've never seen it anywhere I've been."

The family started at the boxing club four years ago, with Andy watching his son Josh and his eldest daughter train.

Andy said: "I was just bringing them, sitting on the seat and watching them to save me going back to Appledore."

Eventually, the father started training with the club to improve his fitness levels, until Richard persuaded him to fight for the first time at the Durrant Hotel in 2013.

"He boxed and he won. Boxed really well, but he said that was going to be his only one," said Richard.

Andy's eldest eventually left the club, while Josh continued to progress until he was ready to fight competitively.

The chance to fight on the card with his son was enough to persuade Andy to box again, and both won their fights at Bideford College last year.

Then Grace joined the club. The 13 year-old has progressed well during the last year – enough to earn herself a fight on Saturday's schedule alongside her brother.

Richard saw the opportunity and persuaded Andy to fight one last time.

He said: "She's been getting better and better and she's ready to box.

"Andy's going to do one more, so if he wins this, he'll have won three from three, and he was never going to box!"

For the family, it's not just about fighting together on the match card.

Andy said: "I feel proud to be on the bill with them.

"It's nice that I can see my kids enjoy it and it's getting them exercise and making friends."

BIDEFORD ABC SHOW

Short story makes history

By Jonny Bonell
jonny.bonell@northdevonjournal.co.uk

ANDY Short spoke of his pride after fighting on the same bill as his son and daughter.

The 37-year-old, who has been boxing for two years, put in a strong performance in his third and final fight to claim a unanimous win against Mark Morrey in their senior heavyweight clash at the Bideford ABC show on Saturday.

After an even start, Short took control with good jab work before hitting Morrey with two big left hooks in the last round.

Earlier in the night, son Josh was strong from the off as he beat St Agnes's Henry Symons by technical knockout and daughter Grace was narrowly beaten on a split decision by Amelia Jarvis, of Mayflower ABC.

It was the first time in the club's history a father, son and daughter had fought on the same bill.

"It was very good, but very exhausting," said Andy. "I was nervous leading up to it but my coach told me what I had to do and hopefully my performance was an impressive one.

"I am very proud, the nerves I was getting in the ring they (Grace and Josh) would feel the same, if not worse, so I take my hat off to them.

"To get two out of three (wins) was very good.

"My eldest daughter and son joined about five years ago and I would go and watch. Telling them to push themselves made me think if I could do better than why not give it a go? So I did."

There was success for five other home boxers at Bideford College – none more impressive than Gabriel Silva's technical knockout in the first round against Shane Skilton.

Silva's work on his feet was second to none and his long reach had already knocked Skilton down once before a second time stopped the contest.

Heavyweight Matt Wade and Trowbridge ABC's Bart Kujana fought in an excellent bout with both fighters landing several big shots before Wade was given the win on a split decision.

The immensely popular Pete Macdonald claimed the fight of the night for his unanimous win against Peter Wills, of St Ives ABC, while Grant Stone also earned a unanimous victory in an all-action battle with Tiverton's Dan Greenwood.

Lewis McKenzie's power shone through against Corey Andrew, of Whitchurch ABC, as he secured a technical knockout.

After a fairly even opening two rounds, McKenzie put the hammer down in the last, landing a big right and getting Andrew against the ropes before the referee stepped in.

Youngster Jacob Stevenson showed some good work despite being unanimously beaten by Jimmy Jordan, Barton Hill's Nile Thomas overcame a tough test in Freddie Wright and Reece Hollingsworth put in a good shift in his skills bout with Kyle Kent.

Heavyweight Billy Stanbury gave absolutely everything in the top of the bill clash with Max Earle, of Mayflower ABC.

The battle certainly lived up to the billing with Earle landing some heavy shots but Stanbury repelled and hit quick flurries of his own. The judges gave the win to Earle on a split decision.

HEAVYWEIGHT CLASH Mark Morrey (left) evades Andy Short.
Pictures: Paula Davies. To order this photograph call 0844 4060 269 and quote Ref: BNPD20160312A-031_C

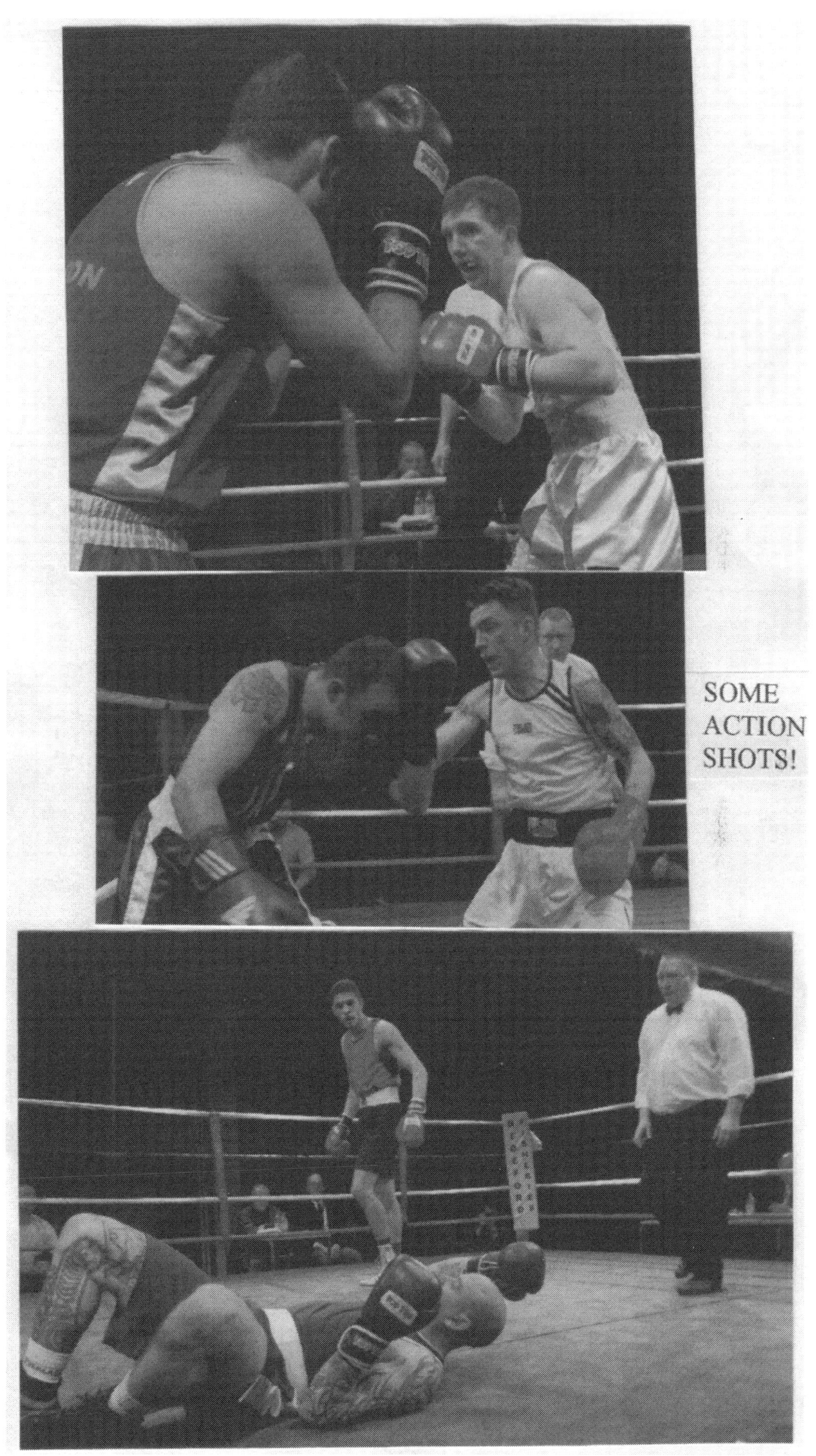

SOME ACTION SHOTS!

GREAT SUPPORTERS of BIDEFORD ABC.

Councillor SIMON INCH.

PRESENTING TROPHIES.

Councillor TONY INCH.

PRESENTING TROPHIES...

DOCTOR ROBIN BUCKLAND,
a TREMENDOUS SUPPORTER of BOXING in NORTH DEVON
for a GREAT MANY YEARS.

DERRY BROWNSON

Farewell fight
for Ben Owens

GARTH GOSS

Barnstaple Amateur Boxing Club

Presents a

Boxing Open Show

at

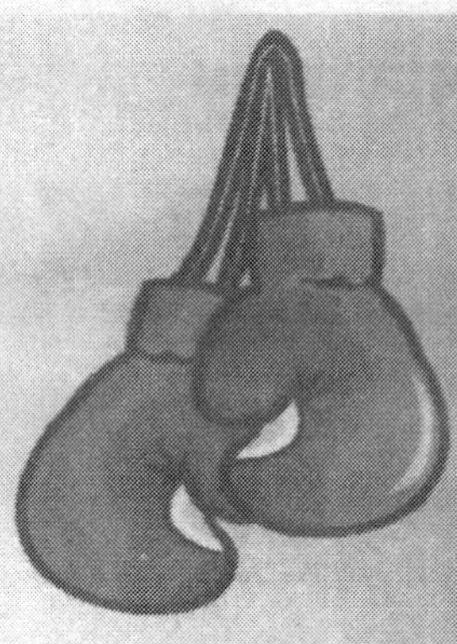

Barnstaple Rugby Club

on

SATURDAY 23rd APRIL 2016
DOORS OPEN 7pm.

BARNSTAPLE ABC SHOW

Silva triumphs in golden bout

By Jonny Bonell
jonny.bonell@northdevonjournal.co.uk

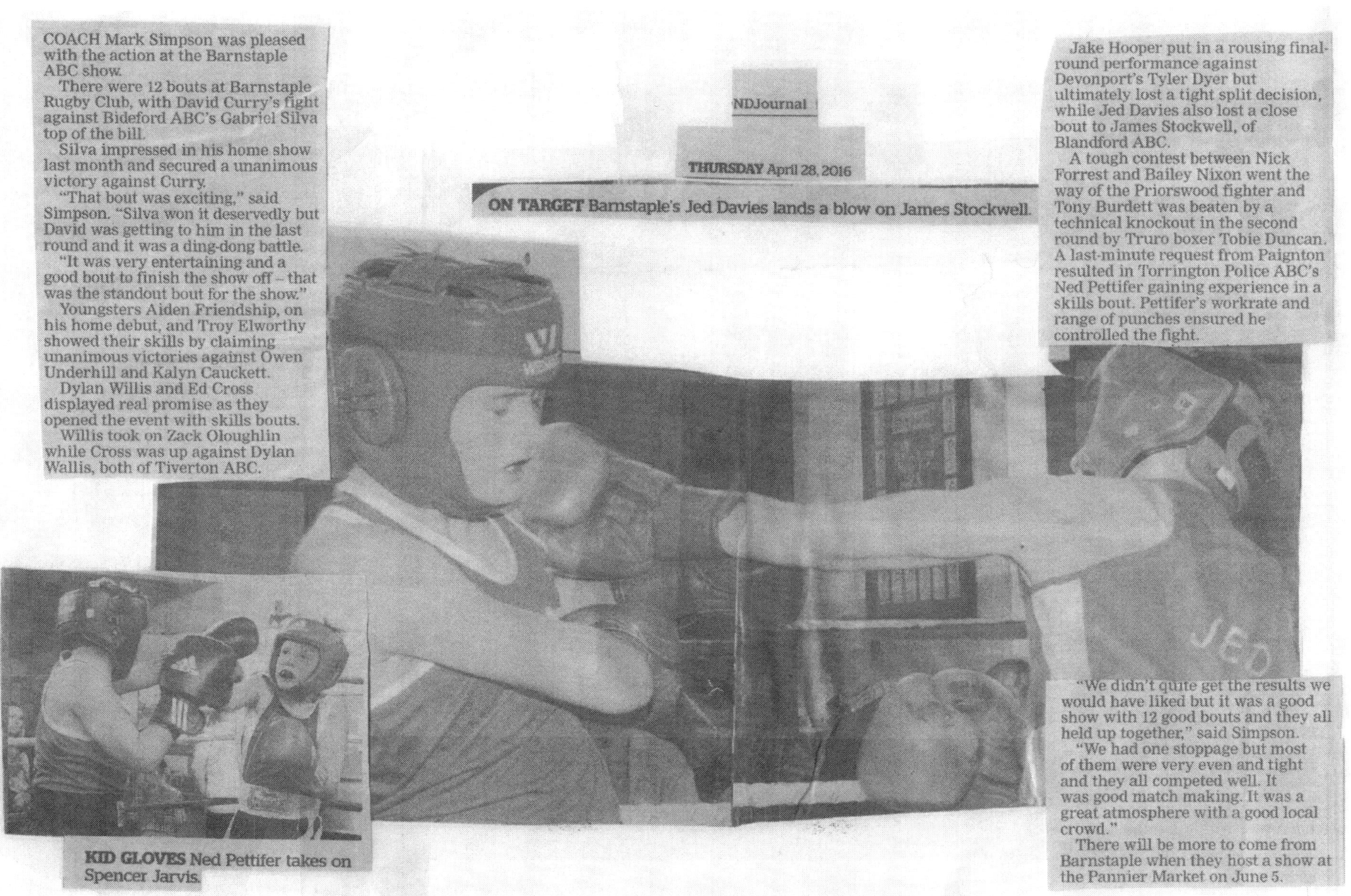

NDJournal

THURSDAY April 28, 2016

COACH Mark Simpson was pleased with the action at the Barnstaple ABC show.

There were 12 bouts at Barnstaple Rugby Club, with David Curry's fight against Bideford ABC's Gabriel Silva top of the bill.

Silva impressed in his home show last month and secured a unanimous victory against Curry.

"That bout was exciting," said Simpson. "Silva won it deservedly but David was getting to him in the last round and it was a ding-dong battle.

"It was very entertaining and a good bout to finish the show off – that was the standout bout for the show."

Youngsters Aiden Friendship, on his home debut, and Troy Elworthy showed their skills by claiming unanimous victories against Owen Underhill and Kalyn Cauckett.

Dylan Willis and Ed Cross displayed real promise as they opened the event with skills bouts.

Willis took on Zack Oloughlin while Cross was up against Dylan Wallis, both of Tiverton ABC.

ON TARGET Barnstaple's Jed Davies lands a blow on James Stockwell.

Jake Hooper put in a rousing final-round performance against Devonport's Tyler Dyer but ultimately lost a tight split decision, while Jed Davies also lost a close bout to James Stockwell, of Blandford ABC.

A tough contest between Nick Forrest and Bailey Nixon went the way of the Priorswood fighter and Tony Burdett was beaten by a technical knockout in the second round by Truro boxer Tobie Duncan. A last-minute request from Paignton resulted in Torrington Police ABC's Ned Pettifer gaining experience in a skills bout. Pettifer's workrate and range of punches ensured he controlled the fight.

"We didn't quite get the results we would have liked but it was a good show with 12 good bouts and they all held up together," said Simpson.

"We had one stoppage but most of them were very even and tight and they all competed well. It was good match making. It was a great atmosphere with a good local crowd."

There will be more to come from Barnstaple when they host a show at the Pannier Market on June 5.

KID GLOVES Ned Pettifer takes on Spencer Jarvis.

BIDEFORD AMATEUR BOXING CLUB

PRESENTS

An Evening of Amateur Boxing

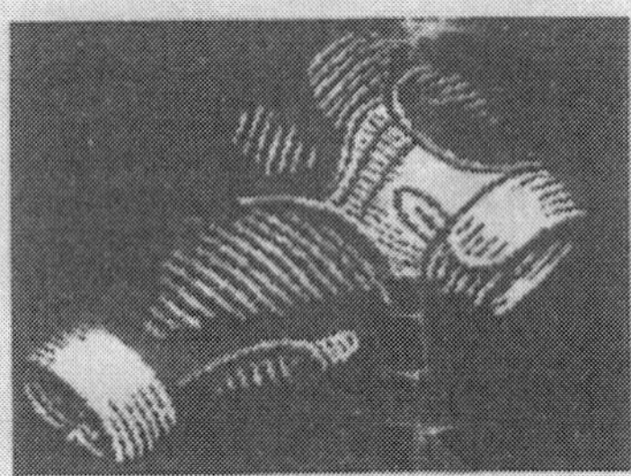

Bideford / South West
V
West Wales

SATURDAY 21 May 2016

Hartland Parish Hall

Thank you for your support

Programme
50P

DICK KERSEY
BRINGS BOXING
BACK TO HARTLAND.

1.	Sammy Heard Bideford	v	Lewis Cornish Bideford	Skills Bout 3 x 1 min
2.	Ashton Lloyd West Wales	v	Billy Heard Bideford	Skills Bout 3 x 1 min
3.	Logan Rees West Wales	v	Finley Symons Pilgrims	Junior 3 x 1.5 min
4.	Kyle Kent St Austell	v	Reece Hollingsworth Bideford	Junior 3 x 1.5 min
5.	Jo Anthony West Wales	v	Finley Dann Devonport	Junior 3 x 1.5 min
6.	Shane Miller West Wales	v	Jacob Stevenson Bideford	Junior 3 x 1.5 min
7.	Hamza Perez West Wales	v	Joshua Kent St Austell	Junior 3 x 1.5 min
8.	James Collins West Wales	v	Josh Short Bideford	Junior 3 x 2 min
9.	Scott Burgess West Wales	v	Ryan Tattersall Devonport	Junior 3 X 2 min
10.	James Parker West Wales	v	Zack Jones Tiverton	Youth Welterweight 3 x 2 min
11	Tyler Dyer West Wales	v	Callum Cunningham Bideford	Youth Bantam wt 3 x 2 min
12.	Rhys Burgess West Wales	v	Lee mcclelland Pilgrims	Senior fly wt 3 x 2 min
13.	Martin Honeywell Devonport	v	Matt Wade Bideford	Senior Heavy wt 3 x2 min
14.	Phillip Jones West Wales	v	Jordan Ruth Devonport	Senior Middle wt 3 x3 min
15.	Bobby Freer West Wales	v	Alex Downie Bideford	Senior Lt Heavy wt 3 x 2 min

Bideford Amateur Boxing Club

Extends a warm welcome to the
West Wales team of boxers travelling to North Devon
for this tournament

Hartland Topics

BOXING TOURNAMENT

An amateur boxing tournament was held in the Church Hall, Hartland, on Thursday, April 19th. It was promoted by Mr. G. Gifford, the local boxer. He himself provided the main attraction of the evening by giving a splendid exhibition of clever boxing. His opponents were Sid Jeffery, three rounds, and P. Smale, the 15-stone heavy-weight. Gifford showed plenty of ringcraft and his footwork was excellent, but he was always ready to receive some hard punches from his opponents.

The tournament opened with a contest between the popular Scoynes brothers, of Bideford, who always provide good entertainment. Raymond displayed fine talent in gaining a points verdict over his brother, who is the elder. F. Wilde and Bernard Bailey, both local boys, provided a hard-hitting affair throughout their four rounds in which Wilde was the more scientific boxer, although Bailey was the stronger man. A draw was a fitting result.

Freddie Squires, of Bideford, gave a clever and entertaining performance against Eddie Brimacombe, of Buckland. The latter put up a good show but was obviously outpointed by superior boxing which contained craft and cleverness.

Most appreciated contest of the evening was that between Micky Guyatt, of Welcombe, and B. Wrey, Bideford. Both boxers showed a great deal of pluck and had had enough at the final gong. Wrey, picking his punches better, did just about enough to gain the points verdict.

In the third round of a four-round contest between L. Ellis and M. Blackmore, the steward rightly stopped the fight to ask the boxers to give a better show. This worked and the last round was exciting with Ellis slightly on top.

Vic Folland gained a points verdict over Derek Berry. The former gave a very clever performance and was an easy winner on points. The evening ended with a very good show by Otto Senik and Denis Bragg, of Kilkhampton. The result was a draw. Senik was the harder hitter and the more scientific.

A competition took place during the interval and the winners were: A visitor, Mr. R. Hollis, Mr. A. Thorne.

Officials were as follows: M.C., Mr. H. Cole, Bideford; time-keeper, Mr. R. Hollis; Medical officer, Dr. Somerton.

Funds were in aid of a ring for the local boxing club. It is hoped to arrange further tournaments.

HARTLAND BOXING, early 1950's.

OTTO SENIK
SAMMY WREY
BOB WREY

SID JEFFERY
P 'PICKLE' SMALE
RAYMOND SCOYNES
F. WILDE
IVOR SCOYNES
BERNARD BAILEY
FREDDIE SQUIRES
EDDIE BRIMACOMBE

MICKY GUYATT
L. ELLIS
M. BLACKMORE.
VIC FOLLAND
DEREK BERRY
DENIS BRAGG

The NAMES of BOXERS who were involved in the LAST SHOW at HARTLAND in the EARLY 1950's.

TOMMY LANGFORD,
a TIRELESS SUPPORTER of NORTH DEVON BOXING.

BIDEFORD ABC trainer, RICHARD GRIGG with SAMMY WREY.
SAMMY took part in the LAST BOXING SHOW at HARTLAND.
In the background, JEFF FACEY and DB.
The VENUE was soon filled to capacity!

TOMMY LANGFORD and DB with the COMMONWEALTH CHAMPIONSHIP BELT.

I served on the COMMONWEALTH BOXING COMMITTEE when a MEMBER of the PROFESSIONAL BRITISH BOXING BOARD of CONTROL LTD., THIS is a PRESTIGIOUS BELT and has been WON by MANY GREAT BOXERS who went on to WIN WORLD TITLES. It was an EMOTIONAL MOMENT FOR ME to SEE and HANDLE the BELT.

THANKS TOMMY.

DB.

Follow us on Twitter
@ndgazettesport

Cunningham is star of show at Hartland

BOXING

Bideford ABC hosted a boxing show in Hartland for the first time since 1958 – and considering the turnout of more than 250 supporters, it was a welcome return in a great night of boxing.

Bideford hosted the West Wales squad in an exciting bill of 13 bouts, along with two skills bouts to start the show.

Bout of the night was a rematch between Bideford's Callum Cunningham and Devonport's Tyler Dyer – a toe-to-toe war that had the crowd on their feet throughout.

Cunningham went in behind his jab and both lads traded flurries in tight.

In the second, a perfectly placed left hook to the body knocked the wind out of Dyer, forcing a standing count. The shot slowed him down as Cunningham dominated the round.

Both lads showed grit in the last, digging in when tired. Both had success but it was Cunningham who had the telling blows, rocking the brave Dyer on several occasions and winning on points.

Matt Wade another of Bideford's big hitters came out fast, swarming Devonport's Martin Honeywell with combinations.

It got too much for Honeywell towards the end of the round as he required a standing count from a hard right uppercut.

Wade relaxed in the second after using a lot of energy in the first; he boxed well off the jab, bringing in right hooks to the body and head, when the opportunity came.

He couldn't resist having a tear up in the last, rallying away until the bell with both lads taking shots in a entertaining bout won by Wade on points.

Reece Hollingsworth didn't need the judges for his bout with Kyle Kent of St Austell.

Despite a tight first round, he upped the gears in the second. He cracked up the pressure on Kent, showing superior power and speed to force a standing count.

Hollingsworth showed the winning spirit as he applied the same pressure and it was a clean right hand that finished the fight, gaining Hollingsworth his first win.

Josh Short kept up his winning ways against West Wales boxer James Collins.

Collins started busy but couldn't find the target as Short proved elusive with good head movement.

Short began countering in the second, coming back with right hands and left hooks which scored all the clean shots.

He backed up Collins with a strong finish in the last round, landing a variety of head and body shots that earned him the win on points.

Jacob Stevenson produced a classy display of boxing as he won all three rounds boxing on the back foot against West Wales boxer Shane Miller.

Miller kept trying but Stevenson showed good feet and fast hands to win on points.

It was not to be the fairytale ending for the hugely popular Alex Downie as he topped the bill against Bobby Freer of West Wales.

Downie started well behind his jab but got tagged with a left hook that sent him to the deck.

He bravely came firing back on unsteady legs but was tagged again, forcing the referee to stop the fight.

Billy Heard and Ashton Lloyd of West Wales both showed potential for the future.

Their skills bout proved to be a great clash of styles as Heard had success on the front foot and Lloyd, a good southpaw boxer, moved and scored well on the back foot.

Lewis Cornish and Sammy Heard also had chance to show off their skills as both Bideford lads went in together to open the show.

Intercontinental and Commonwealth Middleweight champion Tommy Langford was guest of honour giving out the trophies at the show.

OTHER RESULTS:

- **Logan Rees (West Wales) won Technical Knockout v Finly Symons (Pilgrims).**
- **Joe Anthony (West Wales) Lost on points v Finly Dann (Devonport).**
- **Hamza Perez (West Wales) Lost on points v Joshua Kent (St Austell).**
- **Scott Burgess (West Wales) Lost on points v Ryan Tattersal (Devonport).**
- **James Parker (West Wales) Won on points v Zack Jones (Tiverton).**
- **Rhys Burgess (West Wales) Won Technical Knockout v Lee Mcclelland (Pilgrims).**
- **Phillip Jones (West Wales) Lost Technical Knockout v Jordan Ruth (Devonport).**

■ Intercontinental and Commonwealth Middleweight champion Tommy Langford presents the trophies to Bideford's Callum Cunningham (right) and Devonport's Tyler Dyer. Picture: SUBMITTED

■ Bideford big hitter Matt Wade (left) and Devonport's Martin Honeywell are pictured with Tommy Langford. Picture: SUBMITTED

NORTH DEVON JOURNAL

URSDAY May 26, 2016

IN ACTION Bideford's Josh Short, left, takes on James Collings, of West Wales.

Picture: Mike Southon. To order call 0844 4060 269 and quote Ref: BNMS20160514C-022_C

■ **WINNER** Jacob Stevenson, of Bideford, takes the victory against Shane Miller, of West Wales. Picture: Mike Southon. To order this photograph call 0844 4060 269 and quote Ref. BNMS20160521D_010_C

Elworthy in school semis

BARNSTAPLE ABC'S Troy Elworthy has made it through to the National Schools semi-finals in Milton Keynes.

Elworthy will travel to the event on Saturday and if he wins will join fellow Barnstaple member Connor Woods at the finals in Grantham on Saturday, June 4.

That will take place a day before the Barnstaple Pannier Market show.

Tickets are available from the club or by calling coach Mark Simpson on 07749 231121.

■ **FIGHTING WELL** Josh Short (in blue) lands a blow on James Collings, of West Wales. Picture: Mike Southon. To order this photograph call 0844 4060 269 and quote Ref: BNMS20160521D_017_C

Disappointment for Downie in top of bill fight

ALEX Downie was beaten by knockout in his top of the bill bout with Bobby Freer.

The showpiece fight ultimately ended in second-round disappointment for the popular Bideford ABC man, who was caught early with a strong left hook from Freer, of West Wales, and never recovered.

Downie and Freer both came out the blocks quickly but after knocking his opponent to the deck and giving him a standing count in the first, the visiting fighter took control and left his opponent struggling.

The Bideford man didn't give in, but Freer used his range to knock him to the canvas again at the start of the second before the referee called a halt to it.

"Alex got caught with a good left hook and he never recovered," said Bideford coach Richard Grigg. "He was just unlucky and it can happen to anyone.

"He had sold a lot of tickets and helped promote it. He was the main fight and it was a real shame but that is the exciting thing with boxing. You could lose every round and change it with one punch.

"Unfortunately, it went against him. He gave it everything and didn't give up but just got caught."

Heavyweight Matt Wade was in impressive form as he secured a unanimous win against Devonport's Martin Honeywell.

Wade landed some fast flurries and gave his opponent a standing count in the first, before strong right hooks to the body kept him in control throughout the second. The Bideford fighter used his jab well in the final round to keep Honeywell at bay and take the bout.

"Matt wants to impress the crowd," said Grigg. "Since losing his first fight he has come back strongly and won four of the following five.

"He was excellent and always wants to put on a show."

There was a 100% success rate for the rest of the Bideford fighters in action.

Callum Cunningham edged out Devonport's Tyler Dyer on a split decision in the bout of the night.

Cunningham started strongly and landed right hooks on his opponent but Dyer came back into it as both left everything in the ring.

Cunningham's final round performance – in which he caught Dyer with good lefts and rights – swung the bout in his favour.

Josh Short continued his strong form in the ring by outclassing James Collins, of West Wales, to claim a unanimous victory and it was the same for Jacob Stevenson against Shane Miller – also of West Wales.

Reece Hollingsworth overcame St Austell's Kyle Kent by technical knockout in the second round. Hollingsworth hit a series of flurries to give Kent a standing count before the referee stopped the contest.

Sammy Heard, Lewis Cornish and Billy Heard all showed their potential in skills bouts to open the show.

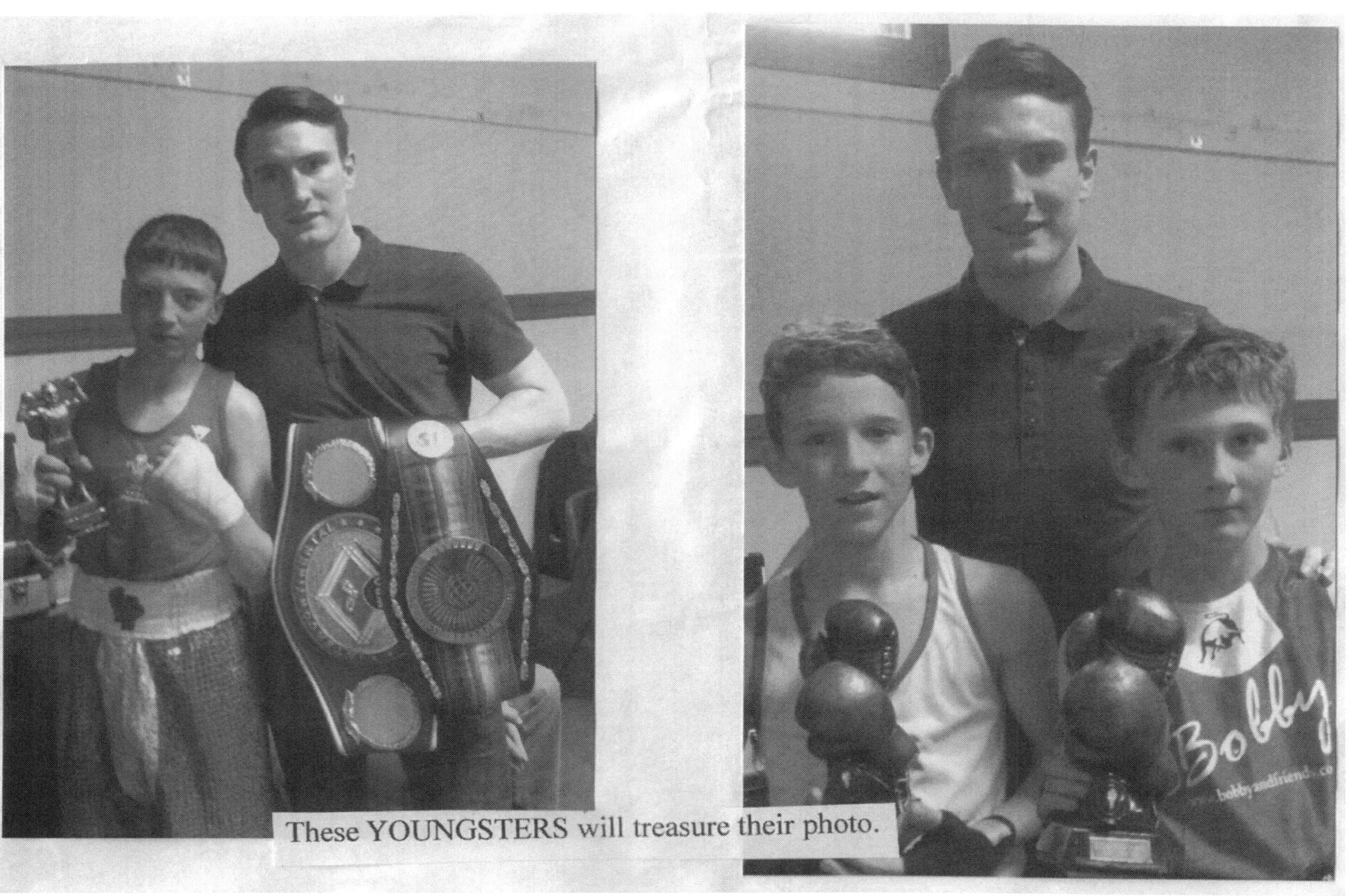

These YOUNGSTERS will treasure their photo.

BIDEFORD ABC SHOW

Boxing back after 58

By Jonny Bonell
jonny.bonell@northdevonjournal.co.uk

BIDEFORD ABC coach Richard Grigg was delighted with the first boxing show in Hartland for nearly 60 years.

Not since 1958 has an event been staged in the village, but Bideford hosted their last home show of the season at a packed parish hall on Saturday.

There were 15 bouts on the bill, with fighters travelling from West Wales, Devonport, Plymouth, St Austell and Tiverton for the show.

Top of the bill Alex Downie sold close to 100 tickets for his bout with Bobby Freer of West Wales – in which he was beaten by a knock-out.

And despite admitting having the show in Hartland was a "gamble", Grigg was pleased with how it turned out.

"It is the first time we have been here since 1958 but we had a few Hartland boys come through our club so we saw the chance and it has paid off," he said. "It was a really good turnout.

"We were going to put the show on not knowing how it was going to go but it was brilliant and we are definitely looking to do one again next year as we had such a great response.

"We didn't expect the turnout at all, we just thought we would give it a go.

"We normally do two shows a season but we said we would put on an extra one. To sell the place out is absolutely brilliant."

It was the third show Bideford have put on this season – following events at the Durrant House Hotel in November and Bideford College in March.

"All the shows have been packed out this season, the lads have performed really well and it is just a credit to the team," said Grigg.

"People only see the boxers in the ring but a lot goes on behind the scenes to help put it all together."

Also at the show was WBO Intercontinental and Commonwealth middleweight champion Tommy Langford.

Langford grew up in Hartland and was at Bideford ABC during his time in North Devon.

The 26-year-old said it was "brilliant" to bring boxing back to Hartland and that it made the sport "more accessible to smaller communities".

"I thought for the event itself to be staged here was great," said Langford. "For such a small community that Hartland is, the turnout and support has been tremendous.

"That is a credit to both Hartland and North Devon.

"Crowds like this in a rural area make for a great night. It is also brilliant that they (Bideford ABC) want to keep doing it here."

Club has the winning formula

BIDEFORD ABC has talented boxers "across the board".

That was the view of coach Richard Grigg, who was speaking after his club's final home show of the season on Saturday.

Five of the six bouts involving home boxers ended with a victory, while top of the bill Alex Downie gave his all but was beaten by a knock-out by Bobby Freer of West Wales.

The show capped off a fine season for Bideford which has seen club members turn professional and included several national titles for others.

"Right from 11-year-olds to Tommy Langford, we have good boxers across the board," said Grigg. "We will always get people leaving the club but we have a good success of turnover.

"For a small town and place like Bideford, we go and compete in championships against fighters from London and Liverpool and we are up with them which is brilliant.

"I am proud to say that.

"You don't have to have millions of pounds to make it, all you have to have is a club behind you with the drive and the boy with the drive. If you have that, it's a winning formula.

"All the lads had the heart and wanted to win for each other on Saturday. What we give the boxers as coaches and committee members all the boys appreciate and they give it back to us by giving 100% in the ring every time."

TOMMY LANGFORD

Applause for all fighters

I ATTENDED the Hartland Parish Hall boxing show at the weekend and auctioned off a signed glove for charity, which went for £550, and I threw in a couple of tickets for my next fight in July, too.

A lot of tickets were sold and it was fantastic to see the local community getting behind the event and showing their support.

The crowd were very lively and appreciative of the sport on display, and really respectful of all the fighters on the show, regardless of whether their boxer won or not, so full credit to the fans for applauding all the boxers that performed.

The fighter of the night for me was Callum Cunningham who was up against a boxer from Devonport Boxing Club in Plymouth. Callum had his opponent hurt a few times, as he can punch a bit, but the other lad fought back tooth and nail.

Callum was the deserved winner in a cracking fight. He's such a quiet kid in the gym but fights like an animal!

I hope it's promoted boxing in the community and that more fighters from the surrounding areas will be looking to take the sport up.

I managed to do my John O'Brien Challenge, which is a minute of non-stop punching, and posted the footage online. One of my nominations has already done their challenge – Jamie Speight.

I'm still waiting for British and Commonwealth super-welterweight champion Liam Williams to do his, and I also nominated the West Brom FC goalkeeper – Ben Foster.

The video has been shared more than 20 times on Facebook with hundreds of likes and dozens of comments, and Jamie's challenge has had over 2,000 views already so it's spreading around and raising awareness for The Devon Autism Centre.

For everyone asking about my next fight, it's likely to be mid-July and I'm back in Birmingham ready to hit the training camp now there's just eight weeks to go. I'll be sparring world champion Liam Smith this week to kick things off.

Follow Tommy on Twitter @Tommy_Langford1 and at tommylangford.co.uk

Champ's glove raises £550 for autism charity

TOMMY Langford helped raise £550 for the Devon Autism Centre.

The WBO Intercontinental and Commonwealth middleweight champion was a guest at the Bideford ABC show on Saturday and auctioned a signed boxing glove.

Langford, a former Bideford ABC member, also took part in a one-minute non-stop punchbag challenge to raise awareness for the condition.

"I felt if I could contribute in any way I would," said Langford. "Putting something up for auction can raise a lot more than a collection probably would have so it is great I have been able to do that for Devon Autism Centre.

"Boxing has always had quite a lot of autism awareness and you learn to understand it a bit more and appreciate the work that has to go in for people working with those who suffer form autism.

"I am so glad so much has been raised as it is a great cause to get behind."

KNOCKOUT GIFT Tommy Langford donated a signed glove which raised £550 at auction.

SATURDAY 21 May 2016

Hartland Parish Hall

BARNSTAPLE
Amateur Boxing Club
Presents
BOXING

★★★

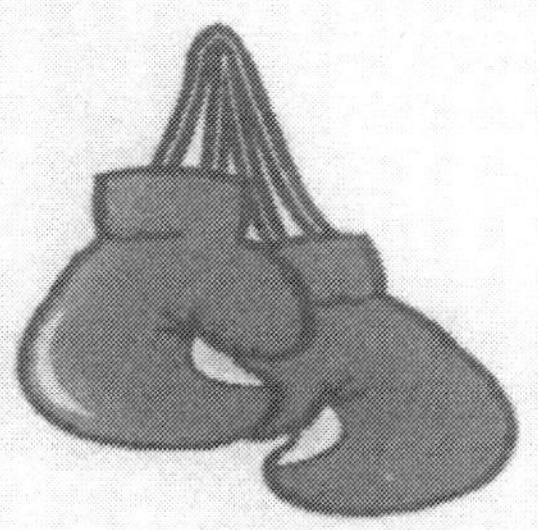

Barnstaple Amateur Boxing Club

Presents an

Open Boxing Show

At

Barnstaple Pannier Market

SUNDAY 5th JUNE 2016
DOORS OPEN 1.30pm

Red		Blue	
Skills 3 x 1			
Dylan Thomas (Barnstaple)	V	Tommy Heyburn (Sydenham)	(32kg)
Schoolboy 3 x 1½			
Jacob Stevenson (Bideford)	V	Liam McCluskey (Torbay)	(42kg)
Schoolboy 3 x 2			
Adam Davidson (Pilgrims)	V	Kieran McMann (Wessex)	(47kg)
Schoolboy 3 x 1½			
Aiden Friendship (Barnstaple)	V	Owen Underhill (Torbay)	(60kg)
Troy Elworthy (Barnstaple)	V	Joe Robinson (Intense)	(47kg)
Jed Davies (Barnstaple)	V	Jack Holmes (Wessex	(54kg)
Female Seniors 3x2			
Rebecca McDonald (Intense)	V	Kate Tinklin (Pantside)	(50kg)
Seniors 3x2			
Peter McDonald (Bideford)	V	Brian Musaruwa (Priorswood)	(59kg)
David Curry (Barnstaple)	V	Chris Banks (Tiverton)	(79kg)
Seniors 3x3			
Liam Laird (Barnstaple)	V	Jake Tinklin (Pantside)	(65.5kg)
Western Counties Challenge Belt 3x3			
Lewis Everson (Intense)	V	James Thompson (Torbay)	(77kg)
Seniors 3x3			
Harry Sugars (Barnstaple)	V	Phillip Price (Pantside)	(75kg)

Barnstaple seniors victorious at home

■ Barnstaple's Liam Laird fights Jake Tinklin of Pantside and (below) David Currey fights Tiverton's Chris Banks.
Picture: MATT SMART

BOXING

Barnstaple Amateur Boxing Club's fighters enjoyed success on home turf.

Seven Barnstaple fighters were in action at the club's show at the town's pannier market across the junior and senior classes.

Sunday's show was preceded by a 10-bell salute for Muhammad Ali, who passed away on Friday.

Harry Sugars, who won the Western Counties Middleweight title at the event last year, was given top billing, fighting Pantside's Phillip Price.

Sugars came out full of energy, putting his opponent on the back foot instantly and landing shots to the body to keep a good pace.

The two traded blows in the second, with Sugars trying to use movement around the ring to his advantage.

Sugars' fitness paid off in the final round, and he was able to land some of his best punches as a result, putting Price on the ropes before the final bell on his way to a split decision win.

Barnstaple also had success over Pantside through Liam Laird, who defeated the Welsh club's Jake Tinklin.

Laird's took some time to settle into the bout, but landed some big combinations in the latter half of the round.

He started the second where he left off, but was rebuffed by some clean punches from Tinklin.

Both boxers appeared to tire in the final round, as both fighters exchanged blows, with Laird doing enough for the victory.

Barnstaple's David Currey fought Tiverton's Chris Banks in a hugely entertaining contest.

Currey started well, landing some cracking combinations in the early stages.

As the bout developed both fighters opened up, with each of them landing heavy blows.

Banks worked Currey's head well, to the point where the Barnstaple boxer required some attention, before both started to tire.

But Currey's first round performance was ultimately what sealed a split decision win.

Pete McDonald was unable to get going against Priorswood's Brian Musaruwa, who defeated the Bideford fighter via a technical knockout.

Barnstaple's junior section had mixed results in the first half of the show's bill.

Troy Elworthy showed plenty of determination against Joe Robinson of Intense, but lost ground in the final stages of the bout to lose by way of split decision.

Jed Davies displayed some excellent counter-punching and landed some good right hands in his match with Jack Holmes of Wessex.

Holmes landed some big hits to give Davies a standing eight in the second.

A spirited effort from Davies in the third was not enough to reverse the unanimous decision.

Aiden Friendship put in a blistering performance against Owen Underhill of Torbay.

Friendship landed flurries of punches in the first, and continued in the same vein in the second to give a standing eight count to Underhill.

The Barnstaple fighter didn't ease up going into the third, continuing to land shots to give Underhill another standing eight and earn a technical knockout in an assured display.

Bideford's Jacob Stevenson was also in action, but lost by a split decision.

Stevenson was on the receiving end in the first round, and was unable to make up the ground in the later stages.

GARTH GOSS, DICK KERSEY, DB and DAVID GRIGG discuss the ACTION.

NORTH DEVON JOURNAL

THURSDAY June 9 2016

Sport

northdevonjournal.co.uk

Trading blows at the Pannier Market

Boxing >> P100

Picture: Rob Tibbles Ref: BNRT20160605C-039_C

DB with former BARNSTAPLE BOXER and TRAINER, 'GINGER' DAVIES.

SUPPORTERS ALL!

MITCH

Sügars settles his bout with a final flurry

By Jonny Bonell

jonny.bonell@northdevonjournal.co.uk

BARNSTAPLE ABC's Harry Sügars admitted his top of the bill clash with Phillip Price "could have gone either way".

Sügars took on the fighter from Welsh club Pantside in the last bout of Sunday afternoon's show at the Pannier Market.

With the first two rounds shared at one apiece, Sügars stepped up the intensity in the last and landed a big left to the body of his opponent before a flurry of strikes had Price on the ropes.

The opening round belonged to the home fighter but Price worked his way back into the contest in the second as he caught his man with straight rights.

But Sügars, fighting in the showpiece of Barnstaple's final home event of the season, kicked on in the third and final round to take the bout on a split decision.

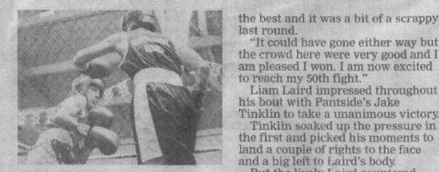

WEAVING Barnstaple's Jed Davies.
Ref: BNRT20160605C-003_C

"That was my 49th fight and it was tough," said the 19-year-old, who has been with the club since he was 11.

"I went out to the Mirror Festival (on Saturday) so my fitness wasn't the best and it was a bit of a scrappy last round.

"It could have gone either way but the crowd here were very good and I am pleased I won. I am now excited to reach my 50th fight."

Liam Laird impressed throughout his bout with Pantside's Jake Tinklin to take a unanimous victory.

Tinklin soaked up the pressure in the first and picked his moments to land a couple of rights to the face and a big left to Laird's body.

But the lively Laird countered with flurries of his own and his fitness and workrate told in the second and third as he left it all in the ring.

There was also success for David Curry, who beat Tiverton's Chris Banks on a split decision.

It was a cagey opening but Curry shook his man with a clean right hand to the face in the first and continued to dominate in the second by using his jab well. The Tiverton man came into it during the last but, despite landing some big body shots, it wasn't enough to take the fight from Curry.

Youngsters Aiden Friendship, Troy Elworthy and Jed Davies all showed their potential in the ring.

Friendship forced a standing count on opponent Owen Underhill, of Torbay ABC, on his way to a unanimous win.

Elworthy and Davies gave their all but came up short against Joe Robinson, of Intense ABC, and Wessex's Jack Holmes, respectively.

Dylan Willis was also in action and performed well in a skills bout to open the show against Tommy Heyburn, of Sydenham ABC.

There were two representatives from Bideford ABC.

Jacob Stevenson could count himself unfortunate to be on the wrong end of a split decision against Torbay's Liam McCluskey, while Peter McDonald was beaten by technical knockout against Priorswood's Brian Musaruwa.

Other results: Adam Davidson (Pilgrims) lost to Kieran McMann (Wessex) by unanimous decision, Rebecca McMullin (Intense) bt Kate Tinklin (Pantside) by split decision, Lewis Everson (Intense) bt James Thompson (Torbay) by technical knockout to win the Western Counties Challenge Belt.

DB with former BARNSTAPLE BOXER, NICK LUXTON.

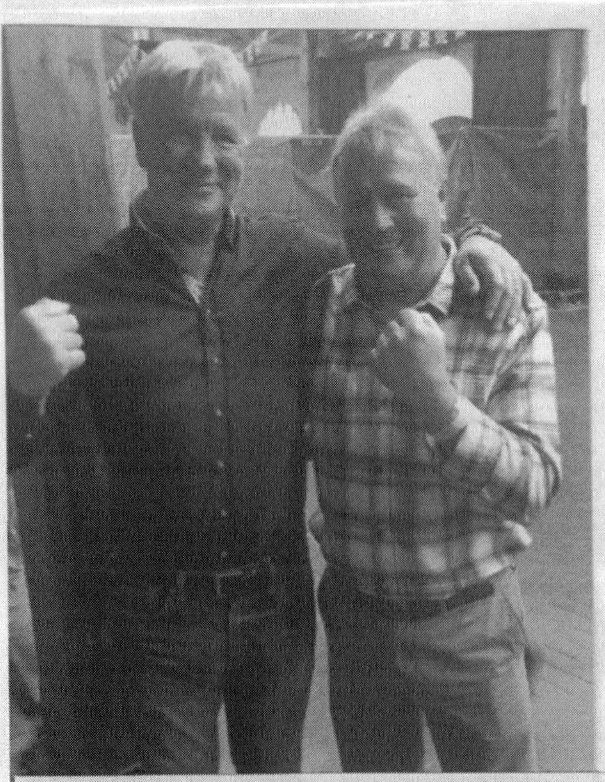

BARNSTAPLE and BIDEFORD. Former boxers 'GET TOGETHER.' PETER MALLETT and DICK KERSEY.

Home boxers make their coach proud

THE Barnstaple ABC boxers who competed at the Pannier Market all did themselves proud.

That was the view of coach Mark Simpson, who watched seven of his fighters take to the ring in their final home show of the season.

Four were victorious, two were defeated and the other – Dylan Willis – put in a great performance in his skills contest to open the event.

The three seniors in action – David Curry, Liam Laird and top of the bill Harry Sugars – all won, while juniors Aiden Friendship, Troy Elworthy and Jed Davies showed their talent.

"Overall it was a very successful boxing event," said Simpson.

"I was pleased with all our boxers who took part and they all did themselves proud.

"It was good to see a lot of the young guys from the club support the guys as they are the future.

"It was a very good selection with the match-ups and they were all very good, close fights."

Tributes to 'golden' Ali

A TRIBUTE to Muhammad Ali was held before the show at Barnstaple Pannier Market.

A 10-bell salute and moment of silence were observed as a mark of respect to the boxing legend who died on Friday, aged 74.

Barnstaple coach Mark Simpson said: "Maybe Ali didn't inspire some of the kids coming through at the club now but he changed boxing in the Seventies.

"All the kids around know of him so it was nice to have the event this weekend.

"I was a huge Henry Cooper fan (who Ali beat in a world title fight) but I grew to love Ali. He was an excellent boxer in the golden era of heavyweight boxing.

"When I was growing up he was a big influence on me and a huge influence on the sport."

BARNSTAPLE ABC

MICHAEL 'MITCH' WARBURTON and JEFF FACEY.

A LINE-UP WELL WORTHY of MENTION!
DOCTOR ROBIN BUCKLAND, DB, HELEN GRIGG, DICK KERSEY, GARTH GOSS, DEAN SAVAGE, ROY SAVAGE.

A quiet corner to CHAT ABOUT OLD TIMES.

BARNSTAPLE ABC

Former BOXER VAL BUMBUL acknowledges the camera!

DB with DAVID GRIGG,
what a GREAT SUPPORTER of LOCAL
BOXING HE IS.

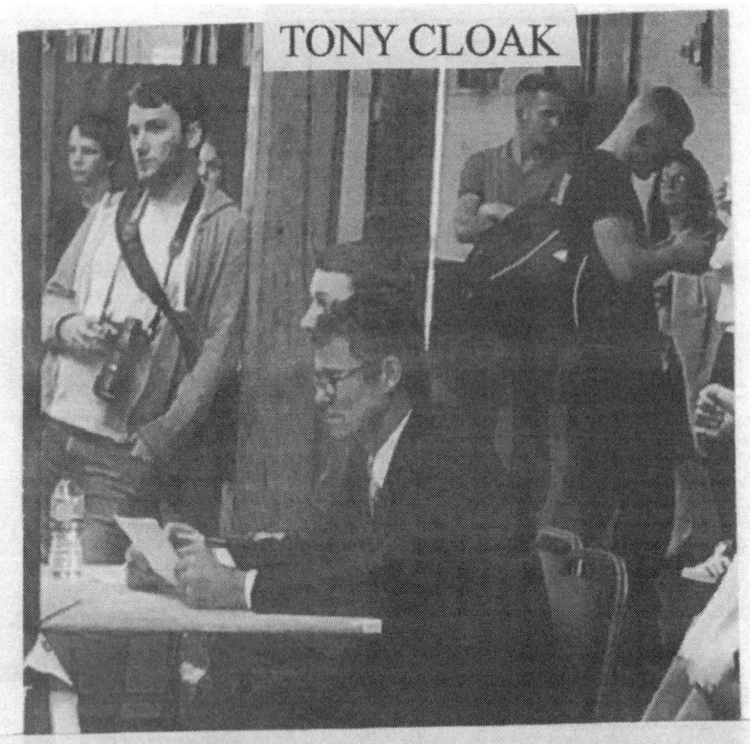

FORMER STAR AMATEUR BOXER for BIDEFORD ABC
who followed with an EVENTFUL PROFESSIONAL BOXING CAREER.
NOW returned to AMATEUR BOXING as an OFFICIAL.

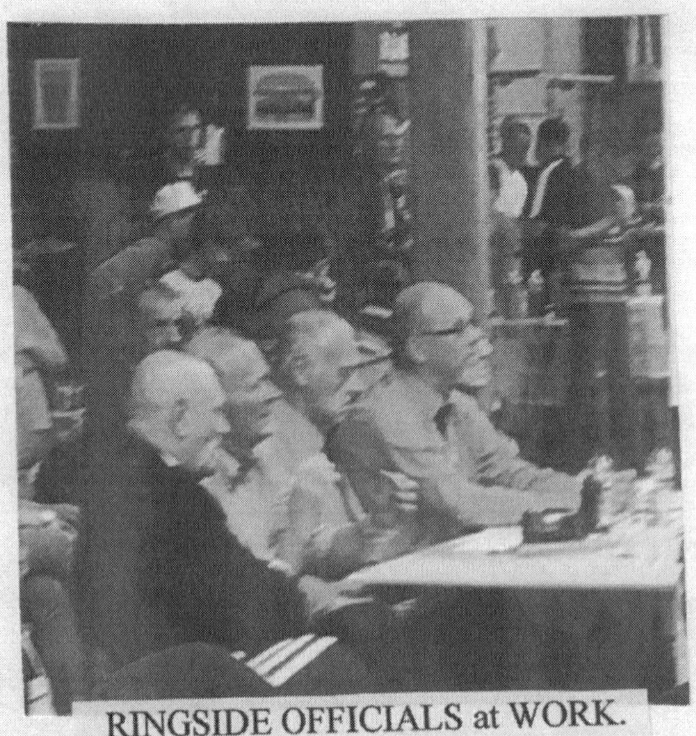

RINGSIDE OFFICIALS at WORK.

BARNSTAPLE ABC

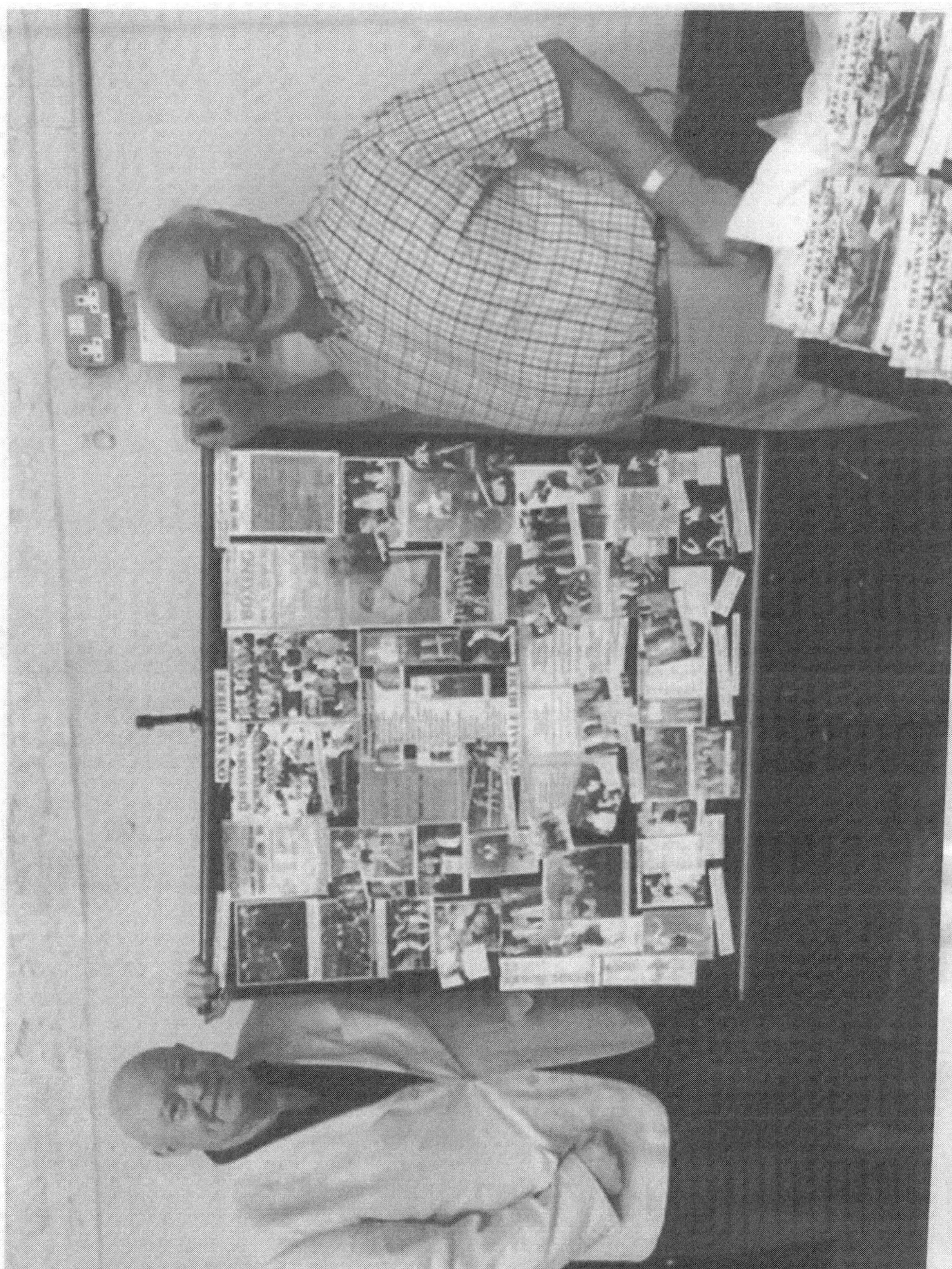

DB gets some help from in setting up the BOOK STALL from DAVID GRIGG.

@NDJournal | fb.com/NDJournal NORTH DEVON JOURNAL

Books sold for club funds

SALES of a book raised £135 for Barnstaple ABC.

Nikki Brownson was at the Pannier Market Show selling copies of The Story Of North Devon Boxing, written by husband Dick Brownson.

The book is normally priced £14.99 but were available for £5.

Volume two is due to be released in October.

Barnstaple ABC also received an anonymous donation of £200 and thanked the donor for their support.

BARNSTAPLE ABC BOSS, MARK SIMPSON, receives the proceeds of the BOOK SALES from NIKKI BROWNSON.

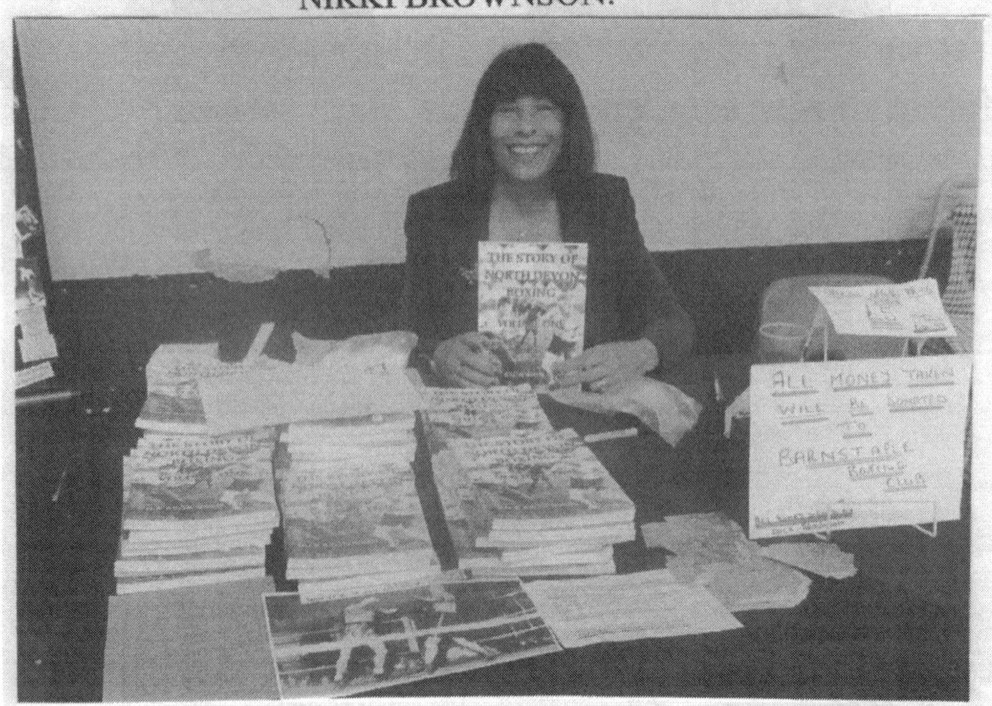

ROBERT PENFOLD'S 'RUMBLIN TUMS'
...looking after the punters!

DB, JOHN FACEY and former BARNSTAPLE BOXER, MICHAEL GRIFFITHS.
JOHN was a stalwart member of the BARNSTAPLE ABC COMMITTEE in the 1970's and 80's. A TIRELESS WORKER for the CLUB.
GREAT to see him at the SHOW !

A BUSY CORNER!

BARNSTAPLE ABC PROMOTION...
The ABA OFFICIALS and others involved in the RUNNING and ORGANISING of the AMATEUR BOXING SHOW.

BARNSTAPLE PANNIER MARKET SHOW, JUNE 5th 2016.
PHOTOGRAPH COURTESY
of the
NORTH DEVON JOURNAL
Picture: ROB TIBBLES.

The ISAAC BROTHERS, JIMMY and RONNIE were both rated in the GREAT BRITAIN AMATEUR RATINGS in 1968 but this is the first time two NORTH DEVON BROTHERS have been rated simultaneously in the BRITISH PROFESSIONAL list and the ENGLISH AMATEUR LIST.
WHAT A BOXING SHOW it would be WITH THESE FOUR on THE BILL!
STANDING ROOM ONLY?

North Devon Gazette | Wednesday, February 3, 2016

■ Write to: The Editor, North Devon Gazette, Unit 3, Old Station Road, Barnstaple, EX32 8PB
Fax: 01271 341665. Email: andrew.keeble@archant.co.uk

Bideford punching above its weight

DICK BROWNSON
Bideford

In the January 2016 issue of the national boxing paper, *Boxing News*, Bideford Boxing Club's former amateur star, Tommy Langford, is number seven in their professional ratings for the British Middleweight Division. Younger brother Jack, still active at Bideford Boxing Club, is number six in their amateur ratings for the English Middleweight Division.

After extensive research, I have been unable to find evidence that this national ranking involving two brothers has ever happened in North Devon before.

Langford is boxer of the night in Wales

JACK Langford made an explosive return to the ring as he secured a unanimous victory against Baglan Bulldogs boxer Thomas Gillheaney.

The Bideford ABC fighter, younger brother of WBO Inter-Continental middleweight champion Tommy Langford, has had a frustrating season with injuries but showed no ring rust as he found his range in the first against the former Welsh junior champion.

In the second round, Gillheaney tried sticking the pressure on, but Langford showed great feet and head movement to control the ring and score at will.

He continued to dominate through the third and did not get drawn into a scrap with his opponent. Langford used his experience to sit back and patiently pick shots which continually found the target to take the win.

His performance was recognised by former Commonwealth light heavyweight champion Enzo Maccarinelli, who gave Langford the award of boxer of the night.

Matt Wade showed he learnt from his split decision loss in Wales two weeks ago as he beat Adam Carter, of Warehouse ABC.

Wade came flying out of the blocks at Carter and landed a good right uppercut and then a right-left combination to send him to the deck.

Carter recovered the count and came back in a tighter second where Wade settled down and used his feet and counter-punching to show his ability.

But the Bideford man was all-out attack again in the last as his superior speed and strength clinched a unanimous victory.

Tickets are available for the Bideford ABC Show on Saturday, March 12, at Bideford College, priced £8, from Dick Kersey on 07841 846552.

Wednesday, February 17, 2016 | North Devon Gazette

Barnstaple's Squires retains English title

■ Rob Squires celebrates a win at the English Youth Championships, and (inset) Squires with his heavyweight championship belt. Pictures: BARNSTAPLE AMATEUR BOXING CLUB

BOXING

Rob Squires rounded off a superb weekend for Barnstaple Amateur Boxing Club by retaining his ABA Youth Heavyweight title.

The young heavyweight was in action at the Magna Science Adventure Centre in Rotherham for the final rounds of the championship, hoping to retain the crown that he won last year.

Saturday evening saw Squires up against New Biggin's Leon Bagley in the semi-final of the championship.

In a dominant performance against an experienced opponent, the Barnstaple boy was able to use his initiative on the way to a unanimous points decision.

The reward for Squires was a match up in the final against Cleary's Amateur Boxing Club's Lewis Williams.

The two young fighters had met before Sunday evening, with Williams getting the better of Squires on that occasion.

Squires was quick to settle in the final, landing some quality shots in the first round before defending some good counterpunching by the Leamington fighter in the second.

Squires took the fight to his opponent in the final round, only to be on the receving end on some good counterpunching. He did not tire, though, and his work rate took the round in his favour.

At the final bell the young fighter was awarded the championship by way of a split decision.

Squires, 17, said: "I got better as the fight went on and was able to start putting on more pressure and landing more combinations.

"It's the best feeling. It's a national title and to win it feels so good."

The Barnstaple fighter is now keen to repeat his achievements at senior level.

He added: "I've won this title twice now as a junior, so next year I'll become a senior and I'll be aiming to do it all again at that level."

Squires wasn't the only Barnstaple fighter to make it to a championship final at the Magna Centre.

Flynn Elworthy was up against Ardwick Lads Boxing Club's Luke Pollit in the Super Heavyweight final.

Elworthy was defeated by Ardwick's Luke Pollit by way of technical knockout.

A GREAT ACHIEVEMENT!
ALL CREDIT to BARNSTAPLE ABC.

Wednesday, March 23, 2016 | North Devon Gazette

English champion is ready for next step

BOXING

English Heavyweight champion Rob Squires is about to begin the next stage of his boxing career.

The 17-year-old Barnstaple boxer, who retained his title in February, is heading to Sheffield for an England selection camp.

If successful, the Barnstaple Amateur Boxing Club fighter will represent the country at the European Championships in Latvia in May.

Squires said: "I'm feeling confident about selection, especially after retaining my national title."

Mark Simpson, coach at Barnstaple ABC said: "I have nothing but respect and pleasure for what Rob's achieving."

■ English Heavyweight Chamption Rob Squires with Barnstaple ABC coaches and David Hunt, of sponsor McDonald's. Picture: SUBMITTED

BOXING

THURSDAY February 25, 2016
northdevonjournal.co.uk

Stevenson rockets past tough test

JACOB Stevenson came through his biggest test to date to maintain his 100% record this season.

Stevenson (pictured) took on unbeaten Josh Brady at his home show in Sturminster Newton and dominated from the first bell to secure a unanimous win.

The Bideford ABC fighter quickly got to grips with Brady's southpaw stance and got his feet in the position to drive down the middle of his guard and leave him with a bloody nose by the end of the first.

That set the trend for the fight as Stevenson's footwork meant Brady failed to land a clean shot.

In the last, the home boxer got frustrated as he fell into Stevenson's shots and was knocked to the deck. Brady survived the count and was saved by the final bell but Stevenson made it four wins in four fights.

He will be next in action at Bideford College on March 12 when Ben Owen will box in Bideford for the last time before turning professional at the end of the season.

Tickets for the show, priced £8 and £5 for U16, are available from Dick Kersey on 07841 846552.

Stoppage for Torrie boxer

NORTH Devon boxers showed their skills at the Camborne ABC Show.

Trai Sheppard and Nathan Board were in action for Torrington ABC – who took Matt Gray, Jack Pledger and Ned Pettifer as spares – while Troy Elworthy, Jake Hooper and Aiden Friendship represented Barnstaple ABC.

Board stopped Falmouth's Lewis Rollason early in the third round after a series of lead hooks and straight rear hands had given his opponent standing counts in the previous rounds.

Home fighter Tyler Andrew narrowly came out on top against Sheppard in arguably the bout of the show. Sheppard did not stop but just came up short.

Elworthy won by a technical knockout over Lewis Penfold in the second round.

Hooper won on a split decision against Mat Curnow but Friendship, making his debut, lost a split decision to St Austell fighter Joe Payne.

All the Barnstaple boxers will be on the bill at the town's rugby club on April 23 (doors open: 7pm, starts 7.30pm). Call Mark Simpson on 07749 231121 for tickets.

Convincing first win for Bideford's Wade

BOXING

Bideford heavyweight Matt Wade has been able to celebrate his first win – and away from home too.

He was competing in his second ever fight against home lad James Anderson at the Intense ABC show in Plymouth.

Wade produced a great jab to stamp his authority from the off and push Anderson around the ring.

In the second he sent in combinations in threes and fours, proving too speedy for his opponent.

He kept the pace up right until the final bell, with some hefty hooks to the body in the last round to seal a unanimous victory.

Bideford ABC's Grace Short stepped into the ring for her first competitive bout and showed great potential against the more experienced Katie Lane of Bulmershe ABC.

Short's southpaw posed problems for Lane as she continually landed the back hand down the middle of her guard to nick a busy first round.

Both girls had a tear up in the last, with neither willing to take a step back and leaving the crowd on their feet at the end.

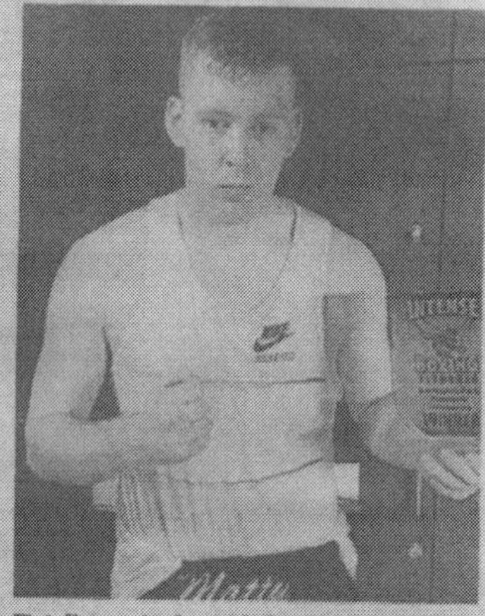

■ A first win for Bideford's Matt Wade. Picture: SUBMITTED

Frank Blackmore lost a split decision against Jack Evans of Intense ABC, a reversal of their previous meeting.

Bideford's Pete Macdonald started fast in his bout against Sam Little, giving him a standing count in the first 20 seconds.

Little came out composed in the second and Macdonald appeared to tire. Macdonald showed grit in the last and found the energy for a last push.

The judges chose Little's speed over Macdonald's power to award a split decision.

He can even the score with a rematch at Bideford's home show on March 12, where Grace Short is also making club history as her dad Andy and brother Josh will be boxing on the same bill. The main event will see Bideford's Billy Stanbury take on Ilfracombe's Tommy Heard.

Thrilling Cornwall clash for Sugars

Barnstaple's Western Middleweight champ Harry Sugars briefly defected to Cornwall on Saturday.

He stepped in to help out the Cornish squad in a match against the Midlands in Newquay.

He was matched against tough West Midlands champ Jordan Thompson of the Birmingham Jewellery Quarter Club.

Neither was willing to give an inch, with Thompson trying to dominate using a long southpaw reach, while Sugars was more than happy to stand and trade.

Spectators felt the last round was probably Sugars' best and at the bell the referee congratulated both boxers on a contender for fight of the night.

Thompson won a unanimous decision but the cheers were loud for both as they left the ring.

Harry Sugars gets to do it all again on Friday in Plymouth as he takes on Troy Elworthy at Plymouth Brickfields on the Devonport show.

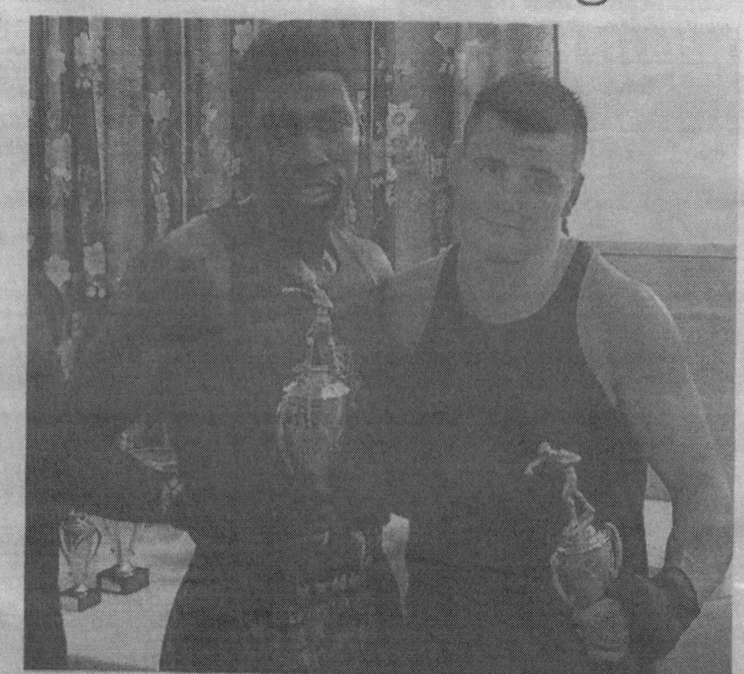

■ Jordan Thompson and Harry Sugars after their fight. Picture: SUBMITTED

Got a story? Contact our sportsdesk
Call 01271 341627 or email matthew.smart@archant.co.uk

Stone and Silva bring home Bideford wins

BOXING

Bideford's Grant Stone topped the bill at Devonport ABC show, featuring in the fight of the night with Dominic Barker of Camborne ABC.

Stone won a unanimous points victory, starting at a blistering pace, his right hand continually hitting the target in a dominant first round.

The pace dropped in the second round but Stone proved elusive. In the final round, Barker came out swinging, chucking everything he had at Stone and landing a few hefty shots.

But the Bideford lad showed heart, weathering the storm. He came back with his own big shots until Barker had nothing left at the final bell, bringing home a victory for the club.

Also at the Devonport show, Bideford's Lewis McKenzie suffered an early defeat against Camborne's Joe Dutton.

■ **Grant Stone and (inset) Gabriel Silva.**
Picture: **SUBMITTED**

Both lads landed big shots but Dutton managed a four-punch combination which caused the first standing count.

McKenzie charged back at Dutton to even things up, but got caught on the way with a clean right hand.

The referee gave a second final count and stopped the contest in Dutton's favour.

Bideford's Gabriel Silva brought home a victory when he travelled to Whitechurch ABC to fight the home favourite Dexy Jones.

It was a stiff test for the 18-year-old heavyweight as he gave away weight, age and experience.

Silva's quick footwork allowed him to land straight shots time and time again on Jones.

Jones had a last big rush in the last round but kept falling short, with a well-timed uppercut from Silva taking the final fight out of him.

Jones ended the fight with his back to the ropes as Silva was firing off with flurries, and the Bideford lad won on points.

BOXING

Elworthy was 'clear winner'

Barnstaple junior Troy Elworthy was in action at Devonport against the home club's Kaleb Caulkett.

From the first to last bell, Elworthy put in some classy boxing, facing the rushing attack in a calm manner.

He calmly turned his man, counter punching and turning defence into a high-scoring domination of the bout.

Going on the front foot in the latter half and accurate punching secured his win for the night.

He put in a great night's work and was the clear winner at the final bell.

The Barnstaple club enjoyed a day trip to learn some sparring skills at the City of Gloucester boxing club.

Laird takes first step toward national glory

BOXING

Barnstaple Amateur Boxing Club's Liam Laird started his pursuit of an English Elite title over the weekend by competing in the Three Counties English Championships in Torquay.

The light-welterweight was one of four competing for the title, and after some initial drama with Laird having to make weight, he boxed Plymouth Mayflower's Ryan Hart.

It was apparent that the two boxers were evenly matched, with both living up to the elite billing.

Laird found success with his southpaw counter-punching and some deft footwork.

The fight went down to the wire, but the Barnstaple fighter took the contest via split decision to progress to the final the following day.

Laird's second fight took place under strange circumstances on Sunday.

The fight took place behind closed doors after a withdrawal, which meant only club coaches, officials and a doctor could watch the contest.

Platt came out in combative fashion, immediately attempting to assert himself over the Barnstaple fighter.

But Laird used his counter-punching well and moved well to keep his opponent at bay, and after three rounds of classy boxing, it was the Barnstaple boy who was awarded the unanimous win to become three counties champion.

■ Jed Davies (left) and Liam Laird fought for Barnstaple ABC on Saturday.
Picture: BARNSTAPLE ABC

Laird's journey to a national title continues next weekend, as he goes to Weymouth Pavilion for the Western Elite Championship.

Jed Davies was another Barnstaple fighter in action in Torquay over the weekend, fighting Reed Carliss in a junior bout.

Davies started the contest imperiously, forcing the referee to give his opponent a standing eight count at the end of the round.

The Barnstaple boy got straight back into his rhythm in the second round, forcing another standing eight count before the referee stopped the contest to give Davies a Technical Knockout win.

Barnstaple fighters Jake Hooper, Troy Elworthy and Aiden Friendship were also in action in Camborne, with Hooper and Elworthy getting wins.

All the boxers will be making an appearance at Barnstaple ABC's home show.

The show takes place at Barnstaple Rugby Club on Saturday, April 23.

N.D.G. 17-2 2016

BOXING

Mixed results for Bideford Boxing Club

Bideford Amateur Boxing Club gained valuable experience with their visit to the Warehouse Club in Swansea.

After all coming off wins in their previous fights, Matt Wade, Gabriel Silva and Freddie Wright tested themselves at a higher level.

Matt Wade came close to upsetting the odds against Swansea's Josh Kaighan.

Wade took the first round with a barrage of punches and displayed his power before the bell.

The Bideford boy continued to be the more aggressive fighter into the second round with good combinations between the head and body.

But a perfectly timed uppercut from Kaighan forced a standing eight count which proved to be the turning point in the match.

Wade eventually lost out by way of split decision, but this was his best performance to date.

Gabriel Silva boxed Swansea's Chris Jones.

There was very much a clash of styles as Silva's tall frame came up against the stocky Welshman.

Silva started strongly and held the centre of the ring, keeping his opponent away with jabs.

But Jones began to find opportunities and was able to get in some good body shots on Silva before the Bideford boy finished the bout with some telling combinations.

These combinations meant Silva was again able to impose his style on the Welsh fighter, and he was able to win the fight on points.

Freddie Wright continued his ring education with an exhibition against Baglan Bulldogs' Dylan Thomas. The Bideford boy was very busy and used his jab well before putting good combinations together as the fight went on.

The lads all received advice from Swansea's favourite Ex World champion Enzo Maccarinelli, who was impressed with all performances.

Wade, Silva and Wright will be in action on Bideford's next show at Bideford College on March 12.

North Devon Gazette | Wednesday, May 4, 2016

Follow us on Twitter
@ndgazettesport

BOXING

Impressive win for Stevenson

■ Jacob Stevenson.

Picture SUBMITTED

Bideford Amateur Boxing Club youngster Jacob Stevenson travelled to Sturminster Newton to box Josh Brady on Saturday.

Stevenson had beaten Brady in the past, but this time the young fighter repeated history in impressive style.

The Bideford boy rushed out of the corner in the first with a flurry of punches to put his opponent on the back foot.

Brady tried to get a foothold in the bout by going out aggressively in the second round, but Stevenson was able to counter and land a straight right to make the referee give Brady a standing eight count.

Stevenson didn't ease up in the third, keeping up an impressive work-rate to eventually take a unanimous points victory.

Stevenson will be hoping to be in action at Bideford ABC's next show at Hartland Village Hall on May 21, where fighters from Bideford, Barnstaple, Torrington and Ilfracombe will take on a West of Wales squad.

■ For tickets, call Richard Grigg on 07949 770616

■ Troy Elworthy

BIDDY BOYS Freddie Wright and Reece Hollingsworth.

Freddie wins

TWO of Bideford ABC's youngest prospects took to the ring at the Torquay Warriors Show.

Freddie Wright dominated from the first bell against Dan Eddy, of the home club, to take the win on points.

Reece Hollingsworth had a skills bout with Torquay's Lorenzo Topaz and showed fast hands, good footwork and a better workrate.

Troy's bid to join Connor at national finals

Young Barnstaple boxer Troy Elworthy has made it through to the National Schools semi-finals in Milton Keynes on Sunday.

The 14-year-old will be hoping to progress in the under 56kg weight.

If he's successful, he'll join fellow young Barnstaple Boxing Club prospect Connor Woods in the finals in Grantham on June 4 – the day before the club's annual end-of-season showcase in the pannier market.

The show on Sunday, June 5, starts at 2pm, with doors open at 1pm.

Wednesday, April 27, 2016 | North Devon Gazette

Barum boxers enter ring for their home show

BOXING

Barnstaple Amateur Boxing Club hosted a home show on Saturday, with plenty of the club's fighters in action.

Dylon Wills and Ed Cross featured in their first show, taking part in skills bouts against boxers from Tiverton – with both showing promise for the future.

At the other end of the bill, Barnstaple's David Currey matched up against Bideford's up-and-coming Gabriel Silva in a thrilling contest.

Silva started well, showing excellent movement and picking off Currey's advances with some well placed jabs.

Currey had it all to do in the last round if he was to turn things around, and found some good shots, but Silva was able to come through with a unanimous win.

Troy Elworthy picked up a unanimous win over Devonport's Kaleb Caucket, in a good warm-up for his upcoming championship fight.

There was also a win for Aiden Friendship, who boxed his way to a unanimous win against Darren Underhill from Torbay in a dominant display.

Barnstaple also had Jake Hooper, Jed Davies, Nick Forrest and Anthony Burdett in action, but the fighters were unable to win their bouts.

The club's next show is on June 5 at Barnstaple Pannier Market.

■ Dylon Willis and Ed Cross took part in their first fights at Barnstaple ABC's home show. Picture: BARNSTAPLE ABC

Wednesday, April 20, 2016 | North Devon Gazette

BOXING

Torry boxers go on the road

Torrington Police Amateur Boxing Club had four boxers in action over the weekend.

Charlie Golder, Nathan Board and Matt Gray all travelled to Weymouth for bouts on Saturday.

Golder boxed well and gained valuable experience in a skills bout.

Board won unanimously with good combinations and a steady jab, but Gray was unfortunate to lose to a split decision in a close fight.

On Sunday it was Fergus McLean who travelled to Downend Boxing Club in Bristol.

The 14-year-old started strong and didn't let up, putting his opponent on the canvas in the first round.

His barrage continued into the second before the referee intervened to give McLean a technical knock-out victory.

BOXING

Langford falls short of title

Jack Langford was in action on Saturday.

The welterweight travelled to Weymouth for his Western Counties title fight against Billy Le Poullin from Guernsey.

Langford had previously won the title two years running at middleweight, but dropped down to have a crack at the welterweight title.

The Bideford boy edged a tight first round with some good combinations, but Le Poullin countered well.

Le Poullin had a big second round as he stepped in with good combinations before landing a big right hand to shake his opponent.

Langford came on strong towards the end of the round to set up a fascinating final round.

Langford gave everything in the last, taking the fight to Le Poullin, and landing a brilliant straight right.

Although the Bideford fighter had the greater punch output, Le Poullin's counter-punching persuaded the judges to award him the title with a points decision.

Coach full of praise for home boxers

COACH Richard Grigg said none of the Bideford ABC boxers let him down at their home show.

There were seven home wins and five victories for visiting boxers, but Grigg, who has been at the club for 15 years, said everyone could hold their heads high.

"They were all very even fights," he said. "A lot of the losses could have been wins and a lot of the wins could have been losses.

"I was very impressed with it, there was a good crowd here and I thought all the boxers excelled themselves.

"There wasn't one person who let me down – overall I thought they all did really well."

The show was held on the same night as former Bideford ABC boxer Tommy Langford became the WBO Intercontinental and Commonwealth champion.

"It shows what can be done," said Grigg. "When we have someone like that right at the top of the game all the lads want to get there.

BOBBING AND WEAVING Pete Macdonald (right). Ref: BNPD20160312A-006_C

"We have a lot of seniors, which is good, because when you have a group like this who all get along they train and push each other through.

"We have a good team who work very hard. A lot goes on behind the scenes but when the night comes off it is all worthwhile."

Owen ready to turn pro

BIDEFORD ABC's Ben Owen signed off as an amateur with a narrow defeat.

Owen took to the ring at Bideford College for the last time before turning professional in a rematch with Tiverton's Bradley Riggs.

The 23-year-old came out on top with a split decision last season, but was beaten by the same result this time as his 92nd fight for the club ended in defeat.

Despite admitting he was "nowhere near his best", Owen said he could not wait to make the step up.

"I had my first bout when I was 11 and have been training at the club since I was eight – which I will continue to do," he said.

"I know I can sell tickets and make money. I want to provide for my family and be someone who makes something of themselves.

"My dad boxed for 26 years so it was always something I have wanted to do. As soon as I came here I loved it."

Owen signs

BEN Owen has signed a professional contract with manager Glyn Mitchell, from Plymouth.

Owen, who fought his final bout for Bideford ABC at his home show last month, hopes to make his debut in the summer.

He will box in shows at Plymouth and Weston-super-Mare to build up his experience.

R&M Utilities and Civil Engineering have sponsored Owen.

Three Counties crown

LIAM Laird became Three Counties champion in the England Boxing Elite Championships.

The light welterweight fought Plymouth's Ryan Hart in Torquay on Saturday, with the winner returning on Sunday to box Jordan Platt, from Launceston, in the final.

Laird's southpaw counters against Hart caught the eye of the judges and he won on a split decision.

The following day, Platt attacked Laird with huge shots in the early stages. But, using all his ringcraft, the Barnstaple man kept the upper hand for most of the contest to reach the Western Counties finals at Weymouth on Saturday.

Also in Torquay, Barnstaple's Jed Davies was dominant from the off against Reed Carliss and caused the referee to stop the contest in his favour.

Top trio claim wins for Barnstaple

THREE of Barnstaple ABC's finest took to the ring in Exmouth and claimed impressive wins.

Ben Stone was named boxer of the night after beating Royal Marine novice champion James Caldecourt in a three-round middleweight thriller.

Caldecourt came out all guns blazing but Stone met fire with fire and showed neat defensive footwork to soak up the attacks.

Junior Jacob Hooper took control against Camborne boxer Mark Curnow with a stiff right jab to set up a dominant display.

After a lengthy layoff, Liam Laird took on Shannon Willy, of Exmouth ABC, and got back to form with non-stop effort which kept his opponent on the back foot.

Ilfracombe ABC boxer Dan Bushell had his first bout on Saturday at Lympstone but came up short in a tight contest against the home club's Dan Birks.

● Bideford ABC hosted a sparring session with Baglan Bulldogs to prepare two of the visitors' boxers for the Welsh Elite Championships.

Morgan and Connor Macintosh are competing in the light welterweight and welterweight divisions and spent the weekend in North Devon to get some quality sparring against Jack Langford and Billy Stanbury. The latter will top the bill at his home show on Saturday at Bideford College.

Thursday February 4, 2016 The Journal

Wade bowls over Anderson to claim first victory

BIDEFORD ABC heavyweight Matt Wade earned his first win at Intense ABC's show in Plymouth.

He beat James Anderson, from the home club, with a unanimous victory thanks to a range of great jabs, quick flurries and heavy body hooks.

Luck was against Frank Blackmore as he lost out on a split decision to Intense's Jack Evans.

The pair met in November and it was Blackmore who came out winner on a split decision, but this time his opponent got the better of him.

Evans won the first round with good boxing and movement, but Blackmore's power came through in the second and third as his right hand began to drive home.

Pete Macdonald started fast against Sam Little, giving the Barton Hill fighter a standing count in the first 20 seconds from a looping right hand.

After being dominated in the first, Little came out more composed in the second and landed with some straight punches.

Both fighters, who will rematch at Bideford's home show on March 12, showed a lot of grit in the last but the judges favoured Little's speed to award him the split decision.

It was a first competitive bout for Grace Short, who showed great potential against Katie Lane.

Short's southpaw stance caused problems for Lane in the first, but the Bulmershe ABC boxer's experience shone through in the second and third to claim the victory.

Short will also feature at the Bideford ABC show where history will be made as her brother, Josh and dad Andy all box competitively on the same bill.

■ OFF THE MARK: Matt Wade.

BOXING

Young fighters enter the ring

Bideford Amateur Boxing Club had two of their youngest prospects in action at Torquay Warriors over the weekend.

Freddie Wright took on Dan Eddy from the home club and put in a dominant performance to take a points win.

Wright wasn't fazed by his southpaw opponent, landing shots early.

Combinations were flying in from the Bideford boy with little coming back his way and a strong right cross sent Eddy to the floor before the bell.

The home boy dug deep in the last, but Wright showed superior skill, power and fitness to win all three rounds.

Reece Hollingsworth had a skills bout against Lorenzo Topaz from Warriors.

The Bideford boy let the combinations go early, showing fast hands.

He used great footwork to make Topaz miss constantly and made him pay whilst hitting the target with clean punches.

In the last round, Hollingsworth went through the gears showing good work rate and skill.

Torrington go to Camborne

Torrington Amateur Boxing Club took Trai Sheppard and Nathan Board to the Camborne ABC open show on Saturday.

Board stopped Falmouth's Lewis Rollason early in the third round after already giving standing counts to his opponent.

The referee intervened after Board worked well behind his jab and used a thunderous straight rear hand and lead hooks.

Sheppard lost narrowly on a split decision to local boy Tyler Andrew, in what was arguably the best bout of the show.

Sheppard used good set piece combinations and never stopped from the first bell.

Owen makes jump to pro

Bideford fighter Ben Owen has put pen to paper on a professional boxing contract with manager Glyn Mitchell.

Owen will continue to box at Bideford Amateur Boxing Club, where he received his amateur grounding.

He has gratefully received sponsorship from local businesses R&M Utility and Civil Engineering, to help kick start his career.

Hoping to make his professional debut in the summer, Owen will box for Bideford for their outings to Plymouth and Weston-super-Mare.

BOXING

Langford misses out

JACK Langford narrowly lost his Western Counties title fight in Weymouth.

Langford, the younger brother of double WBO middleweight champion Tommy, had won the title two years running at middleweight but dropped down to go for the welterweight title.

The Bideford fighter nicked a tight first round against Billy Le Poullin with some strong combinations, but the Guernsey man had a big second round and rocked Langford with a strong right.

Langford gave everything he had in the last and caught Le Poullin with a straight shot which had his opponent dazed, but some flashy counters persuaded the judges to award Le Poullin the title.

There was also a defeat for Barnstaple ABC's Liam Laird in the light-welterweight final in Weymouth.

Barnstaple boxers will be looking to put on performances at their home show at Barnstaple Rugby Club on Saturday.

Doors open at 7pm and fights start at 7.30pm. Call Mark Simpson on 07749 231121 for tickets.

FINAL FIGHTERS Jack Langford (left) and Liam Laird at the Western Counties finals.

BAD LUCK and CLOSE DECISIONS. DB.

Sügars gives his all in a narrow loss

BARNSTAPLE ABC's Harry Sügars was narrowly defeated by Birmingham's Jordan Thompson in Newquay on Saturday.

Western middleweight champion Sügars stepped in to help Cornwall in their annual match against the Midlands, and fought West Midlands champion Thompson, from the Jewellery Quarter club.

Both fighters gave their all in a contest described as the bout of the night as Thompson used his long reach to take advantage.

But Sügars was happy to take the hits and landed many telling blows of his own.

Thompson was awarded the win on a unanimous decision.

Coach Mark Simpson said: "What a contest of two well-match middleweights.

"This was one of those contests where reputations are made, with both boxers leaving the ring to the cheers of a crowd who had witnessed one of the best middleweight bouts of recent years.

"It was not the result we would have wanted but Barnstaple left Cornwall with an immense sense of pride in our boxer."

Sügars will take to the ring again on Friday at Plymouth Brickfields, on the Devonport ABC Show. Troy Elworthy will also be fighting.

■ RIVALS: Harry Sügars (right) took on Jordan Thompson.

Dominant win for Stevenson

Jacob Stevenson took his biggest test to date taking on unbeaten Josh Brady at Sturminster Newton.

The young fighter was a unanimous winner, taking all three rounds and maintaining a hundred per cent record for the season.

Stevenson started in dominant fashion, getting into position and finding the gaps against Brady's southpaw stance.

By the end of the first round, the Bideford fighter had left his mark on his opponent, giving him a bleeding nose.

He continued to dominate going into the second, with Brady unable to find his range to land a clean shot.

Stevenson demonstrated great counter punching, coming back with combinations regularly.

The young fighter was able to knock down Brady in the final round, but his opponent was saved by the bell.

Stevenson will be in action at Bideford ABCs home show at Bideford College on March 12.

I see a GREAT FUTURE for this YOUNG BOXER. DB.

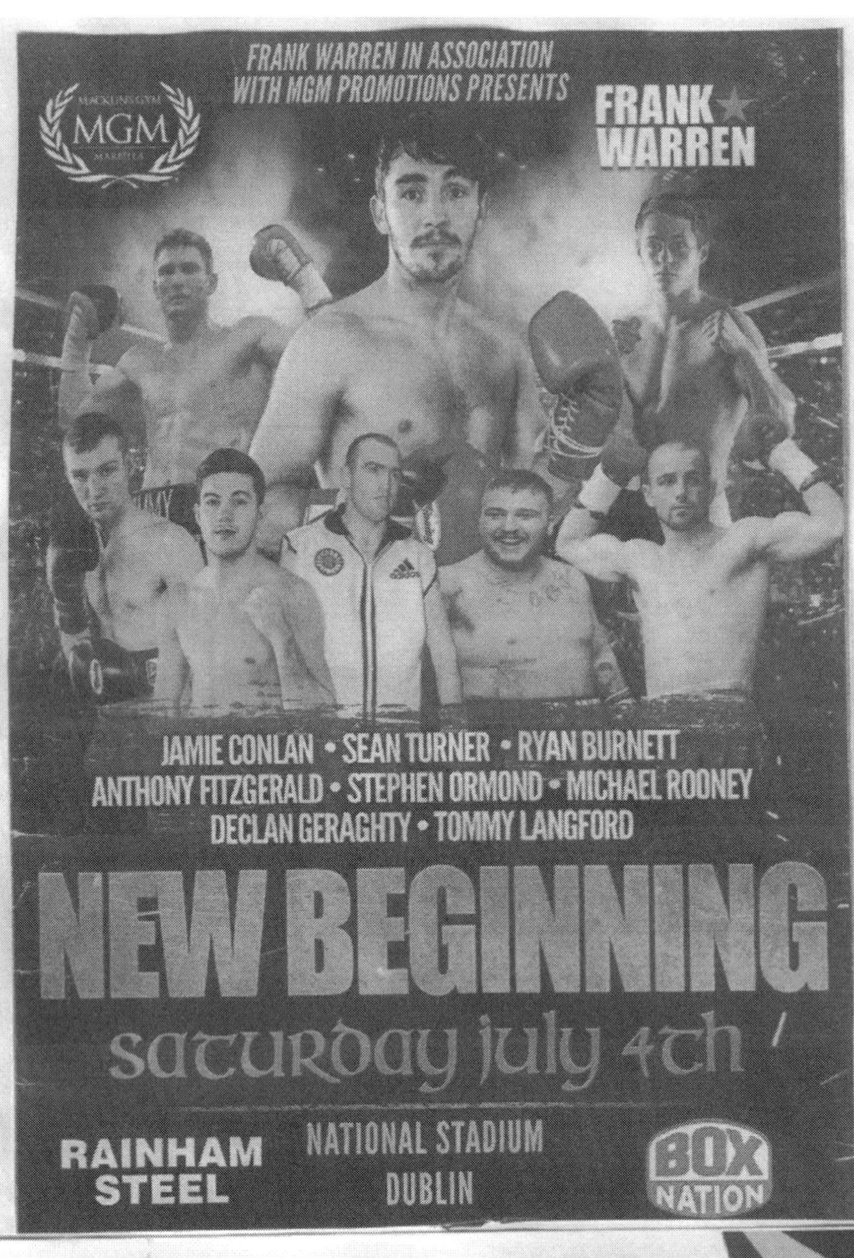

ticketmaster
ENT0407 CASH
BLK A 105.50
F 5
X 7
A-TYPE
725699492747
-50344
890
14:34
TSZ512
18-JUN-15

FRANK WARREN PRESENTS
CHAMPIONSHIP BOXING

NATIONAL STADIUM, DUBLIN
DOORS 6PM
SAT 04-JUL-2015

BLOCK A

ROW F SEAT 5
FLOOR

725699492747

BILL SUBJECT TO CHANGE

105.50 (INC BKG FEE)

TSZ512
45890
18-JUN-15

PROMOTER TICKETS

@NDJournal | fb.com/NDJournal

NORTH DEVON JOURNAL

BOXING: TOMMY LANGFORD

Proud as punch to become a dad

*Despite being **small** he's definitely got the Langford **physique** so he's going to have a good set of **shoulders** on him*

BECOMING a dad is simply the best thing that has ever happened to me.

My son was born on Saturday at 7.18am. He weighed in at a very trim 5lbs 13oz – lighter than was expected.

My wife Leanne and I decided long before the arrival on the name Freddie and I can safely say it suits him.

I know every dad would probably say this but he is an absolute beauty and I'm as proud as punch.

I'll tell you what, though, props have to go out to my wife because childbirth ain't no joke! I actually think that experience has scarred me, I was like a broken man after!

It was longer than expected, more painful than I would ever have imagined and tiring, so Leanne is an absolute hero.

I know I have a hard job and pain comes with the territory but I hope and pray I never have to go through anything like that.

A final note on Super Freddie is that luckily there is plenty of my wife in him, which is great because he will be better looking than me.

But, despite being small, he's definitely got the Langford physique so he's going to have a good set of shoulders on him as he grows up.

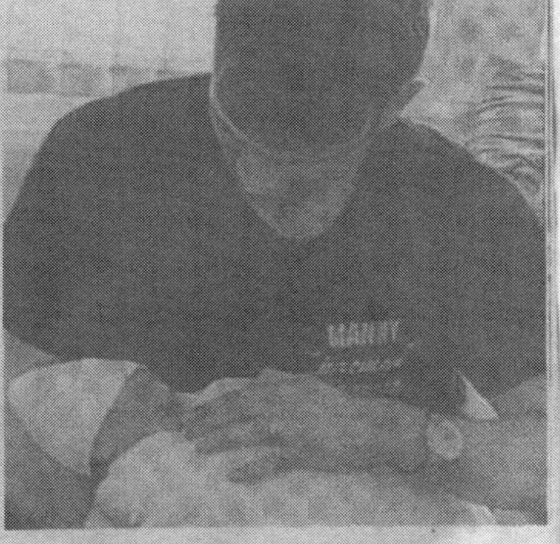

LITTLE KNOCKOUT Tommy and Leanne Langford with Freddie.

Thanks to everyone who has congratulated us, we have been completely overwhelmed by it.

On Saturday night, Chris Eubank Jr challenged Nick Blackwell for his British middleweight title. It was a very exciting fight and incredibly entertaining but, unfortunately, Blackwell sustained a bleed on the

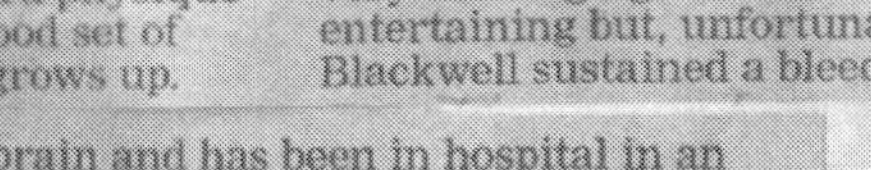

brain and has been in hospital in an induced coma since.

Nick is a friend of mine and we have shared many rounds of sparring so this is a terrible shame and my thoughts are with his family – I wish him a swift and successful recovery.

Follow Tommy at tommylangford.co.uk and on Twitter @Tommy_Langford1

TOMMY LANGFORD, a MARVELLOUS AMBASSADOR for NORTH DEVON and LOCAL BOXING CLUBS.

'I HAVE A LOT MORE SELF-BELIEF'

Hot prospect Tommy Langford emerges from under the radar and talks to **Danny Flexen**

EX-AMATEUR standout Tommy Langford has won 12 straight as a pro (three inside the distance) and is steadily moving up the domestic middleweight ranks. He talks here about sharing a gym with Frankie Gavin and his big ambitions.

Tell us about your impressive amateur career.

I had 106 amateur fights, winning 86. I won two NABC titles and reached two more national finals and represented England from the age of 15 until I turned pro. I captained England in my last year as an amateur and that was the highlight, that and winning my first national title at 15. I started at Bideford ABC in north Devon but when I turned 18 I came to Hall Green; I got myself into Birmingham University so I could train there. I had sparred [Hall Green's] Frankie Gavin at Crystal Palace when he was training for the Commonwealth Games and I was on a junior squad and he was the only one I couldn't hit. I gelled with him. I had family in the Midlands, I had met [Hall Green and Tommy's current pro trainer] Tom [Chaney] a few times before and I liked what he said and did. I finished my degree and got a 2:2 BSc in sports science. I met my wife in my first year at uni.

Why did you turn pro relatively late at 23 and why stick with your amateur coach when you did?

I wanted to finish my studies but I also really wanted to give the [2012] Olympics a crack. I had fought all the lads on the GB squad and beaten and lost to them so I knew I was there or thereabouts. When I didn't make it, I turned pro.

Tom knows me inside out and he knows the sport – he's so knowledgeable. He sees things others do and brings them back to the gym and if he thinks they can work for me, we'll try it out. He's a real winner so he knows what to do to win. We are friendly but in the gym he's the coach and I'm the boxer. We plan training camps together and I write down how I'm feeling in camp – Tom got me to do that – then we assess and make adjustments, like if the sparring tired me or my diet wasn't right. But what he says goes.

STABLEMATE: Gavin trains out of the same gym as Langford, but they spar less now

'MY POWER IS NOT MASSIVE BUT MY TIMING IS IMPROVING'

What are the reasons behind your recent apparent improvement?

I've always believed I had those performances in the tank. My pro debut was a brilliant performance but obviously it was on a small-hall show, not on TV so it doesn't get noticed. I have a lot more confidence and self-belief since signing with Frank Warren four fights ago because someone is really investing in me and I'm getting exposure on BoxNation. I've made improvements in the gym and I'm starting to get stoppages now [two in his last three bouts]. My power is not massive but my timing is improving.

You have said before how much you have learned from sparring your stablemate, Frankie.

We used to do loads but it's less now as I'm a big middle and now I'm creeping up the domestic scene I need to spar more middleweights. We still spar a bit at the start of camp to blow off the cobwebs. But if we spar too much we get ourselves into bad habits – I'm not as defensively minded because he's a welter and he's less confident in his punches because I'm so much bigger and longer, it's more of a gamble.

John Ryder and Nick Blackwell have been nominated to fight for the vacant British title. Who do you fancy in that one and how far away are you from that level?

Ryder is very good and probably technically has a bit of an edge but he's not performed well in his last couple of fights. I've done a bit of sparring with Nick quite a while ago and I think he'll be too strong and busy and will win on points. You can't hurt Nick. Ryder and Blackwell have had about 20 fights [Ryder has had 21], so they're a little ahead of me in experience, but I hope every fight I have now is over the championship distance and I can pick up a few titles. In another two-three fights I think I'll be ready for the British title.

So what's the end goal for you?

Obviously a world title, everyone is going to say that and I'm no different. But I'd like to do it the right way, picking up the British, Commonwealth and European titles as I go through, like Billy Joe Saunders has done. I want to pick them all up.

TOMMY LANGFORD

I just wanted to win, I didn't care how

I ***reverted*** *back to the* ***old*** *Tommy* ***Langford***

I TOLD you I would do it! I defeated English middleweight champion Lewis Taylor via unanimous decision to add the vacant Commonwealth middleweight title my WBO Intercontinental belt.

Taylor was a lot better than I expected and I made harder work of it than I needed to, despite the wide margins with scores of 118-110, 118-111 and 118-111.

Nevertheless, I have picked up my second professional title and I am now undefeated in 16 contests.

Taylor gives Langford his toughest test

TOMMY Langford came through the biggest test of his career to become a double middleweight champion.

The Bideford boxer, unbeaten in 16 professional fights, retained his WBO Intercontinental belt and added the vacant Commonwealth title with a unanimous points victory over Lewis Taylor at Liverpool Echo Arena.

MENTOR Tommy Langford with Bideford ABC's Dick Kersey.

How Dick set me on right road

THE commitment a boxing coach makes is like a full-time job, always matchmaking and thinking about the kids you look after.

My good pal Richard Grigg is head coach at Bideford ABC and has been fortunate to take over a great set-up passed on by Dick Kersey, who is still there in the background overseeing things.

The ethos Dick instilled over many years at the club means it will always create champions.

Dick trained me at the age of 11 and was responsible for all my amateur success, guiding me to two national titles. He gave me so much advice and instruction and helped me win my first national title at the age of 15.

It was Dick banging on the door constantly that got me into the England camp. It was only what I deserved, as I always worked hard in the gym, but he kept on at the England coaches to get me in there.

He was always so calm at fights and could see an opening and told me how to exploit it. It felt natural when I went in there to act out his instruction. He had an expert eye to spot what punch would work and change the fight.

He was so very good in fight situations because he boxed himself and was a good amateur – he was very good at winning.

I had a lot of success with Dick in my corner, fighting anybody all over the UK at the drop of a hat.

I moved away but would have loved to have had my whole boxing career based in Bideford. But he and I knew there wasn't enough competition in the area for me and he was very supportive of my move to Hall Green in Birmingham.

Still to this day, what I have learnt and what I do in the ring comes from what he taught me. I will always be appreciative of how he set me on the right road for later on life. I don't think there are many from North Devon who have gone on to be Commonwealth champion and ranked No 2 in the world.

Follow Tommy at tommylangford.co.uk and on Twitter @Tommy_Langford1

DICK KERSEY, DB, GLYN RHODES meet at the BIDEFORD ABC GYM.
SHEFFIELD BOXING CENTRE brought some strong teams to challenge
NORTH DEVON BOXERS on the
BIDEFORD PANNIER MARKET SHOWS.

GLYN has since been awarded the MBE 'For services to youth and boxing.'

GLYN RHODES, MBE.

SHEFFIELD BOXING CENTRE 2016.

In the centre of photo. can be seen the DICK BROWNSON SHIELD hotly contested for on every BIDEFORD PANNIER MARKET SHOW.
It is now on permanent display in the SHEFFIELD BOXING CENTRE.

North Devon Gazette | Wednesday, June 15, 2016

Follow us on Twitter
@ndgazettesport

BOXING

Boxers fight in Tiverton

Members of Bideford and Barnstaple's amateur boxing clubs were in action on Saturday at Tiverton Amateur Boxing Club's home show.

There were plenty of rematches on the card, with two of the bouts being rematches from last week's show in Barnstaple.

Bideford's Jacob Stevenson was looking for revenge as he took on Liam McCluskey for the second time in a week.

McLuskey edged the contest in Barnstaple, but Stevenson didn't allow such a close contest this time around.

Using his right hand well, Stevenson landed combinations early and didn't let up, maintaining a quick tempo and doing more and more as the bout went on.

Another rematch from Barnstaple's show was David Currey against Tiverton's Chris Banks.

The Barnstaple fighter edged an entertaining fight last week, but was on the wrong side of the decision this time around.

Banks edged the fight with a better work rate in the close and very competitive bout.

Bideford's Josh Short got a second win over Kai Draper of Torbay thanks to a blistering first round.

Short put in some big hooks early on but allowed Draper to come back in the second round before assuring a points victory in the last.

Lewis Cornish showed potential in his skills bout with Dillyn Wallis of Tiverton.

Cornish showed good footwork and punch variety in a well-matched contest.

16 - JUNE 2016

BOXING

Stevenson makes up for market defeat

BIDEFORD BOXERS Lewis Cornish, Jacob Stevenson and Josh Short.

JACOB Stevenson won his rematch with Liam McCluskey at the Tiverton ABC Show.

The Bideford ABC boxer was on the wrong end of a split decision at the Barnstaple Pannier Market Show.

Less than a week later, however, he left the result in no doubt by dominating every round against the same Torbay opponent.

Stevenson started aggressively, landing combinations, and kept the tempo up in the second round when he bloodied McCluskey's nose by using his right uppercut when in tight.

Carrying his momentum into the third, Stevenson put in a big effort and trapped his opponent on the ropes with fast combinations to seal the win, capping a great season in which he has won six of his eight bouts.

Josh Short also had a rematch and beat Torbay's Kai Draper for the second time.

Big hooks rocked Draper in the first round and, after taking his foot off the gas in the second, Short went through the gears in the last to record his fifth win in six outings this season.

Lewis Cornish showed potential in his skills bout with Dylan Willis, of Tiverton. Cornish showed good footwork and punch variety, ending up the stronger of the two in a well-matched contest.

A week on from his Pannier Market victory over Chris Banks, Dave Curry was edged out by the Tiverton boxer's better workrate in a competitive bout.

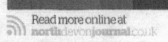

Read more online at northdevonjournal.co.uk

NDJ. 16 - JUNE . 2016

TOMMY LANGFORD

Cardiff is the ideal venue for next fight

THE show for my next fight has been officially announced – at the Cardiff Ice Arena on July 16 – and I will be defending both my Commonwealth and WBO Intercontinental middleweight titles.

I couldn't be happier with the venue as Cardiff is right in the middle between the West Midlands, where I now live, and North Devon, where I'm from.

The date will have no clash with the football season so there should be plenty of West Brom fans in attendance and hopefully all of the lads from Hartland.

Cardiff is a great location and I know a lot of my friends go there from time to time for a big night out.

For my Devon fans, it's a much easier and better journey than coming up to the Midlands, taking just half the distance and time than normal.

I really hope I get a good turnout from both sides as this next contest could determine how soon I fight for a world title. A good performance against tough opposition will set me up for a shot very soon.

Another big announcement is that pound-for-pound superstar Guillermo Rigondeaux will be on the same show. I've dedicated a whole column to the Cuban phenomenon before, all about how proud I was at the prospect of sharing the bill with such a talent.

On that occasion, he encountered issues with his passport and his bout with Jazza Dickens never materialised, but it's back on with El Chacal's WBA world super-bantamweight title on the line.

Headlining the Cardiff show are two of the UK's top prospects – Liam Williams and Gary Corcoran, both unbeaten in 15 fights – in what should be a fight of the year contender.

I spar regularly with Liam, the British and Commonwealth super-welterweight champion – he's a real talent. It's a show not to be missed.

For tickets, visit tommylangford.co.uk. Follow Tommy on Twitter @Tommy_Langford1

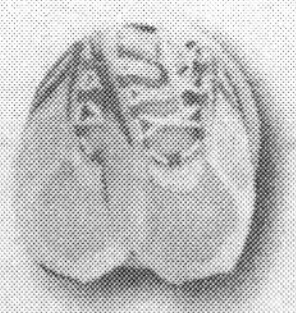

SPORTING BIDEFORD

What's happening in the world of sport

Dick Kersey and Tommy Langford.

Looking back at the boxers of Bideford

Many have passed through Bideford Amateur Boxing Club since it's doors opened. Matt Smart spoke to former promoter and author Dick Brownson about some of the club's biggest names...

Bideford Amateur Boxing Club has enjoyed plenty of success since it's foundation in 1958.

One man who has followed the club's progress steadily in that time is Dick Brownson.

A former promoter, Brownson is putting the finishing touches to the second volume of *The Story of North Devon Boxing*, a 600-page compendium of pictures, cuttings and anecdotes from 1952, right up to the present day.

"The 1950s was an interesting time," said Brownson.

"You had the pros coming back after the war coming back to fight on amateur bills, because no one knew who they were. It wasn't until the mid 1950s when amateur boxing became regulated in North Devon, and the emergence of Bideford came shortly after."

One of Bideford's first fighters to achieve success was Bob Ellis, who became National Sea Cadet Champion in 1966.

Ellis, who is now head coach at Torrington Police Amateur Boxing Club, defeated Earnley's T Arber in the third round to win the bout at Colston Hall in Bristol.

Another young upstart at that time was Dick Kersey.

Boxing for the club for the first time at the age of 11, Kersey went on to compete 200 times for the club until the age of 34. In that time, he had been recognised as the best featherweight in North Devon, winning the Reg New Memorial Cup in 1973.

Bob Ellis in action.

For Brownson, Bideford's biggest star is still in the ring in the form of Commonwealth and WBO Intercontinental Middleweight champion Tommy Langford.

He said: "Tommy now is a superstar, nationally as much as in Bideford. Over the years you can't go further than him to be the main star to emerge from Bideford ABC."

I"n general, the main problem with boxers, is they tend to drift as they get older. I've seen immense talent, and so many have fallen by the wayside. With the Langford boys, they stayed right through."

Part of Langford's success can no doubt be mapped to Kersey, who is still at Bideford Amateur Boxing Club today.

Kersey coached Langford from the age of 11, overseeing more than 100 of his amateur bouts and guiding him to his first national title at the age of 15.

Bideford ABC head coach Richard Grigg was also coached by Kersey until an injury put his career to a halt.

Grigg was then invited onto the coaching staff, where the two now work alongside each other.

Grigg said: "We work together with the coaching, match making and organishing shows. I am coaching the boxers what he has taught me in the past, and it's giving us great success.

"He still has input with all the boxers and there is a buzz in that gym having someone with as much knowledge and experience as him involved."

With plenty of boxers on the books at Bideford, and such experience in their corner, the future looks just as good as their illustrious past. Ellis, Kersey, Langford and Grigg all feature in volume two of *The Story of North Devon Boxing*, due for release in October.

APPLEDORE ABC
BOYS SPORTS CLUB.

The following items came from TOMMY WATERS and I hope at sometime in the future he will be able to give me the full history of the CLUB. They arrived too late to be included in the BOXING CLUB SECTION but are too important a contribution to

THE STORY OF NORTH DEVON BOXING

to have been left out.

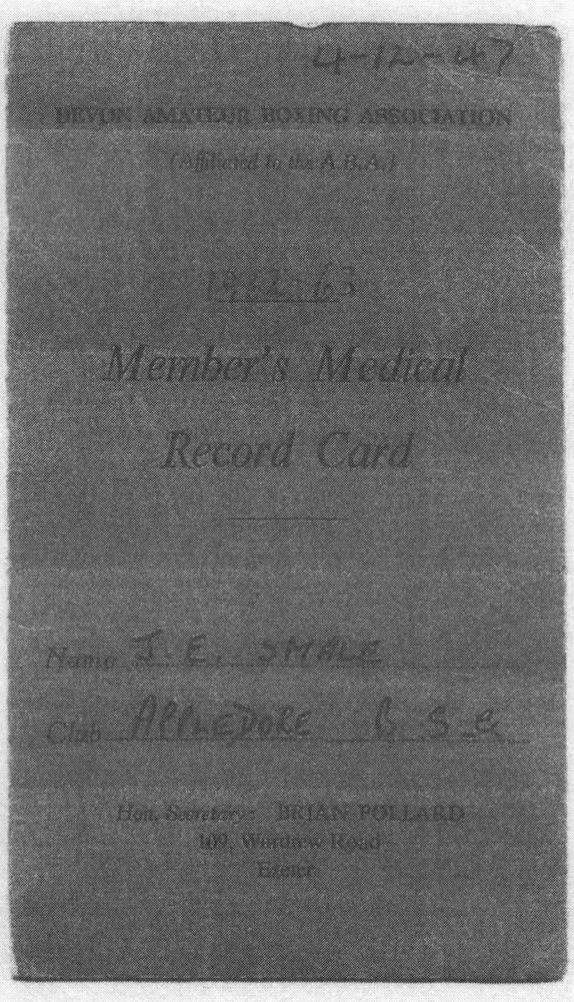

4-12-47

DEVON AMATEUR BOXING ASSOCIATION

(Affiliated to the A.B.A.)

19[illegible]-63

Member's Medical
Record Card

Name J. E. SMALE

Club APPLEDORE B S C

Hon. Secretary: BRIAN POLLARD
109, Wardrew Road
Exeter

APPLEDORE

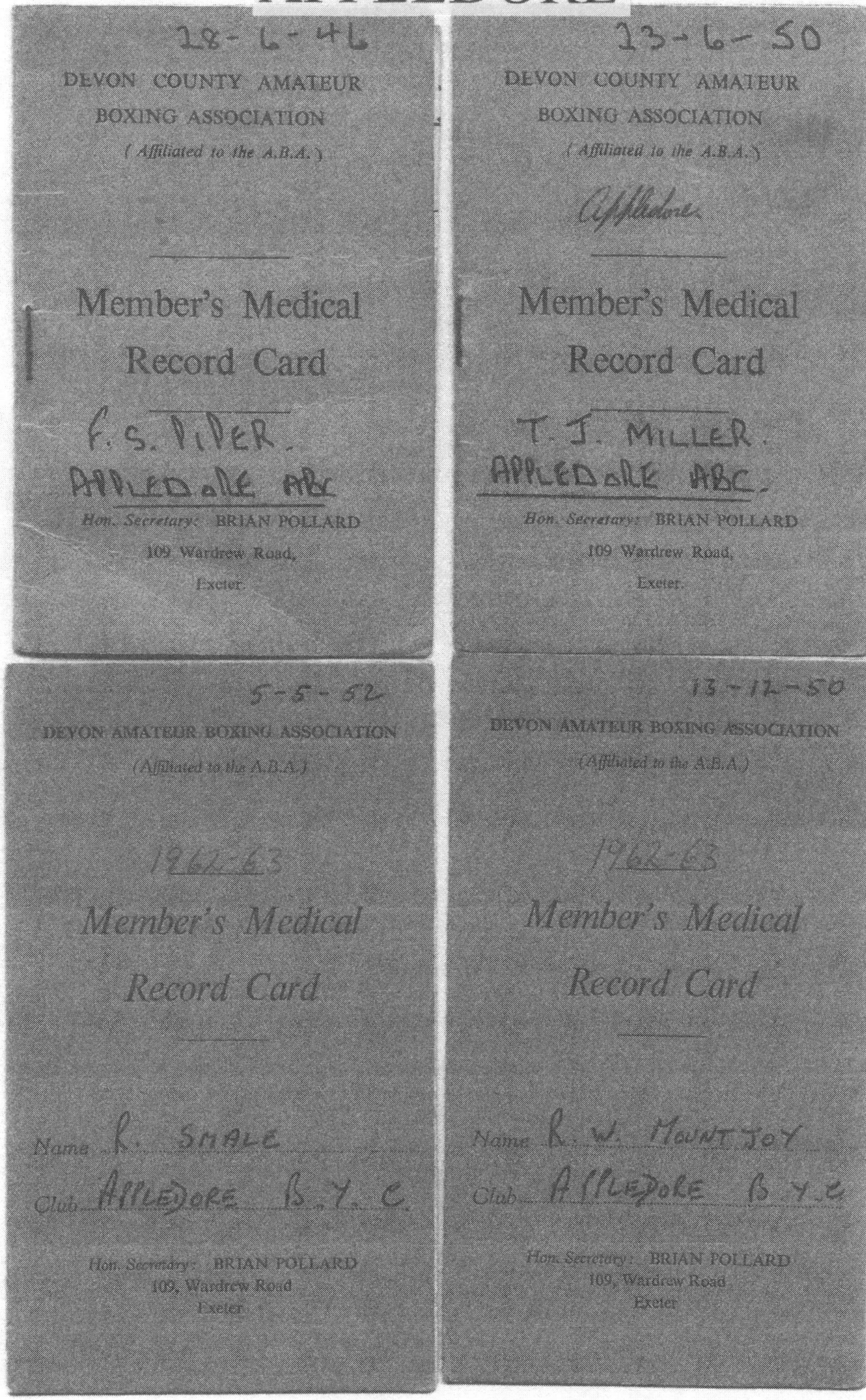

28-6-46

DEVON COUNTY AMATEUR
BOXING ASSOCIATION
(Affiliated to the A.B.A.)

Member's Medical
Record Card

F. S. PIPER.
APPLEDORE ABC

Hon. Secretary: BRIAN POLLARD
109 Wardrew Road,
Exeter.

13-6-50

DEVON COUNTY AMATEUR
BOXING ASSOCIATION
(Affiliated to the A.B.A.)

Appledore

Member's Medical
Record Card

T. J. MILLER.
APPLEDORE ABC.

Hon. Secretary: BRIAN POLLARD
109 Wardrew Road,
Exeter.

5-5-62

DEVON AMATEUR BOXING ASSOCIATION
(Affiliated to the A.B.A.)

1962-63

Member's Medical
Record Card

Name R. SMALE
Club APPLEDORE B. Y. C.

Hon. Secretary: BRIAN POLLARD
109, Wardrew Road
Exeter

13-12-50

DEVON AMATEUR BOXING ASSOCIATION
(Affiliated to the A.B.A.)

1962-63

Member's Medical
Record Card

Name R. W. MOUNTJOY
Club APPLEDORE B. Y. C

Hon. Secretary: BRIAN POLLARD
109, Wardrew Road
Exeter

APPLEDORE

30-3-52

DEVON AMATEUR BOXING ASSOCIATION

(Affiliated to the A.B.A.)

1962-63

Member's Medical Record Card

Name G. GARDNER

Club APPLEDORE Y.S.C.

Hon. Secretary: BRIAN POLLARD
109, Wardrew Road
Exeter

16-4-52

DEVON AMATEUR BOXING ASSOCIATION

(Affiliated to the A.B.A.)

1962-63

Member's Medical Record Card

Name D. BARRETT

Club APPLEDORE YOUTH S.C.

Hon. Secretary: BRIAN POLLARD
109, Wardrew Road
Exeter

14-2-51

DEVON AMATEUR BOXING ASSOCIATION

(Affiliated to the A.B.A.)

1962-63

Member's Medical Record Card

Name T.T. FISHER

Club APPLEDORE B.S.C.

Hon. Secretary: BRIAN POLLARD
109, Wardrew Road
Exeter

16-11-49

DEVON AMATEUR BOXING ASSOCIATION

(Affiliated to the A.B.A.)

1962-63

Member's Medical Record Card

Name S. BARRETT.

Club APPLEDORE A.B.C.

Hon. Secretary: BRIAN POLLARD
109, Wardrew Road
Exeter

APPLEDORE

15-11-49

DEVON AMATEUR BOXING ASSOCIATION

(Affiliated to the A.B.A.)

Member's Medical Record Card

Name B. FISHER

Club APPLEDORE A.B.C.

Hon. Secretary: BRIAN POLLARD
109, Wardrew Road
Exeter

DEVON AMATEUR BOXING ASSOCIATION

(Affiliated to the A.B.A.)

1962-63

Member's Medical Record Card

Name K. SOWDEN

Club APPLEDORE YOUTH S.C.

Hon. Secretary: BRIAN POLLARD
109, Wardrew Road
Exeter

2-10-51

DEVON AMATEUR BOXING ASSOCIATION

(Affiliated to the A.B.A.)

1962-63

Member's Medical Record Card

Name K. R. LLOYD

Club APPLEDORE B.S.C.

Hon. Secretary: BRIAN POLLARD
109, Wardrew Road
Exeter

20-6-53

DEVON AMATEUR BOXING ASSOCIATION

(Affiliated to the A.B.A.)

1962-63

Member's Medical Record Card

Name L. J. FORD

Club APPLEDORE B.S.C.

Hon. Secretary: BRIAN POLLARD
109, Wardrew Road
Exeter

APPLEDORE

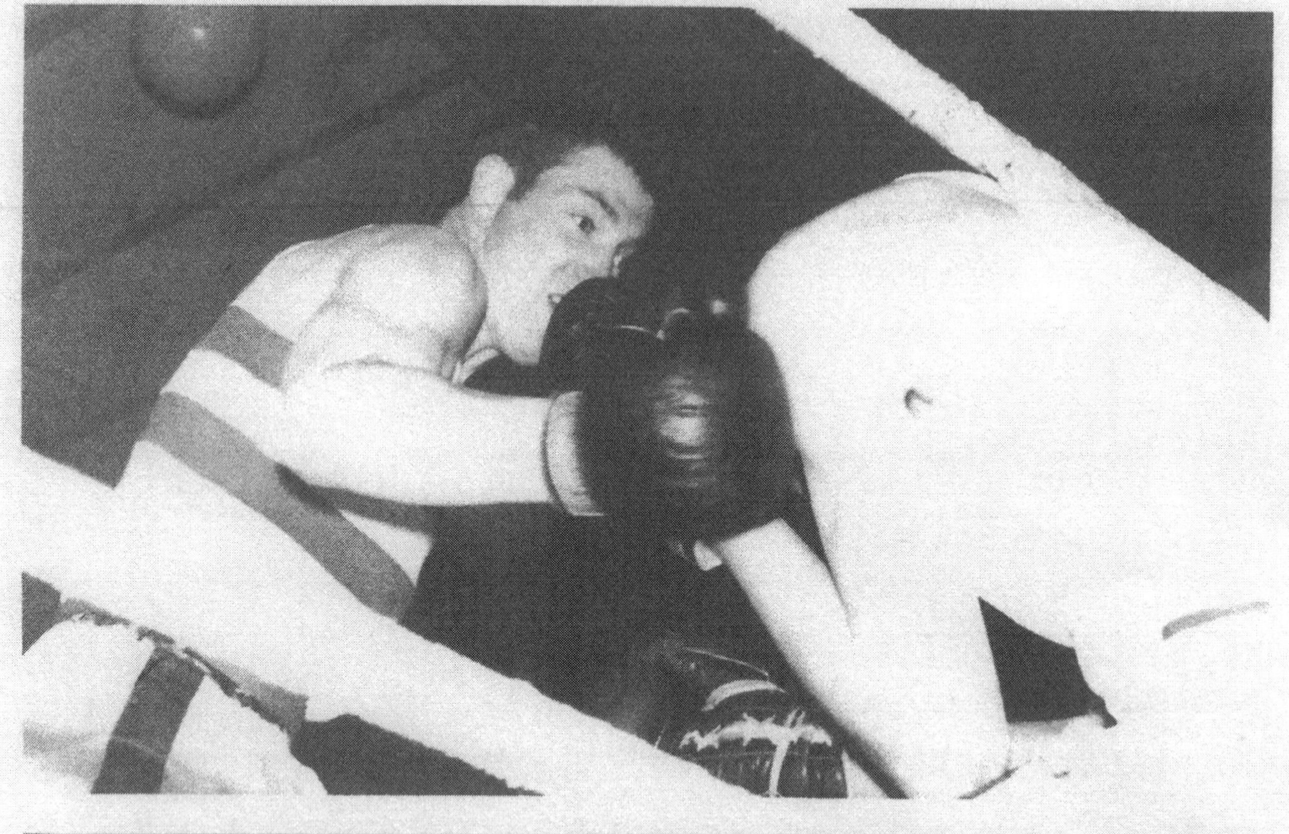

Boxing at Appledore

Sid Craner Appledore Boys Sports Club
Has his opponent on the Ropes
Won in the first Round

Photo Leon Richards
Appledore Lifeboat 1st Engineer.

An early PROFESSIONAL BOXER'S LICENCE issued by the BRITISH BOXING BOARD of CONTROL. This one has a hand written date on it, 25/1/39.

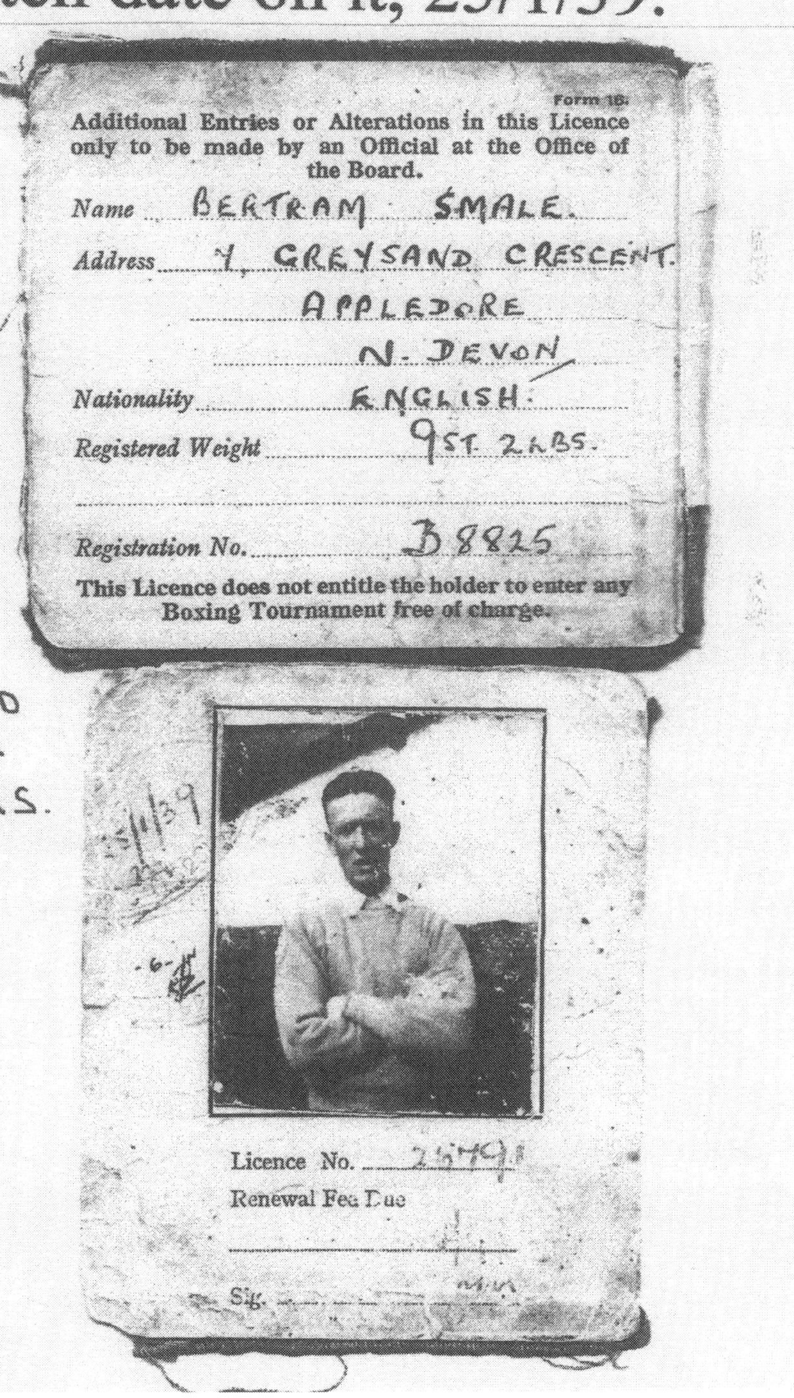

Form 18.

Additional Entries or Alterations in this Licence only to be made by an Official at the Office of the Board.

Name BERTRAM SMALE.

Address 4, GREYSAND CRESCENT.

APPLEDORE

N. DEVON

Nationality ENGLISH.

Registered Weight 9ST. 2LBS.

Registration No. B 8825

This Licence does not entitle the holder to enter any Boxing Tournament free of charge.

25/1/39

Licence No. 25491

Renewal Fee Due

Sig.

FORMAT HARDLY CHANGED IN OVER 70 YEARS.

REMINISCENCES

MICHAEL 'MITCH' WARBURTON

I was flattered when Dick asked me to write of my early memories and introduction to boxing. I moved around a lot as a child and this has been a chance for me to put some of my early life into chronological order.

Luckily my great uncle, Claude Richards of Hammonds farm Berry Narbor was an influence on me, he was a great sports fan, as well as a farmer he played bowls for Berrynarbor and latterly for CombeMartin, and his love of football, cricket and boxing was the beginning of my keen interest in all sport. One of my first memories was moving from Launceston with my mother to Hammond's farm when I was about four years old. We then moved out to Lynton, incidentally where I was born in 1947, we lived with my gran Lock, and then we moved on to CombeMartin to live with my great granny Jewell. After a spell at Berry Narbor where I started school, we moved to Ilfracombe to live once again with my gran Lock, I attended Adelaide College but after a short while we moved once more back to Hammonds farm Berry Narbor.

Uncle Claude and Auntie Gladys were the only members of the family who had television so it was at this time I was able to fix a date to a sports event, and it was the Matthews cup final of 1953.As each goal was scored I ran down to the neighbouring farm called Slowlys to inform Arthur, the young man who was milking the cows, each time a goal was scored. Before the days of transistor radios and modern technology, Children who ran around the village was the way the latest news was spread ,uncle recalled he and a number of men were making hay in the rectory meadows when a young boy ran over to them from the village, and re-laid the news that Jack Johnson had knocked out James Jeffery's, it was a shock as they were all of the opinion that Jeffery's was unbeatable

The 1954 cup final was between West Bromwich Albion and Preston North End and was played on the first of May, I must have seen it but I cant recall much about it . Five days later Roger Bannister Broke the four minute mile at Oxford and I remember that quite clearly. Little was I to know that by the very next year I would become a life long supporter of the Baggies.

My mother remarried and we were off to Redditch in the Midlands to live with my stepfather Ken's mother and grand mother this was in the summer of that year as every day seemed sunny and I can recall the Redditch carnival , By the winter we had moved to 35 Clayton Road, Counden, Coventry. The winter seemed exceptionally cold to a lad from Devon and I had to learn how to stand up for myself as once again I was the new kid in school,. Ken and mum left the house before half past seven to work in the Armstrong Siddely car factory, as did most of the other kid's parents, the play ground of the Counden primary school was full of lads and the site of a massive pre school football match which lasted before school started at nine o'clock. Probably fifty a side and He who had a ball was certainly allowed to play, and that white plastic ball that was pretty flat was preferred to an old tennis ball so I got to play, I was quite often in trouble for fighting, etc, one particular kid pulled a knife on me for several days on the trot and of course I had to back off. The knife was only a paper knife in the style of a silver cutlass I can still see it now, I remembered we had a bronze paper knife at home and so I took it to school, and when the boy threatened me the next time, I was ready, he ran off, and I got the blame of course, this time I was in serious trouble, I cant remember much about the outcome other that it involved the head teacher and my parents, I never saw that bronze paper knife again, nor the kid with the silver cutlass.

VERBATIM from the ORIGINAL.

The Midlands had its advantages to a young lad; once in a while we would be off to the Hawthorns to see West Brom. Ken usually got me down to the front where I got a good view of the match. Amongst many other matches we saw was a repeat of the previous year's cup final, West Brom verses Preston North End .Tommy Docherty was playing left half for Preston and he stood just five yards away from me. . Once the Ford pop broke a half shaft coming out of the cinder car park next to the ground, and we had to go back a few days later to fix it in the freezing cold.
Mums marriage to Ken was a bit rocky to say the least and it was deemed better if I was to go back to Berrynarbor and live with Uncle Claude and Aunty Gladys.
I was not allowed to attend school for some time, as I was run down, I had carbuncles and impetigo and was not allowed to mix with the other kids. I used to sit in a field above the play ground and watch the other boys playing football in the school yard and I longed to be down there with them. This was in the spring of 1955, the cup final was Manchester city v Birmingham the year Bert Troutman broke his neck. A few days later on May the 16th uncle got me out of bed at three o'clock in the morning to listen live from San Francisco, Rocky Marcia no v Don Cockle, it was great, and you almost felt you were there. the noise of the crowd the ringing of the bell and the exiting commentary, Cockle as I recall took a bad beating, It is difficult to say if this was my first memory of boxing as many things associated with boxing began for me at roughly the this time. On Wednesday nights Aunty was banished to the parlour to watch the television while Uncle and I were up in the kitchen listening to the wireless, live British boxing with Eamon Andrews commentating and Barrington Dalby giving the inter round summaries. This went on for many years one of the boxers whose fights I remember listening to was Willie Toweel a South African who seemed to box every other week I believe he fought Dave Charnly for the British and empire champion ship at one time
Other fights we got up early to hear were Floyd Patterson's three fights with Ingmar Johansson. I used to admire Floyd Paterson he had dynamite in his left hook but suffered from a china chin, so his fights had you on the edge of your seat, other nights I recall were the Terry Downs's fights with Paul Pender. We used to listen to the fights live and then watch them the following night on the television.
I was a bit slow with my reading due to going to so many different schools, that uncle tried to remedy that by ordering me a comic. Not the Beano or Eagle but a publication called the Wizard, it was full of storeys not cartoons, this brought my reading on quickly, one weekly serial was about boxing, and foretold the life of John L Sullivan , when that one finished it dealt with James J Corbet and then Bob Fitzsimons. When the series completely finished I changed to the Rover, because that had a fictitious series about a British champion who fought on the booths in the off season, Around this time we used to visit Barnstaple fair once a year , I hardly went on any rides but used to spend the evening. Stood out side the boxing booths with Uncle where we would watch the build up to the show then go in and watch the boxing. At this time there was no wrestling just boxing, There was Sam McGowan's booth, from the Bournemouth area and my favourite booth Mickey Kielys from Plymouth. This booth was really flash with a very ornate frontage; Mickey Himself was always dressed in a dinner jacket and really looked the part. His four boxers stood in line on the platform in front of the booth with Mickey in the middle doing his thing on the microphone. His booth boxers were always immaculately turned out, with clean white towels wrapped around there necks and neatly

tucked in to their posh silk dressing gowns. One boxer I used to admire was a black guy called Bobby Johnson he looked the business, I can still remember his black boxing boots with his white boxing socks neatly turned down over the top of them. Much later when I used to visit the fair by myself, both booths had introduced wrestling this did not flick my switch to much but I still used to go in just to see the boxing. I think that listening to Mickey Kielys great spieling technique, influenced me and my style of delivery as an M.C much later in my life

We had a boys club in the village, and in the winter we used to box each other, the leader of the club, John Valance he was a footballer, not a boxer so we received no practical instruction in the noble art,, just get the gloves on and have a go. I loved it and tried to emulate the peak a boo style of Floyd Patterson, with out much success I might add. But Berry boys club turned out at least one good boxer, a lad I met again many years later called Keith, Pritchard, he joined up and later boxed for the R.A.F.

I sometimes wonder what may have happened if I had lived nearer Barnstaple and was able to attend Barnstaple A.B.Cs training sessions. Instead my path turned to football Berrynarbor boys club also had a football team every boy in the village if he had two legs and could stand had to play. We were regularly thrashed by Combe Martin. Our near neighbours.

My teen age years were taken up with playing in rock and roll bands, I was about twenty when Berry Narbor started up a men's football team that played in division four of the junior league when I got married and moved to Barnstaple my brother in law Stan Bishop persuaded me to play for Fremington. I later moved on to play for Northam Lions were I finished playing when I was thirty two years old .During this time Stan and I used to attend Barnstaple A.B.A, s dinner shows at the Barnstaple motel.

.Much later while working for an engineering firm in Chumleigh I was asked by a work mate Mark Hickey to come and watch him box. Mark at this time was boxing for Bideford and. one or two of us usually travelled to support him. When Mark took part in the A.B.A, s at Bridport. I met up again with an old work mate, Gordon Shaddick who was helping to run Barnstaple A.B.C .He suggested I should attend some of Barnstaple's home shows, that at the time were held at the leisure center.Stan was keen to go as his son Lee Bishop had started boxing for Barnstaple. Lee was a Judo and Karate man and participated at a very high level, he turned to boxing late when he was in his thirties, and consequently only boxed for a few years If Lee was boxing we would travel on the Barnstaple bus to some of the away shows

One evening I had a call from Stan, he said Lee had asked him to ask me if I would like to join the committee of Barnstaple boxing club as they were short of members. I was told all I had to do was shut up and stick my hand up every now and then. I jumped at the chance, but found it hard to shut up. Our shows were not making a lot of profit and we were hiring in rings for each show at £200 a time, we had a ring of our own but the existing members could not erect it as there was to much work to do on the day of a show. After a while I suggested that I should gather together a gang of volunteers who had nothing to do with Barnstaple A.B.C. To put the ring up it was stored at Burrington in Roy Jury's transport yard we did this for many years eventually building our own trailer to store it in as well as transporting it to various boxing venues. At first as I said earlier I did not attend all of Barnstaple's committee meetings; I only went when asked to

make the number up. And in my absence one night it was suggested that I should become the clubs recorder, so once again I had a phone call from Stan.
My first show as a recorder was at the Barnstaple British legion, on February the third two thousand and one, which just happens to be my birthday. Being a recorder got me ring side and the job entailed keeping the boys medical cards up to date and recording the night's bouts on a form that was sent to the A.B.A. This was an official job and you were given a card that you filled in to record your attendance at the show, unfortunately in my opinion since the A.B.A. has been taken over by England Boxing this job has been down graded. I think like many others that this was a mistake as a recorder was quite often a person's first step into becoming a boxing official and heaven knows boxing needs officials. In the early days I used to record for Barnstaple and Bideford and often accompanied North Devon's long time Master of Ceremonies Ron Herniman to shows in South Devon, bearing in mind at this time a recorder had to be registered with the A.B.A. and CRB checked. Ron was a stalwart of North Devon boxing and a gentleman. Years ago he was Master of Ceremonies at pro boxing and wrestling at the Queens hall in Barnstaple; he was the bingo caller at the British legion and served as a magistrate, he was also life long fan of Arsenal and he and his girls attended games when ever possible. Invariably Ron would say they called in for a K.F.C on the way home as it was his girls favourite When Ron sadly passed away I knew the chap who took over his job had his work cut out to come up to his high standard. I volunteered for the task and visited Atlantic village for my first ever dinner jacket and strides. My first show was on the seventieth of April two thousand and four at the pannier market in Bideford. From then on I was out most weekends' compairing boxing shows through out the south west. I found some M.C.s style a little stiff and starchy, adhering strictly to the format set out by the A.B.A, so I tried to bend it a bit to the lighter more personal side. And tried to make my style entertaining after all it is a show we are trying to put on, I very soon realised it was no use trying to hide my West Country accent. So I just spoke naturally. I recon there is a dash of Mickey Kiely in there somewhere with a very small amount of Michael Buffer as well a whole dollop of North Devon.

I believe, to be a good M.C. You must not be afraid to make mistakes, but be big enough to take the blame, and were appropriate make a joke of it. I well remember one evening at Exeter ,not so long ago .In a regional final between Ryan Hart of Mayflower and Liam Laird of Barnstaple, I made a bad mistake, Both the judge who I was sitting by at ringside and myself thought that Ryan had won, and consequently when I came to read out the result I announced that Ryan was the majority winner , but a quick glance at the O.I.C Nicky Kendall made me realise I had made a mistake after quickly re checking my slip, I made the necessary apology and announced Liam the majority winner . The look on Ryan's face is something I will never forget, poor lad, I immediately went over to him and apologised personally to him. And he accepted it with good grace. Another time at a King Alfred's show at High bridge the next bout was not printed on the program. So as I always do I walked over to the both boys corners and asked them for there details, an wished them the best of luck , I announced the first lad with out a problem, but the lad in the blue corner I just stared at him and went blank, I had to walk over and ask his name again. He took it o.k. and for a few years after, and before a show started, the same smiling young man would come up to me and say, you won't forget my name tonight will you.

North Devon has always been short of officials so in the summer of two thousand and nine several Barnstaple members attended a judging course, I also took the time keeping course at the same time, I judged my first show at the riverside in Exeter in the September of that year, Judging is what I enjoy most, what can be better than sitting at ringside relaxed and doing what you enjoy doing the most, watching boxing, and giving it your full attention , there can be no excuses for mistakes, you need to get it right for the boys sake, a mistake in judging is worse than announcing a bout incorrectly as an M.C.s. or letting a round go on for a little to long as a time keeper,

My time as an M.C.s. has to come to an end, it has become too difficult to get in and out of the ring with my old arthritic knees, and I will miss that connection I get. With the boxing crowd, but hope to still be at the shows doing other things.

M Waolton

Barnstaple A.B.C.

MY BOOKS

ALL BOOKS written by DICK BROWNSON are available from...
BOOK SHOPS and AMAZON ON-LINE.

ALSO AVAILABLE DIRECT FROM DICK BROWNSON at...

TORRIDON HOUSE,
CHUBB ROAD,
BIDEFORD,
EX39 4HF,
NORTH DEVON,
U.K.
Telephone..
01237 700901
email..
brownson7@aol.com

ALL books sent POST FREE to U.K. ADDRESSES.

ISBN number given for each book.

Wild Bill Longley

Texas Gunslinger

Dick Brownson

Foreword by Allan Radbourne*

ISBN 978-1-906769-31-4

GRITTY!
EXPLOSIVE!

A Distant Friendly Party

BOXING

A NOVEL ABOUT THE FIGHT GAME

DICK BROWNSON

'It Shall Be As It Was In The Past'

ISBN 978-1-906769-42-0

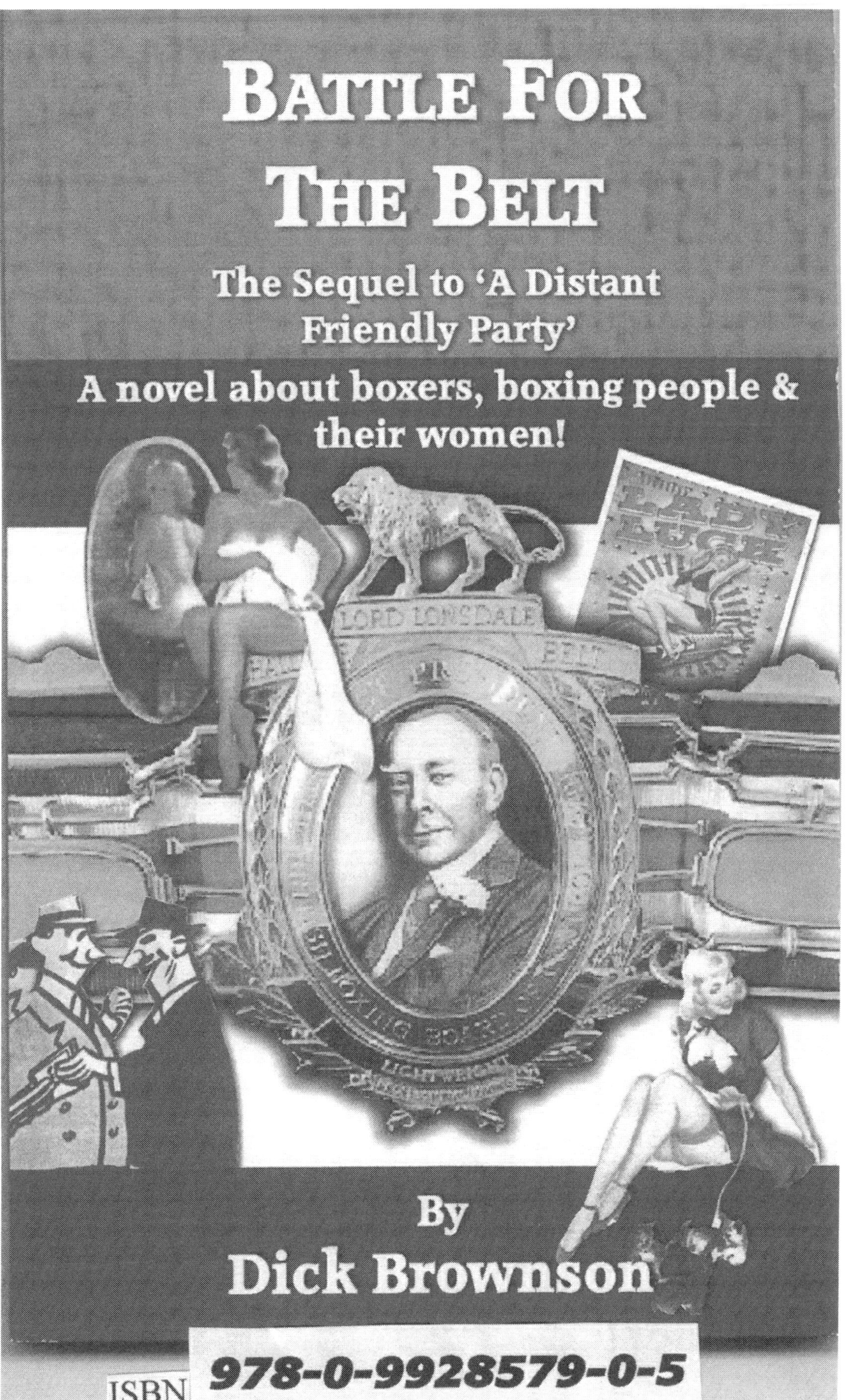
BATTLE FOR
THE BELT
The Sequel to 'A Distant
Friendly Party'
A novel about boxers, boxing people &
their women!
LORD LONSDALE
BELT
LIGHTWEIGHT
By
Dick Brownson
ISBN 978-0-9928579-0-5

THE STORY OF NORTH DEVON BOXING

VOLUME ONE

DICK BROWNSON

ISBN 978-1-906769-58-1

Death Knell For Evil Shadows

Two Bridges
Princetown

Postbridge

Moretonhampstead

By
Dick Brownson

ISBN 978-0-9928579-5-0

THANKYOU and KEEP FIT!

Dick Brownson

Cover design

By

Toby Norton

1200